DON'T CALL IT HAIR METAL

DON'T CALL IT HAIR METAL

ART IN THE EXCESS OF '80S ROCK

SEAN KELLY

ECW

This book is also available as a Global Certified Accessible™ (GCA) ebook. ECW Press's ebooks are screen reader friendly and are built to meet the needs of those who are unable to read standard print due to blindness, low vision, dyslexia, or a physical disability.

Get the ebook free!*
*proof of purchase required

Purchase the print edition and receive the ebook free. For details, go to ecwpress.com/ebook.

Published by ECW Press
665 Gerrard Street East
Toronto, Ontario, Canada M4M 1Y2
416-694-3348 / info@ecwpress.com

Editor for the Press: Michael Holmes
Copyeditor: Rachel Ironstone
Cover design: Michel Vrana
Author photo: Chris Surdykowski

LIBRARY AND ARCHIVES CANADA CATALOGUING
IN PUBLICATION

Title: Don't call it hair metal : art in the excess of '80s rock / Sean Kelly.

Names: Kelly, Sean, 1972- author.

Identifiers: Canadiana (print) 20230154980 | Canadiana (ebook) 20230154999

ISBN 978-1-77041-643-7 (softcover)
ISBN 978-1-77852-134-8 (Kindle)
ISBN 978-1-77852-133-1 (PDF)
ISBN 978-1-77852-132-4 (ePub)

Subjects: LCSH: Glam metal (Music)—History and criticism. | LCSH: Rock music—1981-1990—History and criticism. | LCSH: Rock musicians—Interviews.

Classification: LCC ML3534 .K295 2023 | DDC 781.6609/048—dc23

This book is funded in part by the Government of Canada. *Ce livre est financé en partie par le gouvernement du Canada.* We also acknowledge the support of the Government of Ontario through the Ontario Book Publishing Tax Credit, and through Ontario Creates.

Canada

PRINTED AND BOUND IN CANADA

PRINTING: FRIESENS   5   4   3   2   1

MIX
Paper from responsible sources
FSC® C016245

This book is dedicated to the loving memory of my father, Desmond Kelly, and to my mother, Mary Kelly. Thank you for providing me with every opportunity to live my dream.

I would also like to dedicate this book to Dee Snider for writing the song that inspired a lifelong love of music, and for being a mentor and friend. Dad, Mom, and Dee . . . I'm so glad you all had a chance to meet each other and bring the story full circle.

CONTENTS

INTRODUCTION
MORE THAN THIS

At about seven in the morning on August 20, 2020, our neighbor Karen came to the door of our family cottage just outside Témiscaming, a 45-minute drive from my childhood home of North Bay. There was no mobile phone reception up at our "camp," nor was there a landline installed, so we would often receive messages via the friendly neighbors who were permanent residents of this wooded paradise in the foothills of the Laurentian Mountains.

If someone is knocking on your door at 7 a.m., chances are the news isn't going to be great, and I already knew the reason I was being asked to phone my mother at home.

I hugged my wife and two boys, grabbed my jacket, iPhone, and earbuds, and walked in the rain through the wood clearing between our properties. Upon arrival, I dialed my childhood phone number, and it was confirmed by my mother that my father, Desmond Kelly, at the fine old age of 88, had passed away peacefully in his sleep.

This was no tragedy. Dad had been sick for a long time and had been cared for in his home with incredible love and skill by my mom, who was a nurse. He lived at home until his very last days, when he was admitted to a wonderful hospice. He died perfectly at peace, surrounded by his family, no regrets lingering, and nothing left unsaid. It was as good an ending as

I

one could hope for. The reason that we were up at the family cottage in the first place was because one day earlier, Dad had expressed his last wish. He wanted me to take my sons to enjoy the property he had left as a legacy for his family, now in the loving care of my sister Pam and my brother-in-law Jim. The last smile that I saw part his lips came at the thought of his grandsons jumping off the dock into Lake Temiskaming, the way he himself had done so many times.

I had spent many wonderful summers in my youth on that lake, establishing the architecture of my musical essence and, ultimately, my sense of identity and purpose. With a stack of black wax and chromium dioxide, I'd push the limits of machine and man as the din emanating from the tiny speakers in my battery-powered Radio Shack cassette player sliced through the solitude of my parents' northern retreat.

All of this listening was reinforced with stacks of glossy guitar and general rock magazines. These periodicals were filled with glorious material that would inform my own nascent six string experimentation, helping me crack the code of the shred gods within their pages. With the budget constraints of youth, and the availability of albums in small-town record stores being somewhat limited in comparison to what one might find in a larger city, I often turned to magazines purchased at the local drugstore to get my rock'n'roll fix. Sometimes I would have a fully formed opinion or concept about a band before I ever had a chance to hear them.

The skillful analysis of the writers in magazines like *Guitar World*, *Guitar Player*, *Creem*, *Circus*, *Faces*, and *Hit Parader* allowed me to hear the music through their words, and damn it if those writers didn't manage to bring me pretty close to the reality of the sonics when those records finally did reach my ears.

The music I *did* have access to was pretty common fare for rock-inclined teenagers. With Van Halen, Twisted Sister, Def Leppard, Quiet Riot, Mötley Crüe, Ozzy Osbourne, Triumph, Helix, and Honeymoon Suite serving up a soundtrack that stood in stark contrast to the languid calm of the woods and waters that surrounded me, I would dream of a life electric. The music was a connection to the world beyond the forest that surrounded me. A world of leather and makeup. High-heeled boots and people who didn't care if their hair was grown to the sky. A glorious post-apocalyptic landscape of stacked amplifiers and electric guitars with angles, edges, pointed headstocks, and custom paint jobs, all promising to deliver me from the confines of my imagined preteen imprisonment. I wanted to be part of a band, part of a gang, and I would imagine the deep friendships that must have existed between members of these bands, bonds forged in excessive consumption, loud clothes, and louder music. And make no mistake, for all the hypersexualized flash and posturing that often accompanied the songs, it was the *sound* that drew me back to lift the needle again and again on my seven-inch vinyl single of Ratt's *Lay It Down*, or to sit through the torture of waiting for the cassette to rewind to the perfect space between the last trace of ominous synthesizer in "In The Beginning" to those first Mick Mars power chords in "Shout at the Devil." These analog rituals, perhaps long lost to the fully digitized youth of today, are firmly entrenched in my muscle memory, and have likely contributed to the immeasurable satisfaction I've received from heavy rock. Like the musical hopefuls of Hollywood's Sunset Strip who, I'd imagine, had spent countless nights handing out flyers and slapping posters on telephone poles in order to attract a bevy of beauties and record company A&R execs to their showcases, I had to *work* for my rock'n'roll fix, too, man!

How many hours did I spend in staring out at the lake, imagining the excitement and heat of Hollywood nights and concert performances under the light of a thousand PAR Cans on arena stages somewhere in America's heartland? The dichotomy of all this daydreaming taking place in the grounded purity of my rustic spiritual home has long since been reconciled within me. I have come to realize that I need the storm and the calm . . . I don't do very well with too much of either. And as much fun as the trappings can be, as I have found out in a music career blessed with a taste of various levels of success in the industry, the people involved in the music making and their artistic intention are what continually stoke the fires of my interest.

Just like they did for Neil Young in that town in Northern Ontario he sings about in "Helpless," all of my changes happened at that cottage on the lake, or at least a good chunk of them. And as I changed, so, too, did the music I grew up on . . . evolving, while still retaining strands of connectivity that made it something I could claim as an identity. A magical decade or so of growing up a rocker (or skid, or headbanger, or muso . . . take your pick), faithful to something I always believed to be rock'n'roll, but sometimes, after its initial heyday, to be identified and marginalized as something "other." We'll touch on that later.

My 50 years of life have been charmed. Up to the point of Dad's passing, I had not experienced the grief that comes with the loss of an immediate family member. In the days leading up to the inevitable, I was fearful of the unknown emotions that I anticipated washing over me. It was to be my task to inform other family members who were up at camp, at various locations on the lake, of my father's passing. This included my father's sister, who was now the last remaining member of her immediate family. I really felt that I owed it to everyone to keep it together. I'm not really sure why, but I did.

In an attempt to thwart any maudlin displays, I prepared myself by listening to a song that I had downloaded to my phone, a song I had hoped would steel my courage while also connecting me in a more meaningful way to one of life's inevitable reckonings.

The title track of Mr. Big's 2017 album, *Defying Gravity*, is the song I had earmarked for the moment. The more dedicated rock music fan of the late '80s may remember Mr. Big from the pages of various guitar magazines as a "supergroup" of rock virtuosi: former members of David Lee Roth's solo band, Talas, UFO, Racer X, Ted Nugent, the Knack, Robert Plant, and more. But more likely, if you ask people what Mr. Big means to them, the song that will come to mind is 1991's ever-so-fashionable at the time acoustic ballad (and a number one Billboard hit in 1992) "To Be with You." Their recollection might also be framed by the images of the song's accompanying video, skinny lads in tight pants, carefully coifed flowing locks, billowy shirts, bangles, and hooped earrings decorating gaunt rocker cheekbones. For some, this video might represent one of the last gasps of commercial hard rock that would bother the Billboard charts, and the collective consciousness of the rock-music-buying general public at large.

As guitarist Paul Gilbert's plucky '60s inspired pseudo-raga riff filled my ears, I took a moment to soak in the strangeness of the moment. It was abstract, it was painful, but it was also *special*. Tears flowed freely from my eyes, but when they blended with the rain on my face and the familiar, sweet musk of the wet forest, it all felt quite transcendent. There was an ache, and there was shock and sadness, but I was also connected to a beautiful moment. And when singer Eric Martin's soulful, rasp-inflected voice sang out the first chorus line, I couldn't help but think that my pro hockey–playing, ever fearless, youthful, and joyful dad was embarking on yet another great adventure:

> Time has come when I'll be gone
> Beyond the great unknown
> I'll be flying free, defying gravity
> Cut the strings and say a prayer
> And take off on my own
> Me, I'm flying free, defying gravity

While I knew there would be the inevitable pain from the loss, I couldn't help but bask in the joyous impermanence of it all. With Gilbert's fleet-fingered flights of guitar fancy, the tympanic floor tom drum shots punctuating the rhythmic motif of the main riff, and Billy Sheehan's virtuosic and melodic bass counterpoint framing Martin's soaring vocals and harmonies, I felt the joy of my father's liberation from his pain and suffering. The fear of the unknown that had once terrified me was gone, replaced by a celebration of something noble and inevitable. To date this was the most poignant example of how the rock'n'roll artists of my formative years have provided emotional support and sustenance to me, helping me rise above the fear, loneliness, or pain that life can bring and remember the wonderment. Not that I've suffered much adversity, but we all face these challenges to some degree. Music is often what gets us through. I believe that in that moment, I was able to let go of the things I was or wasn't in my father's eyes, and actually *see* him as his own spiritual entity. Flying free, defying gravity. What a gift. What a song.

I am sharing this very personal story in a book about '80s and early '90s hard rock because it reflects the value that this music holds for me, a value that transcends that notion that an entire genre should be lumped into a one-dimensional, easily compartmentalized relic of an excessive era.

Mr. Big is so much more than one song. This is a band with a nine-studio-album-deep catalog and an incredible amount of collective performance and recording experience. Their influences range from Todd Rundgren and the Beatles, to Motown, Humble Pie, and Free, all framed in a beautiful post–Van Halen sonic modernity. Gilbert and Sheehan are considered architects of a highly technical style of guitar and bass playing that they imbued with the musicality and dynamics of their varied influences, but they have regrettably, in less-informed circles, been lumped in with a group that has become synonymous with indulgence and excess. Labeled as "shredders." I mean, is there anything less musical sounding than the word *shred*? Then again, as I've come to realize in my journey of writing this book, maybe it's not an insult. Maybe that is just my hang-up. I've come to understand that even the artists making the music that would be the soundtrack of my life had differing opinions and views of its artistic merit.

Still, it feels insulting to relegate a band with this amount of human achievement under their belts to one song or one image caught in time. In fact, it is the sting of that perceived insult that initially inspired me to write this book. I have spent my life defending a musical style (I won't say genre; the genre is rock'n'roll music) I love above all others. As a devotee, I've felt the slings and arrows of fellow musicians and fans who stare down their noses at the guitar-based hard rock as they tarred and feathered it with the pejorative label "hair metal." To some people, Mr. Big is a hair metal band, a band that represents a vacuous, indulgent, and unimportant era of music, a style that is best left as a reminder of everything that is wrong with rock'n'roll.

But I know there is so much more. That's because I have put in the time, a lifetime actually, and I have done the research. I've *lived* the research. While the casual listener may have scratched the surface of this music, found a few cheap thrills, and moved on to supposed loftier musical pursuits, I stuck around and dug deep. And through almost 40 years of listening and taking in (that's a Grapes of Wrath reference there, a '60s influenced Canadian guitar pop band that sat alongside my '80s metal quite nicely; a lot of us rock'n'rollers love our power pop, just ask Enuff Z'Nuff!), I haven't budged in my stance that this music has an incredible amount to offer in terms of artistic value. In its aggregate, '8os hard rock is important music. It matters.

I was initially going to call this book *Hair Metal for Hipsters*. My intention was to draw all sorts of clever connections to the critically accepted "cool" music of the past, in an attempt to validate this much maligned iteration of rock'n'roll to the harshest of its critics. It was going to be a real "I'll show *you*" type of vibe, funny and sardonic, but rooted in a kind of defensive academia . . . I think all the years of defending the music's intrinsic value made me want to baffle the critics with science.

But after some heartfelt consultation with my editor and insightful conversation with artists and music industry veterans that were actually living and creating this music, I realized trying to prove someone "wrong" about their subjective taste would be a pointless exercise in my own arrogance. During the course of our conversation for the book, Paul Gilbert introduced me to the concept of the narcissism of small differences, a phrase coined by Sigmund Freud for a thesis that suggests that adjoining territories and close relationships are likely to fight with and mock each other because of hypersensitivity to details that make them different.

I'll explain it and you'll immediately understand. It's when, for example, if you took a person who is not a rock'n'roll fan — [someone] who might know very little about it, somebody from Mongolia who is into whatever, Mongolian music. And we said, "Okay, we're going to play you some heavy metal guitar players. Listen to some Paul Gilbert and now listen to some Steve Vai. Tell me what the difference is." And they'd probably go, "They both kind of sound the same — distorted and they're fast and play up and down and the drums are loud." To them, it just sounded like two of the same things, grape jelly and grape jelly. But to Steve and me, we'd be like, "What? No! I do this thing completely different." To an outsider, what seems like an arcane detail, to us, that's our whole identity and our little territory that we've scraped out where we're like, "This is my little territory where I do it this way," and to me that's like why I'm me.

Engaging in this line of thinking as a motivation behind writing a book just didn't feel right anymore, it didn't sound all that fun, and it isn't a true reflection of who I am as a writer and a person. This isn't really what the music is about to me either. Sure, there are plenty of examples of great "screw you" moments in '80s hard rock, but ultimately this music represents something greater than that to me. It's about the purity of joy and the embodiment of living in the moment.

I also learned some things from the interviews conducted for this book that have challenged some of my own feelings about production value, songwriting, and imagery that I had always believed to be great. Like many of us, I have been guilty of allowing nostalgia to cloud my view of the reality of certain situations, and I feel I've been set straight in a number of cases. Conversely, other convictions have been strengthened and fortified. Amazing what talking to someone who has actually been there can do to one's opinion.

This book is no longer about showing some petulant and self-important hipster "enemy," created out of my own insecurities, how *wrong* they are. It's really about sharing how *right* this music feels to me. And let's face it, most people who pick up this book are already going to have an affinity toward all or most of the qualities embodied in '80s hard rock. For those of us in the know, I think it's about developing a common language to express our love for the music, and the intentions of some of the greatest musicians and songs in rock'n'roll history, in the hope that it can be shared with the general music loving public at large. It's also about diving deep into the sounds, and some of the circumstances, the inspirations, the mechanizations, the settings, and the people behind some of the best of what this style of rock has to offer.

I've been involved in the music industry for 30 years, and I've yet to meet an artist who purposefully set out to be a joke or a pastiche (Weird Al and Spinal Tap aside . . . but that's nitpicking, innit?). There is artistic intention in this entertainment, and I believe that when we get to know the people behind the music, we can hear the music with fresh ears. It has happened to me time and time again, in classical, rap, country, jazz. I learned to love all those genres when I met people who loved those genres and were willing to share with me.

For those who don't see the diversity and artistic intention behind the examples of '80s hard rock in this book, I'm hoping that what I write will help bridge the divide that has kept some people from basking in the glory of what I consider to be amongst the richest and most joyous rock'n'roll ever made. I'll take you through some of my perspectives as a listener, following an admittedly loose timeline of the development of commercial hard rock in the '80s, from the perspective of your basic, rock-obsessed kid.

There isn't a day that goes by where this music doesn't come into my life. It has called me to pursue a career in music as a performer, songwriter, recording artist, producer, educator, and author. It has been the gateway to many different genres of music, while always remaining front and center in my heart and mind as a guiding life principle. To paraphrase a late '80s Van Halen song, it has kept me alive, electric, and inspired. The words are Sammy Hagar, but it reads like Walt Whitman to me. I've punctuated my thoughts and feelings about life with copped lyrics for as long as I can remember, so I don't see any reason to stop doing that as I write (my publisher's legal team may have different thoughts on this).

It's funny . . . there isn't a lot of "metal" in any of the music that gets dubbed hair metal (but as we'll see, there is *some*). However, if that pejorative label is the Trojan horse I need to get through the gates, then I will say this: hair metal matters. But in the end, don't call it hair metal. It's only rock'n'roll. And I like it. I think you might too.

CHAPTER 1
HAIR/METAL

air has been a primary image preoccupation since I was about 12 years old. So many things in my physical appearance seemed out of my control as a preteen pubescent. Too slight of frame for sports, too soft featured for the rugged good looks needed to attract eighth-grade girls, too freckle-faced to look like Vince Neil on the cover of *Shout at the Devil*. But one aspect I felt I could control was the length of my hair. Not to say there wouldn't be obstacles in producing and sustaining a mane suitable for mass adoration.

Let's do a SWOT analysis on the conundrum.

Strengths: the hair was already growing out of my scalp.

Weaknesses: It was curly and auburn, not jet black or bleach-blond. A Nikki Sixx–inspired rat's nest of satanic haystack hair was not a feasible option.

Opportunities: Dee Snider had curly hair. I could grow my hair long and contour or hide the things I didn't like about my appearance, and in doing so make my first steps toward becoming the rock star I yearned to be.

Threats: parental disapproval, and beatings at the hands of minor hockey goons as my aspiring mullet began to push out the back of my helmet.

I felt I had taken my destiny into my own hands when I walked into the Magic Cuts, a small-town mall fixture where one could suffer the great indignity of getting your "budget" cut in plain sight of all the shoppers at the Towers department store. On this, my first solo venture to get my haircut, I came prepared with two pictures ripped out of a copy of *Hit Parader* magazine to present to the stylist. One was of Def Leppard's Joe Elliott, the other of Jon Bon Jovi.

"I want my hair to look like this," I said, with my heart pounding against my denim jacket.

"You have short hair. Why are you coming to get a haircut?" replied the stylist. Touché. Still so much to learn . . .

But this was an issue I had to contend with. My parents made me get my hair cut on the regular. This wasn't negotiable, so what ensued was a laborious process that extended into high school, where with subtlety and ingenuity, I was able to "leave the length at the back" over the course of enough haircuts, and eventually a mullet worthy of consideration began to take effect. I kept it business up front and party at the back, ears were visible, but the waterfall of locks cascading down my neck, tucked under a most Catholic maroon or navy-blue school uniform dress shirt, tickled with the promise of freedom and realization of self-expression. Step one.

In truth, I didn't have too much struggle. There were the usual ignorant guffaws and comments mocking my sexuality, a reflection of the sheltered ignorance that was sadly commonplace in a small town in the '80s. Even more sadly, these hurtful attitudes were often perpetuated in the hard rock community, ironic since so many mid- to late '80s hard rockers fashioned their look on the gender-bending imagery of great glam rock pioneers like Ziggy Stardust–era David Bowie and Marc Bolan of T. Rex and the New Romantics of the early '80s . . . artists who embraced a much more liberated and inclusive view of sexuality. These hurtful attacks were often responded to through an overcompensation in displays of masculinity (or whatever my approximation of that might be, being a coward at heart). I asked a fellow Canadian musician, now making his name on the world stage for his work with Slash, Bruce Kulick of Kiss, and his all-star tribute band Toque, about his thoughts on early identity forged in rock.

Todd Kerns: I remember the distinct conversation over the piercing of ears, which seems so silly now: "You can only pierce your left ear because piercing the right one means you're gay!" What? And at the time — it seems so silly, but because you're just a child — you're like, "So you mean if I pierce my right ear, I'm going to suddenly like dudes?" It just seemed so stupid to me. And then you look at the pictures, like in *Hit Parader* magazine, and all these guys have tons of earrings and big hair. So we just kind of started to emulate all of those people. The lines get really blurred when you get into the glam rock with the makeup and the outfits. It's like when Bill Burr does his stand-up comedy where he's talking about listening to modern techno music and saying, "This isn't music. Music is supposed to be played by men who look like women, singing about the devil." When you look back at those magazines, everybody from Mötley to Stryper were blurring the lines completely.

It didn't take *that* long before I was framed in a mane of my own long hair. It felt awesome, and ultimately fulfilled that most coveted of teenage desires: the acquisition of an identity, one developing alongside my burgeoning guitar skills. I was becoming a musician, taking on the identity of a creator, and with this new look I felt that I at least had a *shot* at becoming a rock star. I had a ticket to the lottery.

Todd Kerns: The tribalism of it all . . . This is punk rock. This is heavy metal. This is thrash metal. There were very defined lines, much like in movies like, say, *The Breakfast Club*, where there's nerds and brains and heads. In a small town, it's sort of all mashed together, and while there are those stereotypes, music appreciation becomes sort of one big stew. Having long hair very much separated you from the norm, which I think is always important anyway. You find your thing, and it's definitely a statement. I think you're trying to connect with whoever your heroes are. I don't know about you, but walking through the midtown plaza mall in Saskatoon and seeing that other dude with long hair and a leather jacket,

you just kind of nodded at each other as you walked by. Or
if he's got a Mötley shirt on or something, suddenly it's like
a "Dude — we found each other."

How many other teens experience this feeling? Has hair always been the
gateway drug to a life of rock'n'roll exploration? Where did this all start?

I guess we could start in the 17th century, when the powdered wig was
all the rage (and oddly enough served as both an antidote to *and* cause
of lice infestation . . . tricky times!). But the fad really caught on when a
syphilitic Louis XIV sported one in order to hide the baldness that resulted
from his unfortunate affliction (I'm not going for the obvious, pre–AIDS
era, rampant sex rock'n'roll penicillin joke here, even though that fruit is
hanging pretty low right now).

Anyway, being a French king and all, Louis was a man of influence, and
when other members of high society caught a gander at the luscious locks
on display, the trend was set. To put a musical spin on it, fast forward to
Baroque cats like Vivaldi and Bach, who both sported some pretty serious
faux barnets. Long hair and musicians go back a long way together. Rock
ahead another hundred years or so, and Romantic era dark virtuosi like
Nicolo Paganini and Franz Liszt would be throwing wild sex and party
favors into the mix and growing their own manes . . . bad boys running
wild. Precedent set.

Shifting this to a popular music context, it seems totally unfair that hair
should come to be the defining element of '80s hard rock. I mean, we don't
call Dylan "bedhead folk." The Beatles were affectionately referred to as
"those four mop-tops from Liverpool," but their hair style wasn't hung on
a definition of their music. We don't call early Elvis (or rockabilly music,
for that matter) "pompadour rock." (Hey, since when is being a hillbilly
cool?) Sure, there were some incredibly outrageous, gravity defying hair
styles in the '80s hard rock scene (Jim Gillette from Nitro, anyone?), but
they were no more outrageous than those sported in the much more critically accepted punk and New Romantic and new wave styles. I mean, did A
Flock of Seagulls have to deal with this crock of bullshit? Well, maybe *they*
did . . . but a lot of others got away with it. It's a look that's even referenced
as cool in today's indie rock culture. And, jeez, even the long-haired freaky

people who couldn't get a job in the '60s still managed to avoid being musically labeled and libeled by their greasy, patchouli-soaked manes. The horror.

I asked my good friend and former Frehley's Comet bandmate John Regan, whose extensive resume also includes playing with David Lee Roth, Billy Idol, John Waite, David Bowie, Peter Frampton, and the Rolling Stones, what his initial thoughts were when he heard the term hair metal . . . did he actually associate it with a particular sound?

> **John Regan:** Yeah, Aqua Net and the hissing of the hairspray coming out of a can. Cause we all did it . . . and that's when I had hair to do it with, but that's another story! I remember, I was in John Waite's band, and we were touring, this was probably 1985, John McCurry was his guitar player, big red hair sticking way up. And around the same time, I was doing some work with Billy Idol, and of course you had Steve Stevens with the three-foot pompadour going. So, one day we're in the dressing room, and I'm inhaling all of this Aqua Net, and it's like, you know, someday we're going to be held responsible for depleting the ozone layer. Yeah, if you want to hold anything against hair metal, that could be it right there. It's very timely with the green movement! I think we depleted the ozone layer more than any generation. And simultaneously, I came up with this wonderful invention, 'cause I used to bust their chops about that, you know, the hair being off into the stratosphere? Yeah. I got this invention: I've retooled a cotton candy machine, and instead of sugar, I'm going to have hairspray going around. And all you gotta do is bend over and stick your head in there and stand up. And it'll be exactly how it looks after an hour of teasing.

All right, the hair was big . . . but still, couldn't that focus have shifted to the outfits? Surely an easier target would have been the spandex? Or the billowy pirate blouses? The chainsaw codpiece? The shoulder-padded jackets that looked like they were borrowed from Siegfried & Roy's wardrobe?

Leather always seemed to be cool, from Elvis to the Ramones to Joan Jett, so that always gets a pass . . . and do you really want to tangle with someone wearing studs and chains?

Even taking a potshot at the clothes doesn't sit right with me. Every one of us has sartorial skeletons in our closet, but are we to be forever branded as "turtle neck man" or "parachute pants guy"? Clothes that have accented the crotch and blinded the eyes of passersby are not the exclusive domain of '80s hard rock. Nor is sky-high hair of incredible volume and length, so maybe we should knock it off with the *hair* metal stuff. People grow their hair for reasons that range from rebellious to ridiculous, but follicle length and volume should not a genre define.

> **Todd Kerns:** I suppose we called it "glam metal" at the time. There was a very specific glitter rock, like T. Rex and Bowie, or the Sweet and bands like that — more of that English glam movement in the '70s. And then glam [metal] was sort of the offshoot. So the term hair metal always struck me as . . . a very arbitrary term to place on an entire genre, because it's pretty far-reaching. And you and I both remember, it wasn't like the next day everybody got haircuts. Pearl Jam had long hair. Soundgarden had long hair. Nirvana had long hair . . .

And now, let's deal with the less problematic, but perhaps misaligned (and certainly more involved) second half of this pejorative "hair metal" designation. The *metal*.

Once again, far better men than I have talked at length about the birth and evolution of heavy metal. My friend and esteemed author Martin Popoff tackles the subject in incredibly well-argued detail in a number of his books, most definitely in his *Who Invented Heavy Metal?* And since what I ultimately want to do is wax prophetic about the more "commercial" '80s hard rock bands (let's face it, thrash metal gets a cool-kid pass), I think we can quickly carve a path (or five) to my destination while still picking up on certain sonic traits and musical accoutrements that will shed light on what constitutes "metal" from an '80s commercial hard rock perspective.

From Mr. Big guitarist Paul Gilbert's perspective, the definition of what constitutes heavy metal has shifted through the decades.

Paul Gilbert: Well the term changed over the years . . . in the '70s, Led Zeppelin, Deep Purple, Aerosmith, Van Halen were all considered heavy metal, where now you'd look at Aerosmith and go, "That's hard rock or classic rock." So depending on when you're asking the question, the answer could be different. Because when I was a kid, I thought I was a heavy metal guitar player, but when I look at what I was playing, that stuff I grew up with, some of it would be like the new wave of British heavy metal — Iron Maiden and Judas Priest and Saxon and, of course, Def Leppard. So really I felt like . . . I got as far as Accept, and then I started going back into the old Beach Boys records and getting into the *Pet Sounds* and sort of went back to pop . . . And then Todd Rundgren, '70s pop, because I was interested in a lot of the keyboard parts that had cool chords.

But as far as just metal, in the late '60s there was Hendrix, Black Sabbath, Led Zeppelin; in the '70s there was Deep Purple and Aerosmith, but also stuff like Cheap Trick, which had a heavy guitar sound but obviously influenced by the Beatles or the Who. When you talk about style, obviously when you label something a style, there's always a blurry edge. To me, Iron Maiden is a great example of what I feel like heavy metal is. Judas Priest, Iron Maiden, Scorpions, but they all have their unique thing. The Uli Roth version of Scorpions added a character that was different from the Matthias Jabs Scorpions. Style is confusing; style labels are confusing. You start thinking, "Where does it fit?" It's a little bit helpful, but I think being a teenager is kind of when you [define yourself by] what you're into, it's really important then, so I think when . . . Like, when I'd go visit my grandparents, that's when I would, with utmost confidence say, "I am a heavy metal guitar player." Because I knew my grandparents were not going to understand.

They used to say like, "How's your orchestra doing?" I could tell there is such a gap in generation in culture that they won't understand, so I kind of enjoyed it. I said, "I'm heavy metal," whereas now at any time a category is put on you, it's like, "Wait a minute, there's more to it."

Electric blues — Willie Johnson, Muddy Waters, and Howlin' Wolf — inspires a goosing of the volume in two environs in particular . . . the garages of America (suburban Texas, Southern California, and the Pacific Northwest) and the council estates of England. The Kingsmen birthed a three-chord piece of nonsense called "Louie Louie," and bands like the Sonics take the formula to ever grungier, nastier heights. A natural inclination to boost the juice is born, and so we pump up the volume. American guitar players like Link Wray and Dick Dale find primal release in the lower register of the guitar neck, spewing surf rock twang and greaser rock with cuts like "Pipeline" and "Rumble," devising all manner of sonic defilation, including, in Wray's case, taking a razor blade to his guitar amplifier speaker to produce a crude, early version of the distorted electric guitar sound that would come to define heavy metal (apparently the Kinks' Dave Davies would take a similar approach to maiming his equipment on "You Really Got Me," another slice of proto power chord nirvana). Single note guitar riffs and power chords. That's a good start.

In the U.K., bands like the Kinks, the Who, the Rolling Stones and the Yardbirds apply art school pretension to volume and introduce a more advanced level of electric guitar manipulation, applying the technological advances of guitar amplifier architect Jim Marshall and fuzz guitar effects maven Roger Mayer. Groovy foot-controlled pedal effects like the Sola Sound Tone Bender, the Arbiter Fuzz Face, the Buzz Tone, the Dallas Rangemaster treble booster, and the Maestro Echoplex are all designed to take the early electric guitar innovations of Leo Fender and Les Paul and amplifiers by Marshall, Vox, Laney, and others into an extreme territory that was stirring the souls and ears of a young audience tantalized by the more rocking elements of the Beatles' post-skiffle rock'n'roll. To that point, credit due to Beatles engineer Geoff Emerick for injecting John Lennon's and George Harrison's electric guitar signals directly into a pair of pre-amps usually used for microphones, thus pushing a tube-powered mixing console to its limits on "Revolution." Further acts of guitar rudeness can be found in the Fab Four's catalog on heavy cuts like "Birthday" and "Helter Skelter."

Clearly, Jimi Hendrix created the greatest change in the way the electric guitar was perceived and played. Arriving in the U.K. in 1967 from New York City after being discovered by manager Chas Chandler, Hendrix transformed and transcended the experimentation with volume and sonic manipulation that was happening in England through feats of feedback and whammy bar derring-do. When matched with the ferocity of his playing, the highly sexualized nature of his stage performance, his flamboyant clothing and showmanship, and a deep understanding of the power inherent in the R&B music he had mastered back in the U.S., Hendrix dropped the jaws of every six-string slinger in swinging London. When watching the highly choreographed stage maneuvers of the many bleach-blond, predominantly white '80s hard rock bands, it seems almost cognitively dissonant to recall that so much of that pageantry came about as a result of a Black man playing super-charged black R&B music through a pinned Marshall stack.

Guitar distortion and feedback, once feared by anesthetic studio technicians wearing white lab coats, is turning out to be a very good thing.

As the guitars got louder, darn it if drummers like Ginger Baker and Keith Moon didn't take notice and start stepping up the power on their kits . . . Baker took a cue from Louie Belson and added a second bass drum to the equation. Baker put his jazz chops and notoriously fiery temper and attitude to good use, cutting through the thick "woman tone" emanating from Eric Clapton's dimed Marshall amps and various Gibson guitars in the heavily improvised power rock of Cream.

The Who's Moon found a way to make himself heard between the thundering din of bassist John Entwistle and the windmilled power chords of Pete Townshend (a man who stared down the virtuosity of contemporaries like Hendrix, Jeff Beck, and Clapton with a rich harmonic chordal vocabulary delivered with ear-splitting volume) via his frenetic forays around his multi-piece kit, and near psychotic performance compulsion to destroy (both onstage and off).

A case can certainly be made for Jeff Beck being one of hard rock's great sonic innovators, perhaps even creator of the hard rock template itself . . . the eastern tinged, effect laden, and volume drenched explorations in Yardbirds' cuts like "Heart Full of Soul" and "Shapes of Things" ultimately led to Beck's groundbreaking *Truth* album with his own Jeff Beck Group, where he and producer Jimmy Page kick up some epic dust on "Beck's Bolero," alongside future Led Zeppelin bassist John Paul Jones and Faces keyboardist Nicky Hopkins. Where Zeppelin's 1969 debut often gets the credit for creating hard rock as we know it, it's hard not to notice that Beck brought the idea of high-volume blues extrapolations, power guitars, a pounding rhythm section, and blues-drenched vocal gymnastics (courtesy of the gloriously mulleted Rod Stewart) to market first.

It's hard to fathom just how fast the changes and evolutions were happening, hard rock and heavy metal being created in real time, with *Led Zeppelin I*, Black Sabbath's debut, and Deep Purple's *In Rock* album happening within mere months of each other, each one bringing new elements that remain in the heavy rock lexicon to this day: Sabbath's down-tuned, gloom-and-doom power chords, Ozzy Osbourne's plaintive wails, and Geezer Butler's schlock horror–meets–hippie worldview satanic lyrics; Zeppelin's incorporation of rhythmic bombast and acoustic and electric guitar textures; and Purple's combination of speed, screech, and classically influenced virtuosity. If we were to trace hard rock or metal's roots based on pure *intention*, *In Rock* may be the first true heavy metal record. After various lineups and varying successes that reflected a diverse stylistic outlook (everything from au courant psychedelia to a full-blown rock concerto with London's Royal Philharmonic Orchestra), guitarist and band leader Ritchie Blackmore took hold of the reins and drove the band into louder and faster terrains. In harnessing the band's inherent virtuosity — Ian Gillan's vocal range, Jon Lord's Bach-inspired harmonic knowledge and classical organ prowess, Ian Paice's lightning-fast way around a kit — and his own highly articulate guitar picking and slurring facility, Blackmore brought together the most crucial elements of great heavy metal: impressive chops, volume, and the threat of violence. Onstage, Blackmore took

Hendrix's more spiritual form of guitar sacrifice to a much darker, literal place. Where it seemed that Hendrix smashed and burned his guitars as an offering to the gods of love and music, Blackmore destroyed his instruments and blew up his amplifiers in a way that mirrored the earlier efforts of Pete Townshend. This wasn't love, this was anger, laced with spite and even hate. It was ominous stuff. And pretty damn exciting. Yngwie Malmsteen, the Swedish virtuoso who would go on to blatantly lift so much of Blackmore's stage mannerisms (and prove to be an incredible mimic of his classic licks, when he wasn't spinning his own innovative classically influenced guitar lines) would sum it up best in a chat with *Guitar Player* magazine.

> **Yngwie Malmsteen:** [*In Rock*] is the one where they go full out the most. Everybody talks about Led Zeppelin and Black Sabbath, and I love those bands too. But *In Rock* is heavier and more metal than any of the other guys. It was just "Turn everything up and play as fast and as loud and as much as you can!" (*Guitar Player*, Vol. 55 No. 2, Richard Bienstock)

> **Rudy Sarzo:** Deep Purple . . . I see it as that balance between Blackmore and Lord. Blackmore being very classically inclined, but also very bluesy at the same time. I think that was a beautiful balance between those two.

From here, I think we can make a case that the early '70s is where divergent musical paths can be taken that lead to the main subject matter of this book. Yes, there are two paths you can go down (well, more like five, depending how thin you wanna slice the ham), but in the long run . . . either just might get you to the '80s hard rock scene I really want to talk about in this book.

One path leads to something that we can view as classic hard rock. You've got your Free, your Bad Company, your Aerosmith. Bands of this ilk keep the swinging drums and vocal phrasing of R&B, add in crunchy guitars that are overdriven but warm, and incorporate a fairly wide dynamic range . . . the quiet makes the loud parts seem more powerful, and vice versa. The song structures on this path are for the most part quite succinct in nature. The keyboard elements, when present, are organic and incorporate piano, Fender Rhodes, and Hammond organ. Thin Lizzy, Bachman–Turner Overdrive, and Wishbone Ash come to mind. AC/DC could be considered a more feral, streamlined travel companion on this path with their dry-as-a-bone guitar tones, leering back-door-man vocal attitude, and Phil Rudd's magical hi-hat cymbal tempering the rock with some swing. Oddly enough, a band like England's UFO could also be here, even though there is little blues content in vocalist Phil Mogg's powerful vocals melodies. The same could be said about guitarist Michael Schenker. He takes traditional rock guitar lines and imbues them with shades of classical music, but it rarely comes across as bluesy or gothic . . . it comes across as very "commercial hard rock," highly melodic in the vocals and rhythm guitar hook department, but not to be confused with "corporate rock" . . . Still with me?

Both AC/DC and UFO can also travel down (albeit as outliers, and really only in their collective late-'70s-and-beyond incarnations) a second path, which I would call your prototypical heavy metal path.

The path that would lead to heavy metal is more streamlined, dramatic, and focused. It doesn't *groove* so much as it *drives*. The rhythms are straight eighth notes (or sometimes equestrian gallops à la Iron Maiden) and incessant in nature, tempos ranging from grindingly slow to freight train fast. The vocals are more theatrical and vibrato laced, melodies more minor key (as a generalization) and gothic in nature, the guitars pushed into a more saturated overdrive and showcasing a little more classical flare and Sturm und Drang alongside the overhyped Chuck Berry licks. This is where we find Scorpions and Judas Priest, two bands that moved very quickly from early psychedelic meanderings into something more concise and cutting. While some might place Black Sabbath on this path (citing a track like "Paranoid"), the jazz influence and swing in Bill Ward's feel and rhythmic patterns set them apart as an anomaly. Sabbath are the defining *mood* of heavy metal, and Tony Iommi's sound surely is the influence for the darkest acts of the genre, but they really are a case unto themselves, far too diverse to be categorized . . . until we get to 1980 and the entrance of one Ronnie James Dio. (More to come on this.) The removal of the swing and R&B elements that are in other forms of rock'n'roll really define heavy metal as a rock'n'roll derivative that is also a legitimate genre unto itself. The heavy metal path ultimately leads us to the new wave of British heavy metal, power metal, thrash metal, death metal, and the myriad metallic subgenres that exist today. It also leads us to '80s hard rock.

A third path leads to so-called corporate rock. Here, the overdriven guitars retain their woolly saturation, but are tamed, the edges rounded with a focus on radio-friendly midrange clarity. The drums are massaged and compressed, still providing energy but not competing for the space with this path's most important feature . . . the melodic vocal line. Keyboards birthed from progressive rock innovation are often incorporated to further frame lush lead and harmony vocal lines. It rocks, but not so dreadfully hard that it can upset the balance of a workday or a Sunday drive. Bands like Journey and Styx start off as adapters of the progressive rock sounds of bands like Yes, Mahavishnu Orchestra, Genesis, and Emerson, Lake & Palmer, but eventually find their stride when the song forms are truncated and the melodic ideas centered around big sing-along choruses. Vocal harmonies come right out of the '60s California playbook, but are recorded with multiple overdubs to provide a rich sonic "glue" that would often function in the same way as a synthesizer pad. There were bands that would deviate off this path into the woods to create power pop, which is a more polished take on '60s garage and U.K. rock, with more concision, attention to melody, and a less fuzzy but very punchy guitar sound. Think Cheap Trick, Big Star, the Raspberries . . . in many ways they resemble hard rock bands, they just seem a little weird.

Foreigner comes along as a result of journeyman guitarist and songwriter Mick Jones's experience with Johnny Hallyday (the man who brought rock'n'roll to France) and '60s U.K. boogie rockers Spooky Tooth. Through application of those early British hard rock guitar tones and the pop sensibilities that were honed as a producer and touring musician in the pop world, Jones created a sound that become the standard for FM radio play–seeking rockers. In Rochester, New York, native Lou Gramm, Jones found a singer who could bring the soul and power of the best English rock singers, and whose vocal timbre would blend perfectly with the crunch of a Les Paul. It was a sound that would resonate through to the early '90s.

One of the greatest influences on commercial hard rock of the 1980s came from Boston's debut album. It's ironic that the album is both heralded and cursed as corporate rock's first, since the only thing corporate about its creation is the fact that leader and founder Tom Scholz worked for Polaroid as a product design engineer. Boston was created in Scholz's basement independently, completely free from any record company influence. But in that basement, through a combination of Scholz's engineering wizardry (he would go on to create numerous music products that would hit the market with great reception after Boston's massive commercial success) and his single-mindedness of vision, Scholz created a classic hard rock masterpiece. The sound of Scholz's richly saturated, harmonically complex guitar tones and Deep Purple–influenced organ sounds worked magic in combination with chiming acoustic guitars and intricate arrangements that seemed effortless but were actually the result of laborious intent. This layered, intensely scrutinized approach would later be adopted on many albums of the 1980s, most famously by Def Leppard as they worked on their star-crossed opus *Hysteria*. The Leps also famously used one of Tom Scholz's inventions, the Rockman, to record their guitars in a very direct and clean (some say sterile, some say shimmering) manner.

Noting some similarities between Boston and one of Canada's greatest and most successful hard rock exports, I asked Triumph's Rik Emmett if Boston's production and composition approach had influenced his band's.

> **Rik Emmett:** How could it not? Yes, for sure it did. Partly, it was because it made such a huge impact at FM radio and we were an FM/AOR kind of kind of act. That's where we hung our hat, you know? And Tom Scholz had built his own model . . . right from the ground up . . . I mean, I actually don't know if you know this, but I got invited to be a member of Boston after I'd left Triumph. And mistakenly I thought that Tom was flying me down because he was looking for a writing partner and a guy to join the band, and so I went and I spent an afternoon with Tom in his basement studio and was singing overdubs on stuff and . . . Now, I can't remember exactly which record it was. I think they'd already

done a follow-up record to . . . Maybe there were two in the main era? But Brad had already left the band, and my friend Mike Shotton ended up being a vocalist on some of the material on that record. Anyways, I went down there and it was great, and we went out for dinner and [were] hanging out and telling stories and . . . I was thinking, "Oh, I'm going to get to write songs with Tom Scholz, this will be so cool." And I got a call a couple of days later from Tom's lawyer, and he said, "Congratulations, Rik, you got the gig."

And I went, "Oh, the gig." And he goes, "Yeah, he's going out for a summer tour and he's looking for a singer to front the band that can play some guitar." And I went, "I thought he was looking for somebody, you know, to sort of be in the band." And he goes, "Oh, no, he's not. He's not." He said, "But you know, why don't you take this job, you know, go out on the summer tour as a sideman who sings the lead vocals?" And I went, "Yeah, you know what? Thanks but no thanks." I know what it's like to be in a band where I'm not really running the show. I go, "It's not in the cards."

As with Jones in Foreigner, Scholz fortuitously found his vocal foil in the angelic, stratospheric vocals of Brad Delp. To think that the universe conspires to work in such ways as to bring these powerful forces of human endeavor together transcends serendipity. For every Eddie, a Roth . . . for every Slash, an Axl . . . for every Page, a Plant.

We are looking at a period of music lambasted for sins of visual excess, yet also often heralded for the "guilty pleasures" of its highly infectious songwriting, and this points to the fourth path, glam rock: that silly, beautiful, pop-perfect confection that was born of '50s rock'n'roll, dressed up like a star-dusted, gender-bending, high-heeled superhero, and baptized with updated '60s guitar power chords, sugar-sweet melodies, and goofy lyrics that brought color to lives of a very gray '70s England, and hope to sexually disenfranchised teenagers and aspiring rock stars all over. Bowie's Ziggy Stardust, Elton John, the Sweet, Queen (who transcend any path they choose to travel down, a path so gloriously rich in tone, power, delivery, and variation they need their own chapter), T. Rex, Slade, and multiple one hit wonders ruled the mid-'70s British charts and ultimately helped carve a hopeful path for aspiring musicians who were daunted by the task of having to learn Yes and Genesis licks in order to be in their own band. Which leads us to path number five: punk rock.

Steve Jones's guitar sound on *Never Mind the Bollocks* alone crops up all over '80s hard rock — more so in the latter half of the decade — thanks to one massive debut offering in particular, as explained by former Guns N' Roses manager Alan Niven.

> **Alan Niven:** One of the things that made me smile was when *Appetite For Destruction* took off, it dragged one record behind it . . . *Never Mind the Bollocks* had just gone gold over its entire history [and] when *Appetite for Destruction* came out, it went platinum.

There is also the reverential treatment given to the more hardcore punk rock scene by nascent thrashers of the early '80s. The punk and metal paths definitely meet at a fork in the road somewhere. If punk's political, anarchist, and antisocial sentiments ever exerted influence, it was in the thrash world, where the influence of hardcore bands could be heard in the Bay Area and Southern California scene that spawned bands like Metallica, Exodus, and Slayer (Anthrax and Overkill on the *Noo Yawk* side). Speaking of the Big Apple, the New York Dolls could travel both the glam and punk paths, but they ultimately have more in common with a punk aesthetic in terms of intention, attitude, and delivery, a little more dangerous than their crossdressing English brothers and twisted sisters. The acts of the '80s that combined elements of a punk more in line with the Dolls, the Sex Pistols, and the Dead Boys with more commercial hard rock and glam rock leanings include Mötley Crüe, Hanoi Rocks, Guns N' Roses, Faster Pussycat, and Poison.

If we have to go down all these paths and jump off at the odd roundabout to get to the fact that this so-called hair metal stuff is actually rock'n'roll music, then so be it. It leads to an interesting question: is heavy metal actually rock'n'roll? It certainly comes from rock'n'roll, but any self-respecting rivethead is going to put the heavy metal designation front and center on the music they love. And fair enough . . . I get it. As I acknowledged in my first book, *Metal on Ice*, I identified as a heavy metal fan as a teenager. If a band had leather jackets, long hair, loud guitars, screaming vocals, and a double-bass drum set, they were "metal" to me . . . even if they also had *keyboards*. It was less of a musical designation so much as it was a social designation.

However, the deeper I look and listen to this music that has accompanied my journey in this life, the more I keep coming back to one thought: maybe there really is no such thing as hair metal.

My friend and esteemed rock journalist and podcast host Mitch Lafon disagrees.

> **Mitch Lafon:** The term hair metal — which the British, by the way, used to call poodle rock . . . a great term — yeah, those bands were represented by their hair being teased up and put up, the same as in the '70s when we called it glam rock . . . And why do we call it glam? . . . They had the makeup and they had the costumes, and it looked glamorous and glammy, but we called it glam rock and you never hear anybody complain about it . . . that's cool. Great. And so hair metal is the same thing, it was the visual aspect. If you look at Cinderella, you look at Bon Jovi, look at all these bands . . . Their hair was teased and cropped, crimped and sprayed to the umpteenth level . . . so hair metal is an adjective to me . . . it's just an adjective.

A good point. And let's face it . . . we all usually come to some pretty similar visualizations in terms of bands when we hear the term. But I'm still not willing to recognize hair metal as a proper genre . . . or even a sub-genre. Maybe we should just tear a page out of L.A. band Great White's lyric book . . . let's call it rock'n'roll.

CHAPTER 2
VISIBLE ROOTS

A rock'n'roll band's sound is obviously a combination of the personal musical influences of the collective. Sometimes, influences are evident and shared in an across-the-board way by all the members of certain acts. For example, the even higher gloss and simpler version of Kiss that was (and still is) Pretty Boy Floyd certainly feels like an agreed-upon ideal, a conscious decision to be the ultimate iteration of what a "Sunset Strip" band would have looked like in the late '80s.

Influences can also reveal themselves in a more subtle, cumulative way. When I see and hear Tracii Guns play guitar, I recognize an artist who channels Johnny Thunders as much as he does Randy Rhoads. His partner in the classic L.A. Guns era, Mick Cripps, plays in a low-slung rhythm guitar style more closely associated with Keith Richards, light on technical virtuosity but heavy on style and swing. In Warren DeMartini, the pervasive influence of Eddie Van Halen's tone and phrasing is mixed with the legato sensibilities of the Scorpion's Uli Jon Roth, and, when coupled with his guitar partner Robbin Crosby's more traditional '70s rock rhythm/lead approach, *Ratt & Roll* is achieved. Fortunately, Nikki Sixx's take on Sid Vicious's "self-destruction as performance art" was also blended with Glen Matlock's ability to construct an anthem, and the ability to actually play the bass.

And then there is Guns N' Roses. Axl Rose's wide knowledge of music allowed him to access Nazareth, Motörhead, and Elton John, and blend it with Duff McKagan's Seattle punk roots, Slash's combustible combo of Michael Schenker chops and Joe Perry slop, Izzy Stradlin's Hanoi Rocks gutter glamour and Keith Richards and Neil Young–approved rhythm guitar stabs, and Steven Adler's "Peter Criss at the Disco" drumming in a heavy metal melting pot that would be the last band of colossal impact in '80s hard rock.

> **Alan Niven:** As far as I'm concerned, it was Izzy's band — I have always said that — and without Izzy, it's not GNR. And the thing about Izzy for me was . . . of all the people I met and knew in my life, he personified rock'n'roll for me, because he had that great right-handed syncopation in his playing. His lyrics had an unimpeachable street vernacular. You knew he had lived the life, and he knew what he was talking about, and he was picture perfect, totally cool all the time, until he had a really bad run with coke at one point and just went down that rabbit hole really drastically, to a point that really scared me. Once he got out of that, he was back to being Izzy. And I think with Izzy, he basically just decided he didn't want to deal with the fame. He didn't want to deal with the pressure. He wanted to get away from that, and that's what he did.
>
> But Izzy actually personified a rock'n'roller to me . . . I have very little that I keep in terms of memorabilia. I don't have a single platinum or gold record — and I used to have literally hundreds of them — gave them all away . . . But I have a photograph in my living room of Izzy and Keith and Ronnie. Three pieces of the same block. All three of them are cut from the same stone.

A serious dive into influence is daunting because the pool is so deep . . . in the '80s, we were already looking at upwards of 30 years of prior rock'n'roll history, thousands of recording acts who had previously vied for the attention of this next generation. The reward, however, is worth the reflection because it provides a new context in which we can begin to feel and hear the humanity within the individual artist and the group as a collective. When we, as active listeners and fans, think of how music has affected us throughout the course of our lives, how it has marked change, growth, love, pain, and joy, we can make a deeper connection to the shared (or different) experiences of the artists we listen to. But even if a connection is made on a human level, does that speak to quality of art? Do we see the greatness, or does it just make the artistic flaws more glaring? Does the artist end up seeming like a pale comparison to the influence? Deep pool, deep thoughts.

I asked some of the players who were making music in the '80s, but were also there in the trenches in the '60s and '70s, how the influence of previous eras differed from the music they were making in the '80s in terms of content and presentations.

John Regan: The '60s to me was the ultimate generation of experimentation and being given freedom by the record companies. And this also goes into the '70s. Obviously . . . my line of delineation is the Beatles on *The Ed Sullivan Show*. That's when it all just took off. But it was fresh, new, experimental, and the labels in the '60s and '70s were owned, a lot of them, by single entities with *vision*. So, if you take Atlantic Records, that was Ahmet and Nesuhi Ertegun, going against the grain and putting race music out, they were real pioneers in that. But they had a vision, a commitment that they stuck with. Same with Berry Gordy [at] Motown. He had a vision. A&M, with Herb Alpert and Jerry Moss.

All of those labels were run by sincere music lovers, and . . . they would give an artist the ability to blossom. I remember being on the A&M lot recording the first album I did with Peter Frampton in 1980 and seeing these big posters of this guy Bryan Adams. "Who's Bryan Adams?" Well, if you look back on his career . . . and the same with Frampton. When he left Humble Pie, he did two or three studio albums that really didn't do anything commercially, but the labels, those people, believed in him. They let his art develop, and they took it and it exploded, and the same for Bryan Adams. I don't think Bryan right out of the gate was as big as he became eventually.

But therein lies the difference. When you started getting into the '80s and you had some of these labels being sold off to the corporations, then the music just became, "Okay, this band is hot right now. Go out and get me 10 more of them." . . . You weren't encouraged to be unique, musically. And visually, too, you know, that that's when MTV took over, right? . . . There used to be a thing called artist development. You saw something in [a] person that was nurtured along and was able to become what now we listen to as timeless music. Once we started getting into that corporate thing. There's a lot of music, especially when you get into the '90s, which is disposable, you know? And that's why a lot of the bands from the '70s and '80s, once they're done — and we're quickly reaching that point, you know — once the Stones are done, once Aersomith is done and . . . you move it into the bands from the '80s, once they're done touring there's nothing to take its place.

Rudy Sarzo is a world-renowned bassist who has toured and recorded with some of the biggest names in hard rock, including Ozzy Osbourne, Quiet Riot, Whitesnake, and Dio.

Rudy Sarzo: To talk about any generation of music, I have to go back to the very beginning of it . . . I'm 71 years old, so I was born before rock'n'roll — the coined term of rock'n'roll — existed. I heard rock'n'roll for the first time when rock'n'roll was *played* for the first time, you know? And it was always cultural. There were cultural shifts around the world, especially in the United States, which is the birthplace of rock'n'roll, and then it emanated to the rest of the free world because there were parts of the world that were not allowed to even play that type of music on the radio . . . So it only impacted really heavily the free world.

I'm so glad that the new Beatles documentary, *Get Back*, put in focus what was actually happening in the room, because nobody does it like that anymore. The Beatles were such an anomaly that it was not an accident, it had to eventually happen. Just like Picasso had to happen, John Coltrane had to happen, Miles Davis had to happen, Mozart had to happen. It had to happen eventually; it was going to happen . . . This is music for the masses, and it really reflected on fashion, society, consciousness, a collective consciousness that emanated from four individuals.

Music is like that, and by the time that we got through the '80s, I think the best and the worst thing that happened was MTV. Now it wasn't really about the music, it was all about the look, the image. It wasn't about the content of the cereal, it was what the cereal box looked like.

And I profited from it; I am still . . . People know who I am because of it, but as far as it being a peak, a creative peak, in the music industry, especially for rock'n'roll, it was not. For example, let's [consider] bands that were successful both in the '70s and [when] they got reinvented thanks to [A&R executive] John Kalodner in the '80s [like] Whitesnake . . . You listen to the Whitesnake records from the '70s, it was more the purity, the essence of what the spirit of Whitesnake was, which was a continuation of Deep Purple. The first version of Whitesnake had three Deep Purple members: David Coverdale, Jon Lord, and Ian Paice. So, you can't get away from yourself, so they still brought in Deep Purple with them, right? And it was very blues-based, very gritty, you know?

By the '80s, the record company and management and David wanted to experience success, because it came down that there was no middle ground in the '80s. You either failed or you were huge . . . you were either an MTV success or a failure, and if you want to stay in the business, you want to be a success [there]. So you put in all the ingredients to make a successful formula for the MTV generation. Was it a better version of the original intent of the band? No. But then again, you could not sell '70s Whitesnake in an '80s era . . . You couldn't.

I maintain that '80s rock is rich with examples of exciting and colorful takes on the music that came before, and the results are diverse and more than worthy of noted inclusion in the tapestry of rock'n'roll's history. But maybe this image thing makes for a more problematic argument than I'd care to admit this early in the story.

In order to place the artists I discuss in a broader rock'n'roll context, we should examine the genetic musical and visual building blocks that brought them into existence. It's a bit of a complicated affair in that, to prove my point, we have to look at some rock'n'roll that faced a fair share of criticism too (pick up an old copy of Creem magazine . . . catch Lester Bangs on a bad, or good, day and an artist could be eviscerated!). But honestly, going on the defensive is not a strategy I'm all that interested in employing. It feels like a waste of printed page to defend the honor of these giants upon whose broad shoulders '80s rockers stand.

So, let's instead make a disclaimer that must be heeded if anyone is really going to buy into anything I say moving forward: You have to rock *at least* this hard to ride.

I suppose that I am asking readers to buy into a recognized gravitas of a few influential musical touchstones and their place of importance in rock'n'roll history, and to acknowledge that these are bands of artistic consequence that have touched almost every facet of the overarching landscape of hard rock of the '80s. If I can sell you on the premise that the influence of acts of quality is instilled in the art of '80s rock, it may be easier to hear and see these *influenced* bands as belonging to a greater rock'n'roll lineage rather than as some ghastly aberration or as "rock gone bad."

As we wander (or strut, or stagger) into specific eras and albums throughout the course of the book, we will see many other examples of rock'n'roll subgenres and artists from the '50s, '60s, and '70s who provided inspiration, but the bands mentioned in more detail in this chapter, to my mind, are the (skull and cross) bones that make up the skeleton of '80s rock'n'roll.

LED ZEPPELIN

Led Zeppelin's recorded output is the industry standard of light and shade in rock'n'roll. It would do their legacy injustice to define a band who so deftly combined elements of blues, world music, folk, and American rock'n'roll as being inclined to lean heavily toward any one musical style. But for the purposes of explaining Zeppelin's influence on the hard rock of the '80s, we have to view them as prototypical hard rock in a number of regards.

First of all, let's look at band lineup and appearance. In Robert Plant, we have a classical model of the lion-maned, golden throated, well-hung (if those close-ups in 1973's *Song Remains the Same* film are to be believed) lead singer. Then there's Jimmy Page, the brooding virtuosic visionary, Les Paul guitar slung low, ambitions held high, a black-magic-dabbling record producer and British studio session veteran who painted in broad strokes of sonic color all while sampling the dark delights of the occult, the needle, and all manner of sexual dalliance and deviance. In John Bonham we discover the prototypical wild man drummer, stocky and powerful, with a reputation for alcoholic excess, heaviness of stick and thunder of foot that at times overshadow the man's dynamic and highly musical approach to the traps. And, finally, there's bassist and keyboardist John Paul Jones: the quiet, reserved journeyman session player, composer, and orchestrator, creating the rich soundscapes that oft go unheralded in Led Zeppelin's panoramic music.

Musically, Zeppelin's orchestrated guitar approach weaves in and out of the '80s rock narrative from the heaviest metal to the most delicate of power ballad picking. And while sometimes the deftness of touch and subtlety of application that Zeppelin employed in the exploitation of Jimmy Page's big, heavy, distorted, blues-based guitar riffs was forsaken, these things were typically used to powerful and musical effect. The same case can be made for Plant's wailing upper-tenor vocal histrionics. It's a fine line between coming off like a Norse god or a hoarse dog. John Bonham's "recorded in an English Manor" reverb-enhanced power grooves have long been a source of inspiration for the sonically adventurous recording engineer, and John Paul Jones's brilliant arrangements for keyboards, and even orchestra, were often referenced (if at times refined to their most rudimentary elements) in the power ballad phenomena of the '80s. Let's face it, "Stairway to Heaven" is the ultimate power ballad (although Aerosmith might have something to say about that!).

Key Albums: *Led Zeppelin II, Led Zeppelin IV, Physical Graffiti*

ALICE COOPER

Like all of the best American rock'n'roll, Alice Cooper found their initial inspiration across the pond in jolly old England. It is universally acknowledged that the Beatles changed the world by bringing the self-contained, self-composing, guitars-bass-drum long-haired rock'n'roll ensemble into the hearts, loins, and collective consciousness of energy-starved American youth. The Beatles, along with the more expansive and electrically charged music of the next generation of British bands, would prove to be a massive influence on a young Vincent Furnier, Glen Buxton, Dennis Dunaway, Michael Bruce, and Neal Smith as they gathered in all-American style to wow sock hops and youth groups in Phoenix, Arizona (initially calling themselves the Spiders). The Rolling Stones, the Who, the Kinks, and the Yardbirds were all writ large over the sounds emanating from the young collective who would ultimately take the regional success of early singles recorded for local independent label Mascot Records as a sign that they were destined for bigger things. Renaming themselves the Nazz, Vincent and friends relocated to Los Angeles after previous road trips had suggested that the City of Angels offered myriad opportunities for a young band. This spirit of adventure would be mirrored in the hundreds (thousands?) of musicians in the '80s who would leave the

Mechanicsburgs and Rochesters of America in search of rock'n'roll glory under the Hollywood sign.

When it was discovered that Todd Rundgren (who would go on to produce the first New York Dolls record) already had a band called the Nazz, the band ultimately came upon the name Alice Cooper (but not from supernatural intervention via a Ouija board, a widely suspected and disseminated idea of the time). Adopting extreme showmanship and avant-garde musical practices (both Furnier and Dunaway were fans of artists like Salvador Dalí), the band was becoming infamous for driving audiences away from venues with their sensory barrage of psycho theater. This impressed Frank Zappa enough to sign them to his Straight Records label and release three albums of experimental post-psychedelic music that failed to make much of a dent. Perhaps the biggest developmental occurrence came with the influence of Zappa's all-female recording act ingenues the GTOs, who inspired the group to experiment with makeup and women's clothing onstage . . . a huge influence on the look of the '80s. Furnier would go on to adopt the Alice Cooper band name as his own, foreshadowing an ambitious future solo career move.

Ironically, it would be the Alice Cooper group's failures in Los Angeles that led to the discovery of the sound that would inspire (directly or indirectly) so many '80s rockers to make their own exodus to Hollywood. Relocating to Detroit, and inspired by the politically driven power chord savagery of the MC5 and the primal performance art by way of self-inflicted violence that was Iggy Pop and the Stooges, Alice Cooper shed some of its more meandering musical explorations for something leaner and meaner. This was brought into even sharper focus when a young Bob Ezrin took charge of the musical direction and production of the band, picking the most anthemic moments of their compositions in order to create a vehicle that could deliver the shock and awe of an Alice Cooper live performance in a digestible hit song format. Of course, Bob would go on to do the same with Kiss's *Destroyer* album, exploiting their individual personae with custom songs designed to seduce middle America.

Cooper classics like "I'm Eighteen," "Is It My Body," "School's Out," "No More Mr. Nice Guy," "Be My Lover," and "Billion Dollar Babies" would combine intertwining rock guitars and a Bernstein-esque sense of orchestration with themes that ranged from the manly to the macabre, all delivered in a half speaking–half singing character-soaked voice by a man with a woman's name. Wearing makeup. With a snake around his neck. Shock and awesome.

Key Albums: *Love It to Death, Killer, School's Out, Billion Dollar Babies*

NEW YORK DOLLS

It could be argued that the influence of the New York Dolls on '80s hard rock bands has more to do with the attitude, image, and theater than anything musical, although we do hear the musical influence play out in bands like Faster Pussycat, Sea Hags, L.A. Guns, Vain, and even Poison in the latter half of the '80s. The Dolls had more in common with the Shangri-Las, Chuck Berry, or the Rolling Stones than they did the tight, succinct, and more overdriven hard rock that bands like Kiss would ultimately create in their wake. In fact, Gene Simmons and Paul Stanley have stated that if Kiss could expand upon what they considered to be the Dolls' very rudimentary musical skill set, while incorporating aspects of their wild image (a combination of glamorous androgyny, stack heels, and avant-garde New York street fashion), their new musical endeavor could take on the world.

In a VH1 interview with Benjamin Smith, dated September 19, 2013, Paul Stanley said, "When Gene and I saw the Dolls you just looked at them and said, 'These guys kill us at looking androgynous.'" Compared to them, he said, Kiss resembled football players. "We went, 'We can't beat the Dolls at being the Dolls, but we sure as hell play better than them. Now let's find out who we are.'"

From the full-lipped "pout and circumstance" baritone of the beautifully grotesque and Jagger-esque David Johansen, the swing and swagger of drummer Billy Murcia — whose baton(s), after his death, would be passed to the equally swinging Jerry Nolan in time for the band's Todd Rundgren–produced debut — to the statuesque superimposition of a Times Square transvestite on an All-American frame that was Arthur "Killer" Kane (a template for both Nikki Sixx and Blackie Lawless of W.A.S.P., himself a very temporary member of the band), the Dolls are the perfect accompanying visual component to rock'n'roll danger.

The band's defining sonic element lies in the primitive interpretation of the Rolling Stones' "art of basket weaving" six string interplay that occurred between Sylvain Sylvain and the tragically gifted lead guitar junkie take on Chuck Berry that was Johnny Thunders. Perhaps more than any other figure in rock'n'roll, Thunders has led some young musicians down a thorny path that drew blood while inspiring magic. The dark romance of this (sometimes not so) elegantly wasted minstrel is forever entwined in the fabric of '80s rock, and arguments can and have been made that this excess and abuse cannot be disassociated with the actual art. But even his co-guitarist Sylvain Sylvain has countered this notion, saying that the band was at its most pure and beautiful before heroin entered the picture, as told to Ian Fortnam for publication in the December 2020 issue of *Classic Rock*.

"At the dawn of the Dolls, Thunders had been a sweet, 18-year-old kid, high on nothing but rock'n'roll and youthful exuberance (witness their court photographer Bob Gruen's excellent *All Dolled Up* movie for the evidence). But shortly before the band's infamous 73 European tour that set Thunders' infamy in stone, he'd discovered heroin.

"'He turned into a fucking monster,' Sylvain admits. '[Heroin] made him aggressive for no reason because everything is boring until you've had a fucking fix. It rules everything and ruins everything.'"

While the performances leading up to Thunder's passing in 1986 would prove to be chaotic, musically disjointed affairs, there were nights when he transcended the limitations of his self-imposed chemical circumstances and shone as bright as any rock'n'roll guitar player before or since. With his rat nest of hair sitting high upon his emaciated, yet beautifully chiselled features, and an arsenal of classic '50s–inspired rock'n'roll guitar maneuvers, Johnny Thunders was the very definition of the rock'n'roll lead guitarist aesthete.

Key Albums: *New York Dolls, Too Much Too Soon*

KISS

When Gene Klein and Paul Stanley Eisen decided to shed the unfocused but promising post-'60s rock of their band Wicked Lester (despite having secured a much-coveted major label recording contract), they committed to losing that band's excessive experimentation and instead brought into laser focus the hard rock influences of bands like Slade and Humble Pie, combining a more raucous riff-based sound with the outrageous visual appeal of bands like Alice Cooper and the New York Dolls.

The Dolls and Cooper were already making waves and major label recordings, and in the case of Alice, already reaping the rewards of combining powerful hook-filled, slash-and-burn, guitar-based rock'n'roll with an image that bordered on the grotesque. In fact, upon attending a Cooper show at Madison Square Garden, Gene and Paul came up with the idea of creating a group with four Alice Coopers (at this point, AC was still a band, but their frontman Vincent Furnier had adopted the group name as his own . . . a move that would prove poignant when he left the group and seamlessly transitioned into a successful solo career). With the courage of conviction that comes with a shared vision, Eisen and Klein cast their nets via a want ad in the *Village Voice* seeking a drummer and dazzling lead-guitar player. Ultimately, they found their final puzzle pieces in Peter Criscuola, a desperate and aging drummer who had tasted minimal success and was looking for one more shot at pursuing his dreams of fame and fortune, and a perpetually stoned lead guitarist named Paul Frehley. Frehley channeled his artistic and inventive inclinations through an infectious blend of Jeff Beck and Jimmy Page–inspired repetitive guitar licks, and mismatched sneakers.

Self-reinvention is a big part of many music industry stories, and through a commitment to black leather, Kabuki paint, and an assumption of new individual personae that encompassed the demonic (Gene Simmons), the extraterrestrial ("Space" Ace Frehley, Paul "Starchild" Stanley), and, yes, even the bestial (Peter "The Catman" Criss), Kiss put a superhero spin on the already established concept of the rock god. The fuel for this fire lay in four individual motivations: Israeli immigrant Simmons's personal "comic book superhero–cum–Walt Disney as American Dream" aspirations; Stanley's desire to overcome the physical and emotional challenges of microtia, a condition where the ear is not formed properly, and become a desired sex symbol; the desperation of an aging Criss to "make it" as rock'n'roll star; and Frehley's desire for interstellar explorations, be they sonic, visual (he designed the iconic Kiss logo), or chemical. All of this would have been impossible to achieve without the element that critics rarely acknowledge, but the kids always knew. Kiss wrote great songs and played with inspired personality. In mixing the New York Dolls' '60s girl group–inspired androgyny with Alice Coopers' horror-show aesthetic, riffs and melodies inspired by Slade and the Raspberries, and Simmons's superhero–meets–American Dream aspirations (a concept that would go on to sell a million lunch boxes), the Kiss legend was born.

Much has been written about how Kiss rose to ascendancy through the aid of visionaries like manager Bill Aucoin and Casablanca Records owner Neil Bogart, defying critics and imminent bankruptcy through unflagging belief, abused credit card limits, and unparalleled work ethic. And while the first three Kiss releases suffered from less-than-optimal production value, the songs themselves translated through the band's thunderous performances as Kiss brought their anthemic take on English glam–inspired hard rock to the American heartland, first by blowing headliners off the stage as an uncompromising opening act, and ultimately as headliners in small to mid-size arenas, buildings large enough to take the bombast of Kiss's pyrotechnic-laced live experience. When it was finally decided that their albums were failing to reproduce the power of their live show, the go-for-broke decision to put out a live album turned out to be the band's "hallelujah" moment. When *Alive!* was released, it would prove to be inspirational ground zero for countless future rock stars to bug their parents for electric guitars. In doing so, they would pollute the solitude of suburban neighborhoods across America with nascent explorations of the riffs, beats, stage banter, and choreography that would populate rock magazines, MTV and radio airwaves, and record store shelves for years to come.

With anthems like "Strutter," "Deuce," "Rock And Roll All Nite," "C'mon and Love Me," "Detroit Rock City," "Shout It Out Loud," and "Love Gun," Kiss would consistently refine the inner-voiced power chord guitar figures of bands like the Rolling Stones, the Raspberries, Humble

Pie, and the Who, combine them with McCartney-esque bass figures and Steve Marriott–approved vocal histrionics, and idiosyncratic drumming that teetered on the brink of collapse, yet always managed to find the groove. *See also:* tongues, spitting blood, fire, pyrotechnics, costumes.

Key Albums: *Hotter than Hell, Alive!, Destroyer, Love Gun*

AEROSMITH

Incorporating the same instrumental-vocal configuration as the New York Dolls, Aerosmith was another band deeply influenced by the Rolling Stones. But whereas the Dolls based their music on a more primal form of early rock'n'roll, Aerosmith injected their blues-based performances with layers of melodic and harmonic knowledge that came from the classical music that was ever present in the upbringing of Steven Tallarico (Tyler) and legit Meters-inspired funk–meets–Jeff Beck fueled guitar chops of Joe Perry. Add in the Berklee education of oft-overlooked coguitarist Brad Whitford (always the bridesmaid . . .), and the rhythm section mind-meld of bassist Tom Hamilton and drummer Joey Kramer, and you have a steroid-enhanced version of the Stones that brought two major musical cornerstones of '80s rock to the forefront: a big vocal hook and a bigger guitar riff. The swing and funk that was evident in so much of Aerosmith's recorded oeuvre would move in and out of prominence throughout the '80s, but the hooks and riffs and the nascent tones of amplifiers being pushed ever harder into cascading harmonic overdrive would remain a constant. Of course, with Aerosmith you could usually count on a piano-based ballad to offset the junkie funk and amped up British hard rock, and these forays into gentler climes would foreshadow the omnipresent '80s power ballad. In the case of the Smith, epic slow jams like "Dream On," "You See Me Crying," and "Home Tonight" would reveal a harmonic depth and melodicism that would be refined (effectively) to its most basic components in songs like Mötley Crüe's "Home Sweet Home."

Key Albums: *Get Your Wings, Toys in the Attic, Rocks*

AC/DC

In my experience as a studio and touring musician, I cannot recall a band that has been referenced as a sonic ideal more often than AC/DC. I've rarely had a producer ask me to get that Nirvana sound, or that Oasis sound, or even that Van Halen sound (although God knows I always try!). But AC/DC? Man, if I had a nickel . . .

And if you've ever whiled away the hours before a concert slamming tall boys in a parking lot outside your local Enormodome, chances are good you have heard AC/DC's "Back in Black" being blasted through the PA speakers as the front of house sound engineer tunes the system, knowing full well that AC/DC is the high-water mark when it comes to what a rock'n'roll experience should sound like.

Founded in Australia by Scottish expats Angus and Malcolm Young, under the production guidance of their older brother George and his musical partner Harry Vanda, AC/DC forged a sound based on the purest of rock'n'roll principles. Backbeat on the two and four. Two guitars moving in lockstep on the left and right stereo channels, employing subtle yet brilliant variance in chord voicing. In Angus, a lead guitarist who conveys the most coveted qualities of the soloist — spontaneity, memorability, control, energy, and technical flash that never crawls up its own arse. In Malcolm, the archetypical rhythm guitarist, sacrificing his own notable lead guitar abilities in the name of a higher ambition, a commitment to purity of intent and groove. The guitar sound is quite deceptive, providing the power that would later come to be associated with heavy distortion but is actually the result of crystal clarity and immaculate representation in terms of equalization, stereo placement, and choice of instruments: Gibson SGs and Gretsch Duo Jets pushing high-volume Marshall tube amplifiers into organic power tube overdrive.

In Cliff Williams, there is a pumping, eighth-note driven bass concept that maintains an illusion of bone-headed simplicity yet can turn on a dime and shift the harmonic underpinning of a song in a life affirming way. When married with Phil Rudd's similarly deceptive rhythmic approach (that snare drum falling *just* behind the beat to create an expanse of time deep enough to bury all the secrets of Sin City), we have one of rock'n'roll's consummate rhythm sections.

I asked Mike Fraser, a Vancouver-based producer and recording engineer who has worked on numerous AC/DC recordings (including their multiplatinum *Razors Edge* album), to describe the AC/DC sound from his perspective.

Mike Fraser: Well, you know it's *tough*. All their music sounds tough. There's nothing wimpy about any of it, even if it's just a hi-hat by itself . . . As you know, as a guitar player, your sound is coming from your fingers and your instrument, but other than that, all I can say is they go for "simple is always best," so when we're doing the drums, it's got to be in a dry room because if the room's all ambient, it might not be the sound of the drum you're looking for, so how can you hear that drum when all the ambience is covering it up? When they do their guitars, it's the shortest guitar lead that they can get away with into their head and then the shortest speaker cord they could get away with, and that's the pureness of the sound. They refuse to use pedals. If the guitar's not distorted enough, well then crank the amp up a bit. If that's not working, well let's get a different head in here. They worked hard at keeping things simple. "Let's not double the guitars." They don't want to cover things up, but everything's got to have a great sound to it. A great sounding snare drum doesn't need reverb on it. A great sounding guitar doesn't need to be doubled [with another recorded guitar]. You can even look at some of the hip-hop stuff, it's just a kick drum, snare drum, and a hi-hat cymbal and it's like, "Well, how did they get those [to sound] so big and punchy?" Well, there's nothing else there [to mask it]. There's no big ambience, there's no cymbals going on. There's not a distorted guitar, it's just a vocal right there and a "boom-chick-boom-chick." Wow, that sounds so huge.

Same with AC/DC; they keep things simple so that the kick and snare drums can punch and you've only got one guitar at each side and a bass underneath. It leaves space for everything to sound huge.

Oddly enough, advents in technology that were meant to create a "huge" sound often went against the sonic principle of leaving "space" . . . or maybe it was just a different kind of "huge"?

Well, when you hear "hair metal," you immediately go to the '80s, and you see these bands with eyeliner and not the Kiss-type makeup, and the giant, giant hairdos and the gallons of hairspray that must've been used in the '80s is just incredible. But if you're not watching it and you don't see the visual of it and you listen to the '80s music, there is some great music . . . It just got a stigma put on it because of the fashion of it, I guess, and then . . . I also remember working in that time and even a little bit further when somebody says, "Hey, we're kind of going for an '80s sound." Well, basically all you do is just reach for all your reverbs, and you put reverbs and effects and everything on everything. Everything had to be bigger then . . . The snare drums are so huge. Well, to get the guitars huge, you had to put them in a room, too, and delays and the vocals were just swimming in stuff, so that, to me, sonically, was the '80s, too, which is as ridiculous as the hairdos. So it was kind of good that we could pull that back a bit. I remember we would be recording drums or something, and I can't even think of which project, but you'd get your snare drums and it'd just be this "um-pah, um-pah," and you think, Oh God, does that ever sound wimpy. Oh, let's put on the AMS reverb and send that into an EMT to play it or something, and "boom-BAH, boom-BAH." Oh, there it is, now that's a big, tough snare drum. And how that perception changes now, when you hear, say, AC/DC, their drums are super-dry and it's just a snare, but it's a great sounding snare drum. Less is more.

AC/DC is also a tale of two incredibly distinctive vocalists who both play a role in the transitional nature of the band's recorded output.

Bon Scott is the bawdy street poet, in possession of a nasal vocal styling and a way with words that conjures menace, leering sexuality, a working-man's pub humor, and a conviviality that belies a deep understanding of human nature. His barrel chested, sailor-tattooed, snaggle-toothed stage image worked weirdly and wonderfully against Angus Young's school-boy gone wild look and the "heads bobbing, feet planted" approach of backline soldiers Malcolm, Cliff, and Phil. His distinctive vocal tone always finding the perfect sonic space in the mix of the richness of tones offered by the band, infusing the songs with a midrange energy that makes every word cut through the power chords with edge-of-the-knife clarity. If you were a tough-guy lead singer with a penchant for a witty turn of phrase, Bon was your man.

Bon's vocal styling was always inherently relatable to those in the know, but it was the Mutt Lange–produced *Highway to Hell* that made it highly palatable to their first million served. While Vanda-Young productions like *Powerage* and *Let There Be Rock* are arguably every bit as strong in terms of raw composition and esprit de corps (and perhaps even stronger in unfiltered rock'n'roll classicism), it was Lange's harnessing of the core elements of AC/DC, and his re-imagining of where they fit within the context of chorus-driven anthems, that helped the band find platinum success for the first time.

We'll see as we progress that every step toward refinement can arguably be construed as a step away from critical credibility, but it is hard to view the advancements made on *Highway to Hell* as being anything other than de rigueur AC/DC. Rather than detract from the credibility, the highly developed background vocal arrangements and tightening of instrumental and vocal performances made for an even more powerful and direct statement.

With Bon Scott's tragic passing, a decision was made to honor his legacy by carrying on, and carry on they did with Brian Johnson. Johnson was the former frontman for U.K. glam also-rans Geordie, who had worked their minor hits successfully enough to have caught the attention of Bon Scott himself, who intimated to his bandmates that Johnson would be the best replacement for him should anything cause him to leave the band.

Johnson's work on the 40-million-plus selling opus *Back in Black* analytically and mathematically places him as the most impactful singer in AC/DC's history, but really this is a result of phase two of the Mutt Lange influence on the early formula. With *Back in Black*, a more sophisticated concision comes to pass, each song referencing an element of the band's Vanda-Young roots while also forecasting a glossier, shinier future for the hard rock of the '80s. Background vocals that once had more in common with skinhead "Oi!" chants would bear the unmistakeable harmonies that we would come to hear later in Def Leppard and the Cars. However, on *Back in Black* they are inserted deep inside the trademark sandpaper screeching that would cause irreparable damage to the larynxes of lesser men (and presumably women) who dared attempt to imitate them. Lange combines vocal tones as deftly as he combines guitar sounds, and *Back in Black* is as much a testament to timbre as it is to attitude, groove, and great songwriting. No album before or since has punched through speakers in all price ranges quite like *Back in Black* did.

Key Albums: *Powerage, Let There Be Rock, Highway to Hell, Back in Black*

VAN HALEN

Van Halen represents two very important things: One: they are a defining example of the American Dream as cultural melting pot, comprising one part wealthy (David Lee Roth), one part working-class Midwestern transplant (Michael Anthony, née Sobolewski), and two parts mixed-race immigrant (Edward Lodewijk and Alexander Arthur Van Halen). And, two: They created the perfect template and high-water mark ideal for '80s hard rock, yet never fell prey to the clichés they inspired. Van Halen consistently ran a parallel path that never actually intersected with the musical content of any of their contemporaries . . . always the influencer, and rarely, if ever, compared unfavorably to their own influences. In fact, they set the bar so high in terms of musical derring-do, showmanship, and overall spirit that it was always out of reach of any acts in the sub-genre they created (of which I won't say the name, but it rhymes with "bear kettle"). Van Halen remain to this day the untouchable and unattainable kings of '80s rock.

If we were going by the first Van Halen album alone, the impossibly high standards are already self-evident and fully formed. And it all starts with *that* guitar sound. Later identified and coveted as "The Brown Sound," Eddie Van Halen created a sonic imprint out of $130 worth of discarded electric guitar wood, an old PAF pickup salvaged from a Gibson Les Paul, a variac light dimmer that changed the voltage of an old Marshall amp, and endless experimentation with vibrato systems that could respond to his string bending abuse.

Eddie's fearless inventiveness and musical wanderlust was a red-hot product of the Southern California hot-rod culture of the 1970s, his family's humble financial situation, and a need to slake the thirst of his tonal desires. It was this same need to satisfy his musical cravings that led him to invent (or at least re-invent and expand upon) guitar techniques that players would emulate with varying degrees of success for the next 40-plus years. Even guitarists like Randy Rhoads, George Lynch, Mick Mars, and Carlos Cavazo, who were concurrently performing in the same Los Angeles clubs that Van Halen were performing in, would go on to bring elements of Eddie Van Halen's technique, style, and sound into their own playing (to be tapped into in greater detail later . . . ouch).

Of course, while EVH is the sonic rock upon which the church of so much of '80s rock is built, David Lee Roth is the high-performance frontman model. A combination of the golden maned, outback wild-man antics of Black Oak Arkansas's Jim Dandy, the chiselled frame and martial arts devotion of Bruce Lee, the aerobic and acrobatic ability of a circus performer, and the pillaging appetite of a conquering Viking, Roth is the patriarchal head of a long line of bleach-blond frontmen.

But while many could cop some of the moves, and the most easily decoded of his many stage raps (Look at all the people here *tonight!*), few, if any, could imbue their shtick with the fierce intelligence and encyclopedic knowledge of American music that Roth had developed from years of listening to all manner of rock, blues, jazz, and Vaudevillian recordings on the radio. Time spent with his uncle, owner of the famous Cafe Wha? in New York's Greenwich Village and undiagnosed ADHD also contributed to young Roth's superhuman consumption and processing of information and artistic stimuli.

Any perceived vocal weaknesses that Roth may have displayed were quickly forgiven when his many strengths were taken into consideration. A huge nod must go to Van Halen producer Ted Templeman for recognizing these strengths and developing the aggregate of them in a way that was ready-made for record consumption (this was pre-MTV, so the music-buying public needed to be convinced of what they heard, not what they saw beyond a flat image on a record sleeve). Without Roth, the world at large may never have come to know the genius of Eddie Van Halen . . . and as history would show, the genius of Roth himself.

And lest we forget . . . the rhythm section. In Michael Anthony, we had one of rock'n'roll's greatest secret weapons. Not only did he have the innate editing capabilities to stay the fuck out of Eddie's way (while still supporting him with powerful and musical bass lines), he was also in possession of a trumpetlike tenor and ear for harmony that could take even the most angular EVH composition and transform it into a sunny musical confection. His voice blended perfectly with Eddie's baritone counterpart and the barely-controlled vibrato-laced howls that would emanate from Roth. Even as Roth's performance musings in concert would see him stray further and further from a song's recorded origins, Mike and Eddie could keep the vocals grounded in the form's origins.

If David Lee Roth and Eddie Van Halen were living, breathing American art installations, the grounding influence of Michael Anthony and Alex Van Halen would often serve as the canvas. But to relegate Alex's drumming to mere foundational support would do a grave injustice to the musicianship inherent in the man. Like Roth, AVH set the visual standard for the drummers of the '80s that came after him. A massive double-bass (later to become quadruple) drum kit, an endless rack of power, myriad cymbals of varying dimension (including the obligatory oversized gong) combined the kit excess of drummers like Ginger Baker, John Bonham, and Carmine Appice and took it all a step further. But for all the razzle-dazzle and sheer grandiosity of presentation, Alex's greatest contribution to Van Halen was a jazz-informed ability to *swing* a groove, and an almost telepathic connection with his virtuoso brother. This fraternal mind-meld allowed Alex to respond with effortless musicality to any of Eddie's whims of composition or improvisation. It is important to note that this swing, with rare exception (Frankie Banali for Quiet Riot, A.J. Pero of Twisted Sister) was not nearly as present in the rock of Van Halen's later contemporaries. In fact, it was all but missing until 1987, when Guns N' Roses' *Appetite for Destruction* changed the game for hair metal fans and bands alike.

Key Albums: *Van Halen, Van Halen II, Women and Children First, Fair Warning, Diver Down,* 1984

Talk about a surface barely scratched . . . how can I not mention the fundamental metal of Black Sabbath, the layered vocal harmonies and polished guitars of Queen and Boston, or the "Van Halen before Van Halen" masterpiece that was Montrose's debut? What justification is there for passing over an in-depth Deep Purple review, when at least 99.9% of the guitarists we'll talk about would count "Smoke on the Water" as one of the first three riffs they ever learned? Not to mention the fact that Yngwie basically copied Ritchie Blackmore's entire stage look and moves (granted, he also combined this with a reverence for the work of Bach and Paganini that ended up inspiring the biggest advancement in guitar playing standards since Eddie Van Halen). Can you really skip Blue Cheer, Cheap Trick, Ted Nugent, the Who, the Sweet, Mott the Hoople, Thin Lizzy, or even Bowie when you are talking about influences? And for every Kiss and Aerosmith, there is a Starz or Angel that changed some kid's life. There is also a wealth of progressive rock influence to be cited . . . Rush, Yes, Pink Floyd, and Genesis encouraged many players weaned on simpler fare to expand into more intricate and developed musical areas; try playing the breakdown that comes after the guitar solo of Winger's "Seventeen" (assuming you can make it through the solo section!), and tell me there isn't some awareness of fusion and prog rock at play. And punk . . . it was supposed to kill the rock'n'roll dinosaurs, but Dead Boys will be boys, and the Sex Pistols were as manufactured as any boy band anyway . . . but what a *sound*. Steve Jones just doesn't get enough credit for what he did with a Les Paul and a Fender

Twin amplifier. I can hear the influence every time C.C. DeVille picks up that guitar and talks to me.

And it doesn't have to be *hard* rock that influences hard rock. Hell, maybe it was *Frampton Comes Alive!* that kickstarted someone's rock-star aspirations and things just went down a heavier path . . . or was that Elton John's *Goodbye Yellow Brick Road*? And really, this also speaks to the ways and the means by which something can be an influence. Let's face it, T. Rex may not have the heaviest guitar sound known to man, but Marc Bolan's corkscrew curls, Les Paul–adorned "Electric Warrior" pose, and penchant for pop hooks were an inspiration for at least half of Def Leppard. Layers are most definitely going to be peeled back as we reel in the years and dig into specific bands, songs, albums, and experiences. All your Beatles, Stones, Badfingers, and Big Stars are going to shed light on where a lot of great '80s songcraft comes from. I think I can even dig up some Elvis Costello in Enuff Z'Nuff records.

It's a long way to the top if you want to rock'n'roll, but it's a short way into the heart of this book if we just get it on, bang a bong, and carry on with it, my wayward sons and daughters. At the end of the day (or the end of the book) it's all looks and hooks . . . or is it? Perhaps there is something more behind this flashiest of musical eras that leads us to take a deeper look at the reasons these long-haired freaky people applied for rock'n'roll gigs in the first place.

CHAPTER 3
ARTISTIC INTENTIONS

Before I make this book all about me and my perspectives, I wanted to share some of the thoughts these artists had on their own artistic intention, in their own voice, and how they have taken initial inspirations and applied these to the creation and dissemination of their art.

Brian "Damage" Forsythe is, alongside Ronnie "10/10" Younkins, part of the guitar duo that makes up Kix, an outlier in the '80s hard rock genre who married a surprisingly diverse set of influences into a highly palatable hard rock sound.

> **Brian Forsythe:** Kix was a little older than some of the other acts of the mid-'80s Sunset Strip–scene, so our influences go way back. In fact, Donnie Purnell, our main songwriter, was four years older than me, so his roots were maybe even further back, but I grew up in the '60s and '70s. Donnie was heavily influenced by the British scene, like David Bowie and that kind of thing. Man, I hear all kinds of stuff in his style, but, personally, I was influenced by the Memphis soul or Muscle Shoals thing, I was influenced by Southern rock, as far as [being] a guitar player. All my main influences were Southern rock and like Billy Gibbons, that kind of thing.

Early on, maybe Chuck Berry even. And that's why I play the cream-colored Telecaster too. I'm a huge Steve Cropper fan.

Yeah, so our brand of "hair metal" or whatever you want to call it was really a mix of like the British Bowie thing; it was the Stones, it was Aerosmith, and then I brought a little bit of the Southern rock thing to it. And I can't forget AC/DC. They came along a little later, but that was huge. Especially with Donnie in his songwriting, because he was very aware of the live energy thing, and AC/DC just had that simplicity . . . it was easy to play, but it was catchy. It's easy to move to, really. Cheap Trick, that was a huge one too. But yes, because we formed right at the end of '77 is when Ronnie Younkins, Donnie, and I got together, and the band formed, and those first few years when we were trying to find a singer and get gigs, we had to play cover songs. At the end of the '70s, it was weird, there was kind of a lull in the rock thing. There was still Aerosmith, but Cheap Trick was huge right at that point, so we did a lot of Cheap Trick. But going into the '80s, that whole new wave thing popped up, and there was the punk scene. There was the Ramones, there was a lot of those little subtle influences. In fact, the Ramones was more of like a road influence. We kind of patterned our [touring on them], the van and the Ryder truck on the road, just playing nonstop.

Paul Gilbert first came to prominence as a young discovery of Shrapnel Records main man Mike Varney, who featured him in a "Spotlight" column he wrote for *Guitar Player* magazine. This ultimately led to Gilbert joining the Shrapnel roster as a member of the tech-metal band Racer X before moving on to commercial success with the supergroup Mr. Big. For Gilbert, inspiration started at home.

Paul Gilbert: Well, my parents had a great record collection of music that I really liked and some that I didn't. I was born in late 1966 — so out of the womb I was already listening to the Beatles' records, the Who . . . Zeppelin wasn't out yet. I was about five when I heard Led Zeppelin, and initially I just wanted to sing because that was sort of the featured part of the Beatles was the singing. You know, they had guitars and I thought guitars were cool, and then my uncle would come and visit and he was — and still is — a really good guitar player. . . . To see my older uncle picking up my junky acoustic and be able to just pull sounds and emotion out of it got me interested in the instrument, and I kind of tried everything.

We had a guitar laying around, and I had a toy drum set, I think. It was the excitement of the Beatles, later on Led Zeppelin, and then to see a performance, like a live performance, was a much scarcer thing because on TV all the rock'n'roll shows were on late at night. So, I was up past my bedtime to watch *Don Kirshner* or *Midnight Special*, and so the only music I could see on TV were the Osmond Brothers and the Jackson Five because they had cartoons on Saturday morning. And I loved both of those. The Osmonds had some great rock songs and great pop songs too. The Jackson Five had great songs. So I really loved both of those, because that was the music that was available. It was just pre-internet so you couldn't just go to Spotify or YouTube and have access to everything. I had access to the radio and my parents' record collection.

I do remember hearing "Stairway to Heaven," and when the end of it kicked in with the guitar jam and Robert Plant starts singing high, that got me excited. I'd go to flea markets — you could get records cheap there, so I got *Machine Head*, by Deep Purple, for like a quarter. You'd have to be kind of scrappy in order to find music, and then you'd find these gems and you'd start putting together what really resonated, and the things that resonated to me were Mountain, "Mississippi Queen," the *Led Zeppelin IV* record, which of course had "Stairway to Heaven," but it also had "Black Dog," "Misty Mountain Hop" . . .

And the Osmonds . . . Even though [they] were a pop band, they had some heavier tunes. "Crazy Horses," "My Drum," "Hey, Mr. Taxi," those were all heavy. And once in a while you'd hear Aerosmith on the radio, "Walk This Way" or something would come on, or Heart. They had "Magic Man" and "Barracuda" . . . It was not easy to find the stuff, that was half the battle, just discovering what it was and then saving up the money to buy a new [record] or having a stroke of luck at a flea market.

Rikki Rockett is the drummer for Poison, perhaps the most famous example of the Day-Glo, neon-lit visual excess associated with '80s hard rock. But we wouldn't be remembering what Poison looked like if we didn't associate that wild image with the amazing songs and enthusiastic performances found on platinum albums like *Look What the Cat Dragged In*, *Open Up and Say . . . Ahh!*, and *Flesh & Blood*.

Rikki Rockett: Our building blocks were varied because of the individual members. We all shared a love for '70s rock, you know? We loved Kiss, we loved Aerosmith, Foghat, all that kind of stuff, and I think . . . I've said this before, and this isn't a rehearsed line, but we tried to be all the things that we wanted to see in a band. We wanted a soundtrack to this whole attitude, you know? This whole larger-than-life sort of live show . . . and we wanted to figure out how to do that, and so it was varied. Everything from the more bluesy rock-based bands all the way up to like Van Halen, more arena-feeling stuff, were influences and building blocks, all the way down to garage rock and things like the New York Dolls, and even some things like the Clash. But with the tones of the guitars and the way it was produced, you may not see that. You know what I mean? Well, the structures of the songs were all those things I just mentioned.

Vivian Campbell has been one half of Def Leppard's guitar team since 1992, when he stepped in to fill the role left behind by the passing of Steve "Steamin'" Clark. Vivian has one of hard rock's finest pedigrees, having been an original member of the classic Dio lineup, Whitesnake's revitalized 1987 lineup, part of the short-lived but well-regarded Shadow King (with Foreigner vocalist Lou Gramm), as well as his own critically acclaimed band Riverdogs. But prior to all of these positions, Vivian was a member of new wave of British heavy metal upstarts Sweet Savage. Here, Viv gives an insight into that band's influences, and ultimately into the inspirations that made him one of hard rock's finest guitar heroes.

Vivian Campbell: I mean, we all grew out of the punk movement, you know? So, in Ireland, my friends and I were listening to Deep Purple albums and Thin Lizzy albums and stuff, but what was really popular at the time was Sex Pistols and the Clash and whatnot, and you had bands like Motörhead that were maybe one of the first bands that had a foot in either camp. I mean, they were a hard rock band, but they were punk, basically. They weren't really technical musicians, and the music was really fast and furious. It had the kind of raw punk energy. I always summed it up as if Thin Lizzy and Motörhead had a baby, it would have been Sweet Savage. But yeah, we were listening. I was more attuned to classic rock because I was a guitar player, I appreciated guys who could really play. I also appreciated the rawness of punk music, like I think Steve Jones from the Pistols was an incredible guitar player. He had great tone, he had great attitude and great energy, but he wasn't influencing me in the way that, say, Brian Robertson from Thin Lizzy was, you know? But subliminally I was influenced by that, so I think the new wave of British heavy metal was all these young bands, young musicians, Sweet Savage included, who kind of were wanting to play more classical sort of hard rock– heavy metal style, but we couldn't escape the influences that we'd grown up through, which was the whole new wave and punk movement.

Rory Gallagher and Gary Moore were far and away my two singular influences. In that order: Gallagher was the first album I had, the first concert I saw. A few years later, when I first heard Gary Moore, he became my focus, and I never, ever heard a guitar player that influenced me more than Gary Moore. Lump in and say Brian Robertson in that category too. There is a certain feistiness in Celtic guitar players, but essentially, I'm blues-based.

Chip Z'Nuff is a founding member of Enuff Z'Nuff, a band whose bright, high-energy power pop confections were colored with just enough Van Halen to establish them as major creative players in the '80s hard rock scene. Chip has kept Enuff Z'Nuff going to this day, continuing to release albums of consistent quality and charm. My band Crash Kelly had the opportunity to tour with Enuff Z'Nuff in 2004 in the U.K., allowing me to witness firsthand the high level of musical ability and sensibility Chip possesses. He is also one of rock'n'roll's great characters, a man who introduced me to the concept of "reverse shoplifting" when our tour bus would stop at various British petrol stops and Chip would proceed to deposit Enuff Z'Nuff's latest CDs into the racks alongside the various megastars on display . . . a wizard, a true star as Todd Rundgren (undoubtedly an influence) might say.

Chip Z'Nuff: The power pop influences that Enuff Z'Nuff carried were very diverse. A lot of stuff was overseas, obviously the Beatles . . . you are what you eat, but we loved bands like Squeeze; we loved Led Zeppelin, they had a pop sensibility about them, very melodic band . . . loved Pink Floyd. Loved Split Enz, another great band.

I was a huge Mott the Hoople fan 'cause I heard about them when I was a little kid when they were on tour with Queen, and I thought, These guys are incredible! First of all, they had great songs. I love their sense of balance as far as songwriting goes — Ian Hunter was just incredible, he was an incredible singer, but then I see him working with Bowie, too, doing "All the Young Dudes" . . . I thought, That's great. And then he was intuitive enough to know to take Queen out on their first tour. And I thought, This is a great band, they've got all the elements of what I'm looking for in music, which was big guitars, great melody lines, wonderful lyrics, good storytelling, and great sounding records.

I love Elvis Costello as well. One of the great things for me as a songwriter and as a musician is to just keep listening to different stuff. It's wash and repeat, whether it be jazz or rock, R&B or hip-hop. I've worked on all that stuff with different cats and I've become, unwittingly, a very diversified musician.

Gilby Clarke was the man charged with filling Izzy Stradlin's very large rock'n'roll shoes when he left Guns N' Roses at the onset of their mammoth Use Your Illusion Tour. Prior to that, Gilby was a Hollywood staple who made his mark with power-pop and new-wave informed acts like Candy and Kill For Thrills. He has since gone on to a successful producing and solo career, as well as being tagged to play with legendary bands such as Heart and the MC5. Weaned on the sounds of '70s hard rock in his native Ohio, a move to California opened Gilby's ears and heart to the sounds of punk and new wave . . . and ultimately brought him back to his hard-rocking roots.

Gilby Clarke: When I moved to California, my musical tastes really changed. . . . I mean, I was such a rock guy, and I was starting to go down what I call the progressive hole . . . As you become a musician, you think you're getting good, you start listening to U.K. and the early Genesis and all that kind of stuff. So, I started to go down that hole and then my [English] girlfriend introduced me to the Clash, and I just went, "This is the greatest rock'n'roll band of all time. This is my generation's Beatles." I just really connected with them for some reason, and that turned me on to, obviously, the Sex Pistols and Generation X and the Pretenders, Elvis Costello. When I got my Candy gig, I was definitely in this kind of pop rock–punk rock thing, and I was kind of losing my hard rock roots, but I had a friend who had a cover band, and they had a gig at Gazzarri's in Hollywood, and they had to do three sets. And basically, their catalog was UFO, Judas Priest, Iron Maiden, all that stuff and . . . their bass player got sick and couldn't do the shows, and since I could play guitar, they go, "Please, we don't want to lose these gigs, can you play bass?" And I go, "Fuck yeah." So literally in two days I learned their whole three-set catalog, but it turned me on to UFO and Rock Bottom and all that stuff. But that's when I kind of started getting back into rock, even Judas Priest. I wasn't a Maiden fan, but I really connected with Judas Priest and UFO, so I became a UFO fan. We're talking in 1980, maybe '79, and I started getting back into that stuff.

Scotti Hill is, alongside Dave "the Snake" Sabo, part of multiplatinum American act Skid Row's guitar duo. For all of their hard rock and heavy metal acumen, Hill also brings a highly melodic and emotional guitar approach to Skid Row's music, particularly on power ballads like "18 and Life," "I Remember You," and "Wasted Time."

> **Scotti Hill:** I guess I came from a more melodic style. I grew up listening to everything. Everything. Like the Beatles, and then I discovered some fusion and I became a Jeff Beck disciple, and I loved guys like Steve Lukather and Neal Schon. I always wanted to play solos you could whistle, and to maybe make a song within a song.

Steve Lynch is the founding guitarist of Autograph, a melodic hard rock band who found commercial success with their 1984 smash hit "Turn up the Radio." I asked Steve, who is a well-respected guitar clinician and author of a book on the "two-hand tapping" approach to guitar playing that pre-dates Eddie Van Halen, what his thoughts were on marrying artistic intention with commercial aspirations.

> **Steve Lynch:** Over the past several years I have severed the tie of thinking commercially while writing. To me, writing is sharing emotion, and you should always be completely honest with yourself before you share what you've created. I like to use bands like Pink Floyd, Led Zeppelin, Genesis, or Emerson, Lake & Palmer as an example. *None* of these bands set out to have massive commercial success, but because they stood by their music alone, without falter, they *became* massive commercial successes. It's because they didn't lie or put on a facade to "make it." They just stayed true to their creativity . . . and people felt it.

Rik Emmett is an artist most famous for his tenure as guitarist, vocalist, and songwriter in Triumph, a Canadian power trio who found great success in the '70s and '80s through a combination of melodic hard rock compositions, highly developed musicianship, and a notoriously over-the-top stage performance that rivalled bands like Kiss in terms of visual effects and sonic power. Rik's diversity as a musician has been a massive inspiration to me, and his incorporation of styles ranging from acoustic fingerstyle and jazz guitar to progressive music in Triumph's anthemic hard rock sound often prompted me to dig deeper in my own listening and playing. Rik speaks with the gentle authority of an esteemed educator, and I asked him about his relationship to his own artistic muse.

> **Rik Emmett:** [American composer] Aaron Copland talked about this in his books a lot, that a composer is trying to find the long line, "la grande ligne," that you're trying to find this thing . . . the spirit, the juice of the idea that you're trying to put across. So, you know, you and I, we're performers, we play. But the music is this . . . It's this thing that we deliver, it has its own truth. It has its own value that you're always trying to adhere to. You know, songwriters will say, "I was

just trying to get out of the way and let the song come out of me." Or a musician will say, "I don't really know what I was doing. It was like I was just trying to remain true to the spirit of what the song was telling me it wanted to be." One of the things that I loved so much about music was that you could perform a song or a guitar solo or a guitar piece, and whoever was listening was now making their investment into this thing. It was becoming part of their narrative, part of their story.

During our conversation, it dawned on me that I really came to know Triumph from the midpoint in their career trajectory, 1985's *Thunder Seven* album. This Eddie Kramer–produced opus, which featured hard rock classics like "Follow Your Heart" and "Spellbound," was very much au courant in terms of what was happening sonically in hard rock at the time. But rather than being a band specifically *of* that time, Triumph was a band that was simply moving *through* that time, creating not in adherence to a set of commercial rules or regulations, but instead creating from the same space of artistic intention, just in the sonic context of the day.

Rik Emmett: I only ever did what I felt was right for me to do at the time. So, it depends on context, like the context that you just described is Triumph being a band that's in with all of these other kinds of bands, and your context is sort of Mötley Crüe–ish, Quiet Riot, Ozzy, that kind of stuff. I mean, when the *Return to Forever* record came out, to me, that was a big record when I was in my late teens and it was like, "Oh, this is the kind of musician I want to be" because it was a fusion kind of sensibility, and never mind that particular type of fusion . . .

Let's talk about being a Canadian musician. The Canadian music scene that I grew up in was guys like Gordie Lightfoot and Bruce Cockburn. To me, Bruce Cockburn was a really important kind of artist, and where he came from on a guitar was a completely different place. He was playing that finger-picky Clarence White kind of thing . . . And he had that shit down, you know? He was so good at it.

I admired that and respected that with as much admiration and respect as I would have had for, you know, Eddie Van Halen or Jimi Hendrix. And you know, Van Halen was not really a big influence on me because I was already sort of a professional recording artist when he showed up. To me, Hendrix probably was what Eddie Van Halen was to you and to younger guys? So, Hendrix changes the vocabulary, but by that time, I'm already starting to listen to Steve Howe of Yes and Steve Hackett in Genesis. And these guys are already doing this thing where one song they're playing 12-string guitar, one song they're playing nylon string. Now they're playing a slide thing. Now they're playing on a Les Paul. There's all this stuff that's going on where they're taking different styles and there's a fusion that's happening, so I was very much a product of fusion. I come into Triumph, and those guys are going, "We're not doing that shit." You know, "We're going to be a heavy metal band. It's going to be hard rock." And I'm going, "Well, there's things you can do with hard rock that . . . " You know, Rush does some great things with hard rock. Led Zeppelin had done some really great things with hard rock.

It wasn't just hard rock, you know? And to me, there was a cleave between, say, Black Sabbath and Led Zeppelin, a whole school of guitar playing and hard rock heavy metal came out of the Black Sabbath model, but Led Zeppelin was this . . . It was a little more fruit-cakey. It had that English folk music-y kind of Plant fucking around, you know? And of course, Jimmy was a studio cat who had this ability to sort of envision a sonic thing that was not going to be as straightforward as a Black Sabbath kind of thing. It was heavy, it had riffs . . . that's certainly where it started, but it's not where it ended up. That thing evolved and progressed. So that had more of an influence on me personally, and on Triumph, and eventually it leads to the Longfellow and Wordsworth

. . . I mean, Neil Peart had already pushed that thing and made that happen, where your lyrics didn't just have to be about . . . "sleep all day, up all night," you know?

George Lynch is one of the most influential and inventive guitarists of the '80s. His work with Dokken and Lynch Mob, and the myriad collaborations that keep him busy to this day, have set a standard for tone, technique, and the pursuit of a unique artistic voice in one's playing.

When I hear George Lynch play guitar, I feel there's a sense of the long line that Rik discussed. I can hear rhythmic variations on themes, idea weaving in and out, yet still somehow connected to a greater overarching artistic voice or concept. Is George seeking la grande ligne when he is creating?

George Lynch: Ah, well, my long line would be . . . my compositional efforts throughout the timeline in my life. So, in the overview, in the macro, you know, the 50,000-foot view, I would say that I've been writing the same song or been attempting to write the same magnum opus since as long as I've been having this stream of consciousness, ultimate song jam solo on a loop in my brain . . . since I was a kid. So, that's kind of what I keep trying to write over and over again. When I listen to other bands, a lot of times I'll hear that in their records over the years. AC/DC . . . Angus and Malcolm are still writing the same song generally . . . Just conveying it in a little bit [of a] different way, with a few little different flavors — it's kind of the same thing. I think a lot of people do that, and not to say there isn't variety stylistically, but there is a kind of a bed, kind of a central theme, to what tells us to be creative. It's just an expression of being alive and being human. I think that's all music, or any creative impulse, is, just a reflection of what our senses [perceive] and how we sort of digest that and express whatever we're expressing as a reflection of that. I think it's all it is. It's not science, it's not that hard to think about. It's pretty simple, really.

In an online trailer for the *Shadow Nation* documentary, a film that follows George and a group of musicians through various First Nations reservations in the American Southwest and Great Plains, he says that one of his life's struggles has been to reconcile his impulses as a musician with his impulse to engage in political activism in the name of social injustice and environmental issues. I asked him if these intrinsic struggles were inherent in the music he created ... were they a part of his incendiary solos in Dokken classics like "Alone Again," "Unchain the Night," "Dream Warriors," or "In My Dreams"? Can we hear them in his signature instrumental opus "Mr. Scary"? Did struggle ever have a tangible effect on his art?

George Lynch: Well, yeah, [they] would have if I were Tom Morello or Bob Dylan or Neil Young and I could integrate my writing impulse with my passion for what it is I care about, the things you just mentioned. But I'm not an accomplished enough or a big enough artist, or not a big enough brain or something to quite do that. The closest I ever got ... the first time that happened to me was when I was a Christian ... When I was, I think, early 20s and I was poor, I was just kind of like living wherever I could live, and I was just sort of hoboing around aimlessly. I didn't have any money or anything, didn't have a car, I didn't have anything. I didn't have any skills. I didn't have an education; I dropped out of school in ninth grade, so I was just kind of floating around aimlessly. I became a born again Christian, an evangelical Christian, and, you know, I would sort of proselytize . . . . And I was playing in a church in Compton, California, and it was pretty awesome, actually. Gospel music and everything. This was the '70s, and I was the long-haired white guy up there, wah-wah pedal, and you know ... I didn't really fit, but whatever, it was cool. But the point being that I was writing some music at that time ... I was Christian and I was passionate about my Christianity, the belief system and everything. It was so powerful that [I felt] my music had so much more depth ... I don't know if that was true for anybody else, but to me it was. And then another time when that happened was when I was working on *Shadow Train* and *Shadow Nation*, and I wrote a good bit of those lyrics, and I don't consider myself a very good lyricist. I can work at it and get it done serviceably, and if I'm lucky I can write some good stuff once in a while, but I'm not a poet most of the time, unless it's an accident. But with *Shadow Nation* and *Shadow Train*, it meant so much to me and it was so genuine that I was writing something I knew about. So that's why they say write what you know. And so again, the music took on an extra dimension for me. I don't think for anybody else, just for me.

Ron "Bumblefoot" Thal may be best known for his tenure in the Chinese Democracy–era Guns N' Roses, but he is also revered for his work as a renowned guitar virtuoso, solo artist, clinician, producer and member of groups like Sons of Apollo and classic prog supergroup Asia. Where there can be an image of a "serious" artist as one who consistently strives for a kind of higher plane of creativity, Ron has been able to reach dizzying artistic heights by acknowledging the value in pursuing higher ideals with the types of social interactions more commonly associated with "hair metal."

Ron "Bumblefoot" Thal: I liked progressive stuff and smart stuff, and I liked the depth of Iron Maiden and Judas Priest and the lyrical content and the historical and intellectual value that it had, and I sort of shied away from the "Let's party all the time" because I personally wasn't that kind of person. I was very introverted. I was a typical struggling teenager, emotionally, and riddled with anxiety and uncertainty. So, for me, I related more toward old school metal, but at the same time, there's a part of you that doesn't want to miss out on the fun and the joy and the good times and getting laid and all of that stuff that a young teenager wants to do — or an old teenager or an old anybody. That never stops. I sort of rode the fence a little bit where I was kind of in the middle. I guess the good thing about riding that fence is you got to be a member of both parties. The deep, introspective party and one that's like, "Let's go out and pick up girls" and "Let's write songs about it" and "Let's be as pretty as we can." And that was a big part of it — it was social.

Mick Sweda came to prominence playing lead guitar for King Kobra (featuring drum legend Carmine Appice) and, most notably, for BulletBoys, a band that struck gold with their 1989 self-titled debut. Mick is a player with a unique approach to melodic phrasing and note choice, and his playing is laced with unexpected turns and high-energy phrases that seem to suggest he's searching for new ground to cover. I asked him if improvisation was an important part of his approach to creativity.

Mick Sweda: Yeah, it's everything to me, and that's why I keep getting drawn back into this band. Or at least up to this point I always have. In my ability to do basic math, I figure our music is like a sketch that's 25% there and the rest of it, I'm improvising, and that's the beauty of it for me. I can be so intimate with these songs; I can play around with them, and I can do things with them that I haven't done before. And when I get ready for our shows, I basically just work on that 25% and, on the night that we play, fill in the other 75%. Essentially, I'm not sure what I'm going to be doing on any given night, and that's the way I prefer it. I don't know if I'll ever be in another band where that'll be possible. When you think about it, there's been a lot of music since the first acoustic guitar was developed, you know, and a lot of songs put down, so at some point, you could say that almost everything's been done. But it doesn't hurt to keep searching and keep trying to push yourself to create something new, something that somebody at least may not have heard in the last 40 years.

Today's musicians have unprecedented access to musical knowledge. With a click, you can essentially access a full visual breakdown of any song or musical technique you wish to learn. Despite this amazing access, I wondered if there was something to the analog days that these players grew up in — days where the information wasn't so instant — that informed their playing. Days before YouTube, where a person had to put in the effort — the time and physical effort — of lifting a needle off a vinyl record from track to track. I asked guitarist Warren DeMartini of Ratt if he felt that there's validity in the assertion that this may have played a part in creating the diverse musical voices we hear among certain players of his era.

Warren DeMartini: I absolutely do. There was something about learning stuff, only listening to it and not getting any visual. When I was figuring stuff out, I would just keep putting the needle back, and once in a while I would switch down to 16 RPM speed where it was an octave down, and that was the only sort of tool that I had for figuring out stuff. Other than that, you'd have to wait for whoever it was to come to town and perform, and hopefully you get close enough. And I could never get closer than 20, 30 rows, you know? But even then, you would get clues. If you were working on a part and couldn't get it, at least you could tell roughly where on the neck he was when he did something, like in the middle or at the headstock or way up high. You know what I mean? I was always getting clues, but I almost never could get close enough to actually see what was happening.

With its obvious visual and sartorial hallmarks, I wondered if there might be a connection between the theatricality of '80s hard rock and the music itself. Twisted Sister frontman Dee Snider is undoubtedly the torchbearer for striking physical presence in an '80s frontman, and the correlation he makes between his compositions and a certain cult classic piece of musical theater goes beyond cross-dressing, glammed up imagery to speak to cross-generational influence.

Did *The Rocky Horror Picture Show* have an influence on theatricality in rock'n'roll?

Dee Snider: I think it had a huge one, I think it brought the glitter rock ethos of the early '70s, because that's when that show started. That's where that show came from. It started over in England, off Broad Street . . . A little show, but this was the early '70s. And another thing about the early '70s is that, just musically . . . we were enjoying a '50s retro era, and in the '80s, it became the '60s retro, kids with Doors jackets and things like that. So, I was in high school, and I chose between joining Twisted Sister or a band called the Dukes, who were a sha-na-na-styled '50s band. They were big, they're doing a big '50s show, and they were guys I went to high school with, and I really loved the '50s . . . but I got a call from them, I got a call from Twisted, and I was like, "Well, Twisted Sister is a career. The Dukes is just like a novelty."

A lot of early '70s music had '50s I-IV-V chord progressions as a [compositional] driver, and you saw bands just using that as their inspiration. So, *The Rocky Horror Picture Show*, a lot of their songs are using this [humming a '50s rock'n'roll guitar figure]. It's Chuck Berry. I remember going with Jay Jay and Suzette to the A Street Theater [in New York], over in the Village, and there were 25 of us in the audience watching a midnight show, *The Rocky Horror Picture Show*. And we were like, "Oh!" We were already into that glitter era, and it just spoke to us, and certainly, I said, "Oh, I got to use white [makeup] under here! Okay, he's using white." And I definitely was refining my makeup from Tim Curry's look, and making adjustments and even some costume moves. I had some garters and stockings at that point. But I think it helped reconnect the '80s rock audience and rock bands with that early '70s glitter, glammier kind of look. I definitely think [*Rocky Horror*] was part of that return to the sensational, very flashy looking performances.

Watching vocalist Mark Slaughter in videos with Vinnie Vincent Invasion or with his more popular, multiplatinum band Slaughter, one might be surprised to learn that the seeds of his creative confidence were planted as much by his exposure to music education in his hometown of Las Vegas, Nevada, as by the music of the rock stars who preceded him to the top of the hard rock heap.

Mark Slaughter: I was really active in school. Las Vegas was a very different place than it is now. I mean, you had all these influxes of jazz players and people that were coming to do the shows in Las Vegas, and it was a really small community, really. So, you have this influx of great jazz artists and great players. It was the entertainment capital of the world . . . In some ways, it still is. I was in jazz band when I was in ninth grade, and Glenn Miller's trumpet player came in and sat with every person in the jazz band and read down the chart. We just would start like at 10 o'clock and then we would go the whole period of going around and letting this guy talk to each person about how to play the chart. It was probably some of the best information I got out of those players and those teachers, and they're just basically helping out. He told me, "Look, you know, you're playing the chart, but some of the things that you're doing are a little timid. You've got to go in there and play it." And he said, "When you play, if you make a mistake, it's about how to get around it and find your way out in a creative way. And that's jazz. . . . Don't be afraid of it — just do it.

And it was an interesting thing that stuck with me my whole life, which is that you just commit. You know, sometimes it's not the best outcome. But the thing is if you *meant* to do it, then it's right. And that way it takes the fear out of it and then you just kind of get this whole kind of like jumping out of a plane. You're not timid about it, you just jump. And I think that was probably one of the better lessons I learned. That's one of the things, and as I progressed through different parts of school, I was really active in choir. I was really active in jazz band. We had like a pop band that went to Disneyland and did, you know, all the pop hits at the time. And then I was the president of the barbershop choir . . . My whole day was music. My whole evening was music, and then I'd basically go home, eat, do my homework, go to bed. And that was the next day, as well.

Jason McMaster is the lead vocalist for Dangerous Toys, a Texas band that came swinging out of the gate with their raucous self-titled 1989 debut. Jason explains that Dangerous Toys were a band that explored contemporary '80s hard rock and earlier blues-based influences in the same measure, to create their signature sound.

Jason McMaster: I feel like musically it really kind of starts with Scott Dalhover's guitar playing. He loved Van Halen. He still worships Van Halen. You hear his solos and you, you go, "Yeah, that guy is into George Lynch and Eddie Van Halen and Randy Rhoads and Yngwie Malmsteen and all of the classic guitar hero guys from the '80s." But he's also into Tony Iommi. He loves to drop tune, which is interesting because you have this dirge-y, heavy guitar thing going on, but he's also adding a little flash. He's doing all kinds of two-handed tapping riffs, but he won't make the tapping part a show-off thing, he'll make it a riff for the song. He'll make it be a repetitive, fun thing to hear when it comes back around, like a chorus, you know? There is also the funk and the Motown and the blues influences, and the boogie and us being from Texas. I always described it [like], if for some reason Foghat became a heavy metal band, it would sound like Dangerous Toys.

Scott Dalhover also likes Warren DeMartini from Ratt. He likes that kind of writing. He loves that. And I like Stephen Pearcy's voice, and I love John Bush of Armored Saint. He was somebody I got into in the mid-'80s, and, you know, they're *bluesy*. They're coming from a bluesy place just as much as Ronnie James Dio was. He's just a bluesman. Steven Tyler and Dan McCafferty [of Nazareth] and guys like that are guys I was really kind of going for. I was stealing as much as I could from those guys . . . and even Janis Joplin. And you can hear it in my voice.

Suffice it to say, there are as many different artistic intentions and inspirations as there are artists creating, no matter what genre or discipline. But perhaps the intention that resonates most with this participatory branch of the rock'n'roll tree is *connection*.

Mark Slaughter: What you want is your art to be a part of people's lives. It's not about the money. Obviously, it's the music *business* — you need to make money — but it's not driven completely on that. When you're an artist, you're all about heartstrings, man. You want it to resonate. You want it to be somebody's soundtrack. It's got to be the opium for that person who needs it, or their laugh when they need it, whatever it is that moves them emotionally, you have to provide that in music. And the only thing that takes you back where you were, you know, when you're in ninth grade or whenever . . . is music or the sense of smell . . . They are the only two things that'll take you back to that. You hear a song and you go, "Oh man, I frickin' *love* this song." And you think about the car you drove at the time, where you were at the time, what the city looked like, because it was totally different than it is now. I mean, you start to reflect. Who your friends were . . . I wonder how these people are? Your mind just starts to wander in the fabric of that song. And that is *your* song and it relates to you and that's part of your life. And that's the beauty of what music has done for me, because I think that's really the art form. That sharing and universal feeling . . . ultimately what you're trying to do [is] make it universal.

Paul Gilbert: From being a clinician as well, a lot of times I'll perform with musicians that I've never played with until that afternoon. I'll go pick up bands through Italy and in every imaginable venue — good, bad, and in-between — and so there's a lot of situations that are less than optimal, and I'll find there's one cure for every difficulty, and it's one word, and that word is *connect*. If I'm onstage and something is not going right, you feel it. Something's not going right, there's no secret, so I'll go, "What am I going to connect to?" Step number one is the drummer. If I can connect to the drummer, that usually solves it already. If it's still . . . If something's still squirrelly, okay, now I've got to connect to the audience. That might help. Just take a look: Who's here? What's their expression? Look at some eyes, see what they're doing. Connect to what's inside of myself. What am I hearing? Am I being honest about what I'm playing? Am I just playing finger patterns, or am I actually playing something that I hear or feel in my soul? And is there anything there in the first place? You start searching for those things to connect to, and the more you do, the better it feels and the more it works, and that's why the harmonies are so wonderful, because you're connecting to the voices of other people, and that's a very human thing to do.

Root inspirations, aspirations, and ambitions aside, the symbiotic relationship between artist and audience really lies in connection. Looking at how these artists connected to their delivery of the music has informed how I connect to '80s hard rock on a variety of levels . . . sonic, harmonic, lyrical, visual, and ultimately spiritual. As we go through the progression of "hair metal"'s sound, look, and cultural impact, I hope that the artistic voices we hear throughout this examination of an era help to give shape to why this music has more to offer than may appear on the surface. Now, let's see if we can connect the dots that connect the years that brought us some of rock'n'roll's most exciting music.

CHAPTER 4
1978 TO 1980

CUMIN' ATCHA LIVE!

We are going to make a few pit stops on our way to the '80s . . . we've got some Scorpions and Priests to contend with, and a few new waves to surf before we get to the heart of the matter and the heat of the moment. I'd like to start by rolling a big fat theory on a few double gate-fold albums that I feel may have helped inspire the sound and spirit of '80s rock.

If you consider some of the more bombastic elements of '80s hard rock record production, a point could be made that bands, producers, and engineers of the era were trying to capture the energy and excitement of the live hard rock experiences of the '70s, musical experiences that took place in massive reverberant hockey arenas and auditoriums. The live albums we'll talk about can also be seen as a foreshadowing of a number of the musical approaches we would come to hear in the commercial hard rock of the 1980s, and study of these records makes for a pretty convenient road map of how we arrived at the sound of pop metal.

For the young music fan on a budget, live albums represent incredible value for the money. They sometimes get a bad rap as contractual filler or throwaway cash grabs, but when executed in the right spirit, they can capture the rock'n'roll art form in its purest state. A great live album represents the spiritual communion between artist and audience, an emotional contract that bonds band to fan as a result of transactional energy. In a live album we hear the sounds our hearts make as we listen to studio recordings amplified, the roar of the crowd reflecting our own enthusiasm for the music. To my ears, a great live album was (and is) the rock'n'roll dream made manifest. When I hear the crowd's affirmations being showered on the artists in these recordings, I am able to engage in both sides of the dream and am reminded that artist and fan are two sides of the same coin.

A live album is essentially a time capsule of what the artist considers to be their best work at the time. As a cash-strapped teenager, a live album was a way to get a "cooler" version of a greatest-hits album and a chance to better connect with songs that I read about in those glorious rock magazines. The first two live albums I purchased were W.A.S.P.'s *Live . . . In the Raw* (1987) and Great White's *Recovery: Live!* (1988). The use of the ellipses and the colon in the respective titles added to the anticipation I felt taking these cassettes home in a brown paper bag from the Records on Wheels shop on Main Street in North Bay, fingers fumbling with the tight shrink-wrap that kept me from the treasures and pleasures within.

Live . . . In the Raw was recorded as the band toured to support their *Inside the Electric Circus* album, and it's still burned into my brain as the template for how a hard rock concert should begin. The "most outrageous band in the world" is introduced to the audience at the Long Beach Arena by a carnival barker (send in the evil clowns?) as a staccato sixteenth-note rhythm-guitar slices the air, punctuated by eighth-note bass, drum, and guitar power chord "shots" (that I could only imagine cued a blazing display of hundreds of synchronous PAR Cans). It's the sound of the caged animals of this circus being held back until they are finally set free to attack the audience by drummer Steve Riley's explosive fills and "on top of the beat" grooves. Primal and exciting stuff.

I was pleasantly surprised many years later to find concert footage from this era that lined up incredibly well with the images I had concocted in my younger brain, visuals pieced together from album art that featured the band's garish stage props, and individual pictures of the band onstage in various states of maniacal grin and grimace. These sounds and images served as foundational inspiration for my own songwriting, as I would often think of songs as serving a different point on a timeline of a concert.

Each choice of tempo, riff, groove, and feel designed to add to the emotional arc of an overall experience. These early ideas about songwriting have broadened through the years, but somewhere in my brain, I'm sure I am still trying to sneak in a riff that will sound great as I'm angling my guitar neck to the ceiling of a venue, backed up by a wall of towering Marshall amps and a fiery pyrotechnic display.

With the Great White album, the major benefit to my young development was the fact that half of the record was cover songs, recorded "live," direct to two-track. This ended up serving me very well, as it was here that I was introduced to covers of songs by bands like the Who, Led Zeppelin, the Beatles, and Humble Pie. My first professional music experience involved phoning the numbers found on flyers in that same Records on Wheels shop where I purchased the album, and ultimately joining bands that featured musicians much older than I . . . armed with "unique" takes on "Immigrant Song," "Money," and "Substitute," all gleaned from *Recovery: Live!*

It's fascinating to note that both this album and *Live . . . In the Raw* feature covers of Humble Pie's "I Don't Need No Doctor," from their famous *Performance Rockin' the Fillmore* (1971) release. Years later, I would play in a band called Four By Fate with the legendary John Regan, longtime bassist for Humble Pie's Peter Frampton (no stranger to a great live album himself). When "I Don't Need No Doctor" was called out at our first rehearsal in Long Island, New York, it's safe to say that I can thank Great White and W.A.S.P for my quick response in recalling the chords and riffs, saving face in front of the other rock legends in the band, vocalist Tod Howarth (Frehley's Comet, Ted Nugent) and Stet Howland, drummer for Metal Church, Impellitteri, and others . . . but maybe most famous for his stint in (wait for it) . . . W.A.S.P.

Live albums are concert documents that can ultimately be seen as a summation of a chapter in the band's existence, and in some cases represent an end to one chapter in a band's history and the beginning of another.

Ron "Bumblefoot" Thal: In the '70s, there was no MTV, there was nothing visual. There was no VHS, there was no anything, so all you had was a live album, and you filled in the blanks with your imagination to put yourself there. And these live albums were done so well that they achieved that easily for the listener. So all the great live albums, there were so many, they're iconic. They're legendary, and they launched a thousand music careers for inspired young kids. And one of the biggest ones that did that was Kiss *Alive!* For me, I was five years old, about to turn six, when that album came out. I had just moved in the boroughs of New York from Brooklyn to the next one over, Staten Island, which was a lot less gritty. It was more nature, deer and rabbits, and nice neighborhoods, and the block that I moved onto, there were all these kids my age, and we all had older brothers and sisters a few years older, and between our parents that would have Beach Boys albums and Four Seasons albums that we would just pull out and look at, to our older siblings that had Elton John and Beatles and Sex Pistols and Ramones, and all kinds of stuff. I would go over to my neighbor's house and there would just be albums, just these 12-inch-by-12-inch squares of art lying all over the floor around the house, and we would just pick one up and we would go into the bedroom and we would put one on, drop the needle and just sit on the bed and stare at the speakers, like we were watching TV or a movie or something like that.

And one day, I remember picking up this unusual look-ing one, and I didn't know what to make of it. What were these beings on there? I remember looking at the back, and it had four people holding this banner and surrounded by fans and this huge crowd. I remember they had long hair and they were young, and I couldn't tell if they were boys or girls because I was only five; and I was curious. I was like, "What is all this? This is some other world," and put it on. And from the very beginning, "You want the best. You got . . ." Just the crowd cheering, the energy coming out of that music that just infected you. As soon as I heard it, I was . . . There's very few words to describe the feeling. You were there. You were transformed. You were inspired. You were lifted . . . It changed you.

When I heard that, even at the young age, the inexperienced life, the age of five . . . As soon as I heard that, it's like, "That's what I want to do with my life. I want to do that. This is so incredible. This is just so cool. This is so exciting. This is so invigorating . . . . This is what I need to do with my life, I need more of this." And I immediately started, after hearing that album, I said, "Okay, I need to put a band together, I need to write songs, I need to make recordings, and I need to play gigs, need to make merch. I need to do what these guys are doing."

Gilby Clarke: It's simple for me. Kiss *Alive!* It was the first Kiss record I got . . . and it just blew my mind. I was young, everything about it . . . from their costumes to the way the cover looked . . . you studied it, visually, and then you listen to it, and it's just so exciting. I got it way before I ever went to an actual concert. I had been to a couple club shows, but I'd never been to a concert.

The last years of the '70s gave us a number of such transformational and inspirational concert recordings, albums that have gone on to be acknowledged as career-makers. I've already talked about the power and influence of Kiss *Alive!*, an album that (alongside Peter Frampton's massive *Frampton Comes Alive!*) not only elevated Kiss to rock god status, but also increased the industry awareness of the lucrative nature of such commercial offerings. Let's look at four albums, all influential and universally admired for their quality and artistry, all a crucial link in the chain of great rock'n'roll that would lead us to the '80s. Two of these albums served as springboards for even loftier heights of career achievement and creative accomplishment for their creators, and two proved to be the best things that the artists would ever go on to do.

Recorded over two nights in April of 1978 at Nakano Sun Plaza Hall in Tokyo, Japan, Scorpions' *Tokyo Tapes* is an album of incredible depth and warmth. It is striking to hear the roar of approval of the Japanese crowd dramatically decrescendo as the band kicks into "All Night Long," a stand-alone single that hadn't appeared on a full-length album prior to *Tokyo Tapes* (there's that value for money!). This scream to a whisper response is a testament to the respect, graciousness, and self-control that has long come to be associated with Japanese culture.

Throughout the '70s, Scorpions were a band that were growing from strength to strength, building off their Battle of the Bands–funded 1972 debut *Lonesome Crow* (an album strangely embraced by certain factions of the musical hipster elite for its nascent psych rock leanings). The album featured a then 16-year-old Michael Schenker, who would leave the band at the end of the tour supporting the album to join UFO, an act who had followed a similar trajectory of stylistic change by abandoning earlier journeys of musical exploration for a more focused and refined melodic hard rock style. The ballad "In Search of the Peace of Mind" is the only remnant from that debut on *Tokyo Tapes*, but its dark melodicism would be a strand of sonic continuity throughout the Scorps' career. The addition of Uli Jon Roth and Francis Buchholz for 1975's *Fly to the Rainbow* brought a Hendrix-ian flair and a degree of lineup stability. Of the two tracks from this album featured on *Tokyo Tapes*, it is "Speedy's Coming" that would foreshadow the influence that Scorpions would have on '80s rock.

From the first vibrato bar "divebomb" (a guitar technique where the strings are slackened by the depressing of a steel whammy bar that is attached to the bridge of the instrument, allowing the player to subtly or dramatically alter the pitch of the strings), you can hear Uli's influence on a young Eddie Van Halen, as Roth demonstrates a trademark guitar move we would come to identify as idiosyncratic to EVH's style. In the song's myriad guitar breaks we hear articulated high-velocity picking of chromatic melodic figures, wailing unison string bends, and the whammy bar being used in a more controlled, melodically intentional manner. Roth can be seen as an evolutionary guitar-playing bridge between Hendrix and Van Halen.

Tokyo Tapes reveals Roth's virtuosic control and an almost classical elegance on a sampling of tracks from 1975's *In Trance*, 1976's unfortunately titled *Virgin Killer* (featuring the most egregious album artwork in a catalog of album art that suggests either an ill-informed commitment to the purity of artistic ideal, or a deep-seated sexism that would make Spinal Tap blush), and 1977's *Taken by Force*. That album's "Sails of Charon" is an early example of the neo-classical style of highly technical guitar playing that was made popular in the '80s by Swedish guitar virtuoso Yngwie Malmsteen and adopted by many guitar players in both progressive and commercial hard rock settings.

One of those players is Warren DeMartini of Ratt, who explains the impact Roth had on his own playing, and how his fascination with the music compelled him to connect with his hero in the days before social media.

Warren DeMartini: Jake [E. Lee] and I were huge Uli fans, and he could play at very high speeds, but he didn't do that all the time. He used it very, very elegantly, and that probably had something to do with . . . guitar, lead guitar, seemed to get more and more popular — there were more notes to what people were doing, you know? In the same space, you know what I mean? So with Uli, there was always a very lyrical quality to his lead playing that would be composed of also very blistering fast stuff, but it just wasn't all . . . I don't know how to explain it other than, just . . . It wasn't all the time. It seemed like later on in the '80s there got to be more notes in the leads in general.

Uli was a huge, huge influence. There's a crazy story . . . tell me if you've heard this one. On the first Scorpions record, it was the strangest thing, there was a phone number on it. There was never anything like that, I had never seen that before, just an address to the record company, and that always felt pretty futile to try to get in touch with an artist that way. But this one had a phone number, and this guy that worked at Guitar Center called it incessantly and said that he was Floyd Rose and he needed to talk to Uli because Uli was going to want this device that he invented. Totally made up, right? But whoever it was [answering that number] gave him Uli's home phone number . . . This circulated around us guitar rats. I worked it out with the time change and everything, [figuring] he probably sleeps till 12, so at four in the morning, man, California time, we'd start calling. And of course, he's not like that at all. He's up at eight and doing stuff. But every time I called, he wasn't home. It was 12 o'clock. But we kept trying, and eventually he did answer, and this was back when it was five bucks a minute, and my mom got that bill!

By this point, Klaus Meine and rhythm guitarist Rudolf Schenker had forged a songwriting partnership that was becoming ever more refined and would come to commercial fruition in the decade to follow. The combination of Schenker's disciplined adherence to simple but effective rhythm guitar patterns (power chords and cleanly picked Beatles-inspired open-chord arpeggios) and Klaus Meine's highly pleasing combination of warm yet nasally midrange vocal tone and throaty rasp support the ambitious compositions in a way that helped them cross over to mainstream acceptance. Japanese audiences were the first to embrace the band, to the extent of honoring them with their first gold-selling discs for *Virgin Killer* and *Taken By Force*.

The rhythm section of drummer Herman Rarebell and Buchholz would never again sound so warm, swinging, and free as it did on *Tokyo Tapes*. Scorpions' move toward heavier rock and catchier, more easily digestible song form in the '80s would come at the expense of the richness of bass tone, roundness of drum resonance, and the expansiveness of musical composition that are associated with the best '70s hard rock. These refinements would ultimately cost the band Uli Jon Roth, who had already decided prior to the Japanese shows recorded for *Tokyo Tapes* to leave the band to follow his more adventurous artistic muse. Fortunately for all involved, Roth was convinced by Meine's sincere and impassioned plea to return to the fold for these final shows, a testament to an enduring respect and friendship that sees Roth join the band sporadically onstage to this day as a guest performer.

Tokyo Tapes is a wonderful summation of the first chapter of a band that would go on to be a commercial juggernaut in the '80s. Still, when listening to the driving early metal of "He's a Woman, She's a Man" or Roth's thematic, legato flights of guitar fancy on "Pictured Life" and "Backstage Queen," one can't help but wonder what shape '80s hard rock would have taken if Roth had remained with the band as they embraced a more condensed hard rock structure.

Fortunately for Scorpions, there was a third German virtuoso waiting in the wings to man the lead guitar position. Matthias Jabs would forsake his law school studies to be brought into the Scorpions' fold for 1979's seminal *Lovedrive* album, only to be abruptly ousted for original guitarist Michael Schenker's return and then begged to come back (which he did begrudgingly) at the behest of Rudolf when his younger brother left the band high and dry for a concert performance. This was a theme that would recur throughout Michael's career as he struggled with alcoholism and mental health issues, although he would attain sobriety and conquer stage fright later in his career.

In truth, Michael Schenker and Matthias Jabs share many stylistic traits in their guitar playing; technical facility that allows them to execute fast runs, a European classical sense of melodic phrasing that also embraces the English rock influence of players like Beck, Page, and Blackmore, and the ability to craft memorable lines that serve as independent compositions within the songs themselves. On later Scorpions albums like *Animal Magnetism*, *Blackout*, and, one of the '80s-defining albums, *Love at First Sting*, Jabs would apply a post–Van Halen approach to modern guitar technique (including finger tapping) in conjunction with an "in and out in eight bars" concision that was happening in the radio-friendly hits of bands like Billy Squier, Survivor, and Toto. Alongside Bon Jovi's Richie Sambora, it could be said that Jabs was perhaps the most effective practitioner of this approach. On *Lovedrive*, Schenker handles the lion's share of leads, and the result is something that feels slightly freer and more adventurous, a lead guitar style imbued with more of the player's personality. Like Ulrich after/before/after him, Schenker is a guitarist in pursuit of musical purity, one that is an expression of a singular vision. This is wonderful for creating art, but not necessarily for embracing and capitalizing on formula. The term "formula" often comes with negative connotations, and an implication that all heart, soul, and artistic intent has been removed from the creation. However, as *Lovedrive* and the three (or four, or five, or six, depending on your taste) albums that followed show, formula can also come to suggest an internal affirmation of artists' collective and individual strengths, an acknowledgment that the defining traits of individuals can be harnessed to create a stronger identity for the whole. The fact that the 2022 released *Rock Believer* is an album that rivals the best of their '80s output in terms of youthful rock delivery speaks to the effectiveness of holding fast to this ideal, and the appetite for bands who effectively deliver brand identity.

Michael Schenker jumped ship from the Scorps and into UFO just as the British band were finding their way out of the fog of some early attempts at '70s space rock, which were actually received well in Japan, though they certainly weren't keeping bands like Hawkwind up at night.

When Schenker joined forces with vocalist Phil Mogg, bassist and loveable rock'n'roll pirate Pete Way, and drummer Andy Parker for UFO's 1974 major label debut *Phenomenon*, the result was an embrace of a classic and classy hard rock style that blended clean electric and acoustic guitars with distorted power chords (a combination introduced and perfected by Led Zeppelin, and a sonic trait that would become hallmarks of recordings by bands from Boston to Def Leppard). Two stone-cold hard rock classics from this album, *Doctor Doctor* and *Rock Bottom*, would find their definitive versions on *Strangers in the Night*, a live album recorded at shows in Chicago, Illinois, and Louisville, Kentucky, on the band's 1978 tour. The album also featured cuts of prime hard rock from 1975's *Force It* (cue yet another sexually questionable album cover, this time courtesy of Hipgnosis, the company that would bring you the high art of "bubble gum on boobs" for *Lovedrive* by the Scorpions), 1976's *No Heavy Petting*, and the pièce de résistance of the band's recorded oeuvre, the glorious early Def Leppard template that would be 1977's *Lights Out*.

Like *Tokyo Tapes*, *Strangers in the Night* is a beautifully recorded album . . . the guitar and drum tones are warm and punchy, and Mogg delivers his deceptively melodic vocals with a workingman's sincerity. The roar of the blue-collar American audiences that filled the concert halls on the evenings captured here stands in slight contrast to that of the Japanese audience on *Tokyo Tapes* . . . more whistling, more hootin', more hollerin' . . . and more consistently raucous throughout the songs. This reciprocity of energy between audience and band also gives *Strangers in the Night* a vibe that feels more in line with the hard rock and metal that would be inspired in its wake . . . and one of the reasons why Iron Maiden uses that album's version of "Doctor Doctor" as their preconcert intro music.

UFO manage to sound both thoughtful and urgent at the same time, perhaps a reflection of the diametrically opposed personalities of the tough-as-nails Mogg and the fragile and sensitive Schenker. The pop sensibility and roguish bonhomie of Pete Way serve as both musical and interpersonal glue that allowed UFO to weather storms that can arise out of such disparities. Worth mentioning here is that the addition of keyboardist and rhythm guitarist Paul Raymond elevated UFO's in-concert representation. As with the clockwork precision of Rudolf Schenker's rhythm guitar work in Scorpions, Raymond's playing grants Michael Schenker the license to roam wherever his fleet-fingered muse takes him. The tasteful application of his keyboard work is something that we would come to hear (even if self-identified "true metalheads" would be loath to admit to liking) in '80s hard rock acts like Los Angeles's Autograph.

> **Steve Lynch:** The keyboards added a whole new level of melodic texture . . . and I loved the way it played such a huge part in Autograph's overall sound. The keyboardist, Steve Isham (RIP), was absolutely brilliant at composing a variety of innovative layers and melodic interludes that created a uniqueness that set the band slightly apart from most others at the time.

As wildly inventive and adventurous a soloist as Schenker is, he was also a purveyor of catchy and addictive hard rock rhythm guitar licks and riffs, the kind that force your hand out of the pocket of a faded jean jacket, ball it into a fist, and pump it in the air in a sign of solidarity and connection with every heart-on-sleeve lyric pouring of out of Mogg's mouth. And lest you consider any of Mogg's streetwise sentimentality to be a sign of weakness, the pugilistic frontman could turn (and has) "heart-on-sleeve" into "fist-in-face" faster than a Michael Schenker guitar lick.

Strangers in the Night has connected with critics and fans alike as one of the greatest concert recordings of all time, a unifying, primal hard rock experience caught in vinyl grooves, and an influence on bands like Iron Maiden, Tesla, and Mötley Crüe. When you see Nikki Sixx circa 1985 in stripey attire sporting a Thunderbird bass, you are seeing an iteration of 1978 Pete Way with slightly more makeup and significantly more hairspray, but likely just as inebriated.

While *Strangers in the Night* was UFO's greatest commercial achievement, it would be disingenuous to say that the band didn't enjoy success after the fact, and enduring success at that. With the addition of guitarist Paul "Tonka" Chapman, the band recorded some very strong albums (some that rank as favorites amongst UFO diehards) including 1980's *No Place to Run*, a U.K. silver-certified disc recorded by legendary Beatles producer George Martin. Other legendary musicians who have done time in the ongoing saga of UFO include Billy Sheehan, "Atomik" Tommy McClendon, and guitar virtuoso Vinnie Moore. Having said this, *Strangers in the Night* differs from *Tokyo Tapes* in that it represents UFO's defining moment as a band. For Scorpions, *Tokyo Tapes* set the stage for heights yet to be achieved, and an even stronger identity to be forged.

After "Mad" Michael Schenker cemented his nickname and reputation by dramatically departing UFO at the height of their powers, essentially throwing a brick wall up for the band on their road to superstar status, he proceeded to demonstrate further instability with his hasty departure from Scorpions after his stellar work on the *Lovedrive* album. 1980's Michael Schenker Group (MSG) debut is a wonderful consolation prize for the loss of what could have been had Michael remained with UFO and Scorpions. Schenker enlisted topflight players like keyboardist Don Airey, drummers Simon Phillips and Cozy Powell, and vocalist Gary Barden (cut from the same vocal mold as Phil Mogg) to create an album that served up meat-and-potatoes power rock alongside more exotic musical fare. It all serves to highlight Schenker's fluid and melodic guitar work, with the instrumental "Into the Arena" being a textbook example of his mastery of a catchy rhythm hook and impeccably phrased and executed lead lines.

Just as *Strangers* will remain a picture caught in time of UFO in their prime, Thin Lizzy's *Live and Dangerous* opus also stands as the ultimate portrayal of what many believe is the world's *classiest* hard rock band. If ever there was a frontman who captured all ranges of aspirational manhood, it was Philip Lynott. Born a perfect outlaw (out of wedlock and half Black in very Catholic, very white Dublin, Ireland, in 1949), Lynott developed two essential survival skills: great charm, and the ability to handle his fists. When talking failed, fighting would do just fine. Blessed with cinematic good looks and an easy manner, Lynott worked his way through the ranks of the Irish music scene, ultimately forming Thin Lizzy with drummer Brian Downey and guitarist Eric Bell. In much the same way as did Scorpions and UFO, Lizzy enjoyed the latitude that came with the experimental nature of the times to work out their own unique musical style, forging a sound that blended R&B and hard rock influences (both European and American), and notably implemented the Celtic melodies of their native Ireland.

As was the trend in the tempestuous days of the ego, chemical, and alcohol fueled '70s, Thin Lizzy's lineup changed until ultimately coming together in its defining form. Lynott and Downey, along with guitarists Brian Robertson and American heartthrob Scott Gorham, had two kicks at the studio can with 1974's *Nightlife* and 1975's *Fighting* before breaking through the barriers of anemic guitar tone to deliver 1976's monumental *Jailbreak*, defined by its wailing siren attack and ubiquitous hit of a title track. But even here, the sound is not quite where it would end up, and after another strong outing with 1977's *Bad Reputation* (guitar recording handled primarily by Gorham, as Robertson had been given short-term walking papers after cutting his hand in a barfight), the ferocity of the Lizzy sound was finally harnessed on the *Live and Dangerous* album, which captured dates from as far back as 1976 in London, and shows from the Bad Reputation Tour in '77 in Philadelphia and Toronto.

As hard as *Live and Dangerous* rocks, there is also a romance about the proceedings, a swagger that resides in the space between Lynott's poetic, back-phrased vocals and the strutting, stiletto-heeled click of his plectrum-articulated bass playing. Make no mistake, these were pirates out to take the night and all that belonged to it, but they would do so slowly, with charm and civility . . . if they were going to break your heart (or your nose), they let you know in advance, as they do on Lynott's ode to bad romance, "Don't Believe a Word." If there was going to be a breakout into the city zone, they made sure that their women (yup, that's going to be a problem down the road) were staying some place safe that night. Sexist as all get out, but it played as sentiment back then, and Lynott sold it with those droopy eyes and that "aw shucks" grin.

There was wonderful wordplay at work in Lynott's lyrics, and the best of it made his audiences feel as if they themselves were part of a grand adventure, pirates on the high seas of a rock'n'roll journey . . . he brought American imagery, a Celtic mix-up of First Nations strife and cowboy folklore, not only to European audiences, but to North Americans themselves, largely due to the fact that he himself bought in. It is the same kind of connection that Bon Jovi would effectively make years later, making the audience part of the narrative . . . or making an audience of Tommy and Gina's the central stars of said narrative. This is where hard rock music found its purest soul, an earnestness that often transcended "cool" and wandered a good distance into the area of innocent corniness (for example, going to the pictures and getting chocolate stains on your pants in "Dancing in the Moonlight" while on a date . . . jeez, I sure hope that's innocence, anyway!).

No matter what message Lynott was delivering, it was always backed by the impeccable swing and fluidity of Downey's drums, and the greatest hard rock guitar team of all time, Robertson and Downey. Together, these two forged a dual lead-guitar harmony style that would be a main inspiration to Iron Maiden, Helloween, Tesla, and countless twin guitar bands to follow. In fact, it's almost impossible for two guitarists to play single-note, overdriven guitar melody lines an intervallic third apart without immediately calling to mind Lizzy.

Bad choices and bad blood would go on to plague Lizzy, and Robertson would ultimately leave the band for good, to be replaced by Irish virtuoso Gary Moore, who had popped in and out of the Lizzy camp for previous scattershot live and recorded appearances. He would help the band deliver what many people consider to be their last truly classic album, *Black Rose*, in 1979, a record that showcases the fiery playing and Celtic melodies on stun that would come to define his later successful forays as a solo arena rocker. As with MSG, he would make more of an impact in Europe and Japan than he would in the U.S. Moore ultimately found his greatest success as a renaissance bluesman in the early '90s with his multimillion selling *Still Got the Blues*. Moore abandoned Lynott and Co. without warning on the tour for the album, forcing the ushering in of new foils for Gorham that include Ultravox frontman Midge Ure and U.K. session ace Snowy White. Lizzy would go on to deliver strong albums that edged toward a more polished hard rock sound in 1980's *Chinatown* and 1981's *Renegade*. Always one to keep abreast of current trends in rock music, Lynott took inspiration from the burgeoning heavy metal sounds coming out of Europe and the U.K. and delivered a surprisingly solid effort in 1983's *Thunder and Lightning* (featuring a young John Sykes, who would go on to define the heavy guitar sound of the late '80s on Whitesnake's 1987 self-titled album). But the heart of the great Thin Lizzy beats strongest on *Live and Dangerous*.

Unlike the other bands in this quartet of defining live-album creators, Judas Priest managed to spend less time meandering in the fields of psychedelic rock, and were quicker to create something that is closer to what came to be known as heavy metal. While their 1974 debut *Rocka Rolla* reveals a few "twee" moments of plinky, clean guitar and decidedly less-than-menacing guitar tones, 1976's *Sad Wings of Destiny* is an undeniable heavy metal masterpiece, with the band's twin guitar team of Glenn Tipton and K.K. Downing moving in lockstep to create heavy metal riffs of ominous gravitas and beauty. Vocalist Rob Halford's mile-wide vibrato and banshee-like wail are vocal traits that would become idiosyncratic in the world of hard rock vocals for years to come. The evolutionary trend toward heaviness continued on through 1977's *Sin After Sin* and 1978's *Stained Class* (both produced by Deep Purple bassist Roger Glover), with the guitars becoming ever crunchier, the harmonies becoming tighter and more cleverly arranged, and drumming beginning to straighten out and drive harder with complex double-kick patterns. Even ballads like "Beyond the Realms of Death" mix the direct and the epic with striking affect, light and shade working toward a common metallic goal.

It was a second 1978 release (no rest for these poor bastards!), *Killing Machine* (*Hell Bent for Leather* in the U.S.), that to my mind is the best example of an album on the cusp of two eras. Two worlds are straddled in a battle between the warmth and dry precision of '70s production aesthete, and a brighter, shinier, and more richly saturated sound that highlighted both the efficiency and the state-of-the-art musicianship of the metal that Priest was forging ahead with. Tracks like "Delivering the Goods," "Hell Bent For Leather," and "Running Wild" are definitely pushing forward into territory that would be aggressively mined in the thrash metal and power metal scenes that would follow, while anthemic melodic fare like "Evening Star" and "Take On the World" would foreshadow the merging of FM radio rock melodic hooks and propulsive metal guitars and drums that we would hear in the commercial hard rock and metal of the early to mid-'80s.

And in terms of live albums, *Unleashed in the East* collects songs from all of Priest's catalog (at least from '76 on) with even more power, speed, and ferocity than is represented on the studio albums. Ah, the energy of that totally live experience . . . or is it totally live?

You see, the problem with live albums is that they are not recorded under ideal circumstances.

A recording studio offers architectural environments that are acoustically designed to create the perfect environ to capture a performance, where every sonic element can be isolated, managed, and massaged. Add in the rigors of the road — fatigue, vocal wear and tear, human exuberance (or boredom) — and various technical ghosts in the machinery, and you could have a recipe for disaster. *Unleashed in the East* was often dubbed *Unleashed in the Studio* in its time, with rumors (now confirmed by the metal god himself in his recent biography) swirling around that much of the album was indeed doctored in the studio, especially in the lead vocal department.

Having been involved in a number of commercially released live recordings, including albums by Lee Aaron, Coney Hatch, Nelly Furtado, and Howie D. from the Backstreet Boys, I'll say that the experience can be harrowing. Performing live in front of an audience can be stressful enough. There are so many technical aspects that can go wrong: malfunctioning amplifiers and PA speakers, broken drum skins and guitar strings, and the perils of personal illness that arise from less-than-ideal living conditions on the road. Most of the time, things go off without a hitch, and even when there are hitches, they're overcome fairly quickly and forgotten as the show goes on. But performance anxiety can be greatly compounded with the feelings of pressure and expectation, knowing that your performance is being recorded in microscopic detail for a release that will live far beyond a singular 90-minute concert experience. You see, we musicians are generally a highly self-critical lot. To get everything technically perfect in one go in a live setting is a big ask, even if it is what many musicians aspire to. My most successful personal performances on live albums have happened when I had no idea we were recording, and I'm proud to say that most of the live albums I've been associated with have had little to no enhancement. But yes, there have been times when I've had to enter the confessional booth and seek penance in the form of an overdub on an out-of-tune guitar part or a flubbed vocal line.

But in the end, who cares? The same rumors plagued *Live and Dangerous* and Kiss *Alive!* (to which Paul Stanley famously and rightly retorted that "It's as 'live' as it needed to be"). And while it is surely noble when a band delivers a live performance that is chock-full of energy *and* note-perfect precision, a live album is ultimately a document of what it felt like to *be* in the audience on a given night of a performance. In the confines of the concert bowl, no one gives a shit if Pete Way doesn't perfectly nail the gallop in "Doctor, Doctor" . . . or if Paul Stanley accidently frets that B power chord in strutter a half step up while jumping around on seven-inch leather heels. It's about the *feeling* and interaction between performer and the audience, and the power of congregating in the name of a shared passion. As Lemmy Kilmister sings in Motörhead's "On the Road," it's about being part of the new religion, the electric church, the *only* way to go. The intention of any great live album is to capture the feeling of the live concert experience, where imperfections are often masked by volume and viscera. In some cases, the unvarnished sonic truth of a recorded performance doesn't necessarily reflect the emotional truth of the concert experience as a whole. If a bum chord or sour vocal note reveals itself in a recording, and it takes the listener away from the magic of the moment, why wouldn't an artist take the opportunity to fix it? I say that if the odd cosmetic enhancement on a live album is too much to bear, perhaps you should get season tickets to the symphony. Classical musicians of that caliber rarely screw up, but then again, they don't have to jump around or dodge pyro explosions either.

If you were to listen to these four albums back-to-back, you would traverse a pretty solid bridge to where hard rock music was going. From the emerging new wave of British heavy metal that was sweeping the U.K. and Europe (a combination of the DIY ethic and rabid energy of punk with the musical chops and sense of loyalty to the first wave of heavy metal bands like Black Sabbath, Deep Purple, Budgie, and Uriah Heep), to the more sunshiny (at least on the West Coast), melodic, yet still hard-rocking fare being developed in the U.S. by bands like Van Halen, Quiet Riot, and Twisted Sister, bar bands were developing into concert acts, and as ambitions were fueled, new sounds were emerging.

It makes sense that we take a look at a few of the places where burgeoning new musical movements were taking root. Lots of different shades of influence to be sure, but one could argue that all of these scenes mirrored some combination of Kiss, Scorpions, Judas Priest, UFO, and Thin Lizzy (along with the myriad influences that make up the hard rock lineage), if not directly, then at least in terms of what they elementally represent (larger scale ambition, refinement and focus of sound, concision of arrangement, coalescing of artist and audience members), and that their live albums were a strong representation of the aspirations of a new wave of hopefuls vying for a spot at the top of the rock'n'roll mountain.

Late '70s Los Angeles is really a mash-up of the decade's glitter rock from the U.K. and the dirty American rock'n'roll you'd find smeared between the pages of *Creem* magazine. Tastemakers like music publicist Rodney Bingenheimer had successfully raised awareness of the glam rock movement he witnessed while in England and brought it back home to Hollywood. His club English Disco was a Sunset Strip landmark that took sex, drugs, and rock'n'roll clichés to new highs and lows, with a focus on catering to the underage groupies that were so appealing to the many elegantly wasted musicians of the day. Legendary groupies like Pamela Des Barres and Sable Starr would compete for the attentions of the rock stars from both sides of the pond, and in doing so created their own hierarchy and star system within the tiny clubs' walls. From a 2021 perspective, this scene — built on hair, makeup, skin-tight clothing, and feigned underaged ennui — reeks of perversion. And yet, for those who love the rock'n'roll from the era, it holds an air of high romanticism or a freedom to rise above restrictive societal norms. The dichotomy can almost be summed up in the formation of the band the Runaways by longtime L.A. producer-publisher slash con artist–scene-maker Kim Fowley. Was it the abusive, manipulative, lecherous work of a predator on the hunt for drugged-out Lolitas, or was it a gateway to the emancipation of women in rock'n'roll, a chance to show the boys club that the desire to make it and the ability to do so was not contingent on having a cock and balls? Like the answers you would get if you were to interview Joan Jett and Lita Ford, or Cherie Currie and Jackie Fox, the truth is probably found in a mixture of both perspectives.

What can't be denied is that this scene was highly motivational for a number of the musicians we will come to look at as we progress through the book. This scene, which also included clubs like the Troubadour, the Starwood, the Whisky, and Gazzarri's, was where members of bands like Ratt, Great White, BulletBoys, W.A.S.P., Dokken, and others would start their journeys. But the late '70s L.A. scene is largely a tale of two guitar players from the humble suburbs of Pasadena and Burbank: Edward Van Halen and Randy Rhoads. This actually makes sense, when you think of the audience that truly connects with '80s hard rock. It isn't the hipster elite of the big cities, or the music critics who fell most deeply under the spell that emanated from the fingers of these players, it was suburban kids . . . kids who dreamed of the hot rodded and customized cars, surfboards, skateboards, and ultimately guitars of sunny California.

Eddie and Randy were very aware of each other, and of each other's status as guitar kings of their respective scenes. Reports of mutual admiration and jealousy sprout up in equal amounts, depending on who you ask, as each player demonstrated a prodigious fluidity on their instrument and the ability to make a guitar and amp sing with an accentuated midrange sustain that had really made its first mark on American listeners with the first Boston record. The difference between Tom Scholz's playing and that of Eddie and Randy was in its ferociousness. Whereas Scholz was a fine player with a laid-back, melodic approach that threw out the odd technical flourish, both Randy and Eddie played with a pick attack that brought out the more aggressive harmonic content that would become associated with '80s guitar. We hear this same sound in the playing of contemporaries like George Lynch, Warren DeMartini, and Jake E. Lee, players who were circulating in the scene at the same time, playing customized and modified instruments by luthiers like Grover Jackson, Wayne Charvel, and Lynn Ellsworth, amplifiers modified by Jose Arredondo, and components like pickups and tremolo bar systems (whammy bars) by Seymour Duncan and Floyd Rose that accentuated these rich harmonic qualities and allowed the player high-performance tools with which to push the boundaries of electric guitar tone and technique.

For years, I have benefited from the expertise of my good friend, '80s guitar afficionado, and guitar modifier par excellence, Jay Hlady. Jay works out of the Twelfth Fret guitar shop in Toronto, and he has helped me to understand how changes to my instrument can facilitate my access to creativity. Jay takes into consideration factors like my personal touch and playing dynamics when modifying my instruments, which gives me the confidence and ability to tackle the challenging guitar-playing techniques found in '80s rock. I asked him what the most common modifications were for players in the '80s.

> **Jay Hlady:** If a player likes to use a lot of whammy bar tricks like fluttering [rapidly raising and lowering the pitch] and dive bombs, adding a Floyd Rose tremolo can definitely add to their expression. For certain types of playing, like two-handed fingerboard tapping, having a flatter radius and larger frets on the neck makes that style of playing easier. The most common mods back in the day are basically what you still see on rock guitars today . . . changing the neck and also changing pickups are still very popular choices. Back in the day, you couldn't buy a guitar with those features already — you had to modify. However, since the late '80s, manufacturers started making production models that you could buy off the rack with these details.

I asked a few players who were active in the California music scene of the late '70s–early '80s what their perspective was on this hot-rod culture happening in the guitar and amplifier world.

Warren DeMartini: The explosion of Van Halen was the liberation, the idea that you could make something awesome at home. It didn't have to be an off-the-rack guitar, and that just opened up [possibilities] . . . Everybody knew about the back pages of the magazines where you could mail-order a guitar body or a neck or anything, stuff like that, but it wasn't until that white Strat that Ed made [that guitar modification] became an absolute craze. I knew a guy, Dave Jellison, he played bass in Ratt for a while. He got a job at Charvel because he was one of the guys who lived in San Diego and L.A., he would go back and forth, and he worked at Charvel. Once in a while there'd be a "second," a neck that's fine, but it's got a little burr in the wood or something that when they sanded it down it appeared, so now they would have to throw it out. Well, guys like me were happy to pay 50 bucks for a "second." It's like, "Burr? What burr?" You could make something killer that you couldn't afford to buy new. And Charvel guitars were never cheap . . . like two, three grand. That was just way out of the question for me.

Billy Rowe: I would say California played a big part in it. DiMarzio pickups started in New York, but then you had Seymour Duncan on the West Coast. The first really boutique amp company, I could say is Boogie, which is Northern California. Guitar-wise, it would be Charvel in Southern California, and then you had Mighty Mite, and all the Eddie Van Halen–influenced stuff. Those are the original boutique guys, you know? Yeah, I mean, to me, everything that changed with the music and from the '50s and '60s into the '70s and '80s was that the [amplifier] gain got stronger . . . If you listen to old Priest and Iron Maiden's first few records, and you listen to the guitar tones, and they're not even [Marshall] JCM800s at that time [one of the earliest "high gain" amplifiers]. You know, we're talking about '79 [Marshall] JMP with a distortion box in front of it to give it more of that bite and smooth crunch, you know? When the pre-amps [modifications designed to drive an amplifier further into overdrive] came in and everything, the gain started going up, up, up, up in each genre.

Gilby Clarke: I worked at a music store and we had a really great repairman, and he was into all that stuff, and he turned me onto the Blackface Bassman thing, which I still use to this day. And he had a master volume, he used to call it a B-plus master volume. He said "Gilby, it'll sound better than any Marshall you ever had." And I had one, and at that time, gain wasn't [that high]. I wasn't a gain monster. I didn't need all that gain, but he could get it out of amplifiers. Like I said, my Bassman had so much gain. I actually had one of those Mark I Mesa Boogies, the first generation ones. Same thing, that had so much gain. I didn't know what to do with it, but I could hear all those local players and they [have] that Kiss, Ace Frehley, ch-ch-chang. They had a lot of gain in their sound. So yes, I definitely think it was a California thing. I definitely didn't hear that coming out of Ohio, that's for sure.

Kinda crazy to acknowledge that the heart of the guitar sound that would dominate MTV, radio airwaves, and stadiums throughout the '80s has as much to do with the ingenuity of woodworkers and electrical repair technicians in dusty shops in California as it does with the musicians playing them, but just like the magic and fire that was found in the grooves of those classic live albums, true musical reciprocity erases the delineation between frontline and backline.

It's strange to think that the names that adorned so many flashy, pointy, and angular guitar headstocks belonged to humble craftsmen waking up every morning and popping into their little shops ensconced in the Valley. It's something to keep in mind the next time you hear a guitar player talking about throwing a set of (Seymour) Duncan humbuckers into their (Grover) Jackson Flying V that's loaded with a Floyd Rose whammy bar and running it into a "Jose" mod-ed (Jim) Marshall Plexi.

I find it fascinating that at the same time that Eddie Van Halen and Randy Rhoads were carving out their reputations, other guitarists who were right there with them, playing the same clubs, soaking up the same influences, sometimes teaching at the same music schools, and vying for the same opening slots and recording contracts, have been cast in a secondary role in the history books. A narrative has been constructed that Van Halen and Rhoads are the first great innovators of late '70s–early '80s hard rock guitar playing in L.A., with players like Jake E. Lee, Carlos Cavazo, George Lynch, Warren DeMartini, and Autograph's Steve Lynch coming afterwards to further the advancement. But, in fact, other players had been developing techniques like the two-handed tapping approach before being exposed to Van Halen . . .

Steve Lynch: I was at the Guitar Institute of Technology back in 1978 creating my own particular style of tapping. I'd been influenced to experiment with it previously after watching guitarist Harvey Mandel and a local guitarist named Steve Buffington, who incorporated the technique into their style during the mid-'70s while I was still living in Seattle. While attending GIT, I stopped listening to other guitarists to concentrate on my own sound. Except for one . . . Allan Holdsworth. I thought much of the sound he was creating was by incorporating both hands on the fingerboard, so I tried to figure out his legato-style licks with both hands. I later found out that most all his technique was played with just his left hand on the fingerboard, but it surely gave me a lot of interesting ideas transcribing it with two. Most all the guitarists attending GIT at the time were jazz or fusion players, so I didn't have any exposure to the local L.A. talent. I was intently focused on creating my own style and became very reclusive, which I have a tendency to do every now and then. This enabled me to write the material for my first book on the two-handed technique titled *The Right Touch*, which was completed at the end of 1978.

Gilby Clarke: I moved to California in '77 and I, like I said, I was just getting into bands, and I had friends, we had our little bands, and we played . . . Like I said, we didn't play covers, we played originals, but we were playing school dances and parties and things like that. And there were other bands, but I had a friend who was a guitar player, too, and he was telling me about Van Halen. He goes, "You got to see this local band, they're playing the Starwood." He goes, "They're called Van Halen. He's the greatest guitar player, he's better than Hendrix, he's better than anything I've ever seen." And I went, "He's no Rick Derringer." Like, I didn't want to believe it, you know? So I never saw Van Halen live, but I did see Randy Rhoads quite a few times.

And yeah, so in L.A. at that point . . . Van Halen was just getting signed, and they played for a little while and then they stopped, because they were doing their record. But definitely, Van Halen. Randy Rhoads, but also George Lynch, Carlos Cavazo. He had a band called Snow that was unbelievable. I mean, they were just unbelievable. And like I said, George was in a band . . . Xciter, it had a girl singer. To me, every guitar player that I saw was just way beyond my ability, and it was a whole different realm of what was coming in at that time.

George Lynch: Everybody was doing something different back then, to an extent. I mean, there was Eddie, obviously, he was the king, and then there was the other guys — everybody else was the other guys. There was me and there was Warren, but Warren didn't come up yet. But there were some other local cats in the late '70s that were just fucking amazing. Kevin from A La Carte, oh my God, he was . . . But he was, you know, he played a Junior. I think he was like a heroin addict or something. They'd come out . . . They were a three piece, but they sounded like ZZ Top but looked like they were the *Rocky Horror Picture Show*. They came out in lingerie and makeup and would be all just drugged out on smack, and he was fucking awesome. I mean, he was really super greasy blues rock. He was . . . Great tone and a great player, slow hand, but it was awesome. But I put him right up there with Eddie.

For all the accolades all of these players would command for themselves in the '80s, they would ultimately exist in the shadows of Eddie and Randy, onetime peers who are often seen as acolytes in the history books.

To simplify matters for the sake of forward motion, let's say this: Eddie as a guitarist and Van Halen as a group were truly "first to market" with this new turbo-charged hard rock sound and approach. And for all the hotshot guitar players out there vying for record company attention, it was Van Halen who embodied the entire package that would represent hard rock's next evolutionary wave, and the most developed sense of innate artistry. When producer and Warner Bros. vice president Ted Templeman caught Van Halen playing to a half-empty Starwood on a rainy Monday night, he saw two things: a guitarist whom he ranked alongside Charlie Parker and Miles Davis as a true genius, and a band that was playing to 10 people like it was a crowd of 10,000. Together, they harnessed that artistry and intention and delivered it through that rarest of musical commodities — great songs. After that, it was just a matter of getting the sounds on tape, and within a few days at the fabled Sunset Sound Recorders, engineer Donn Landee was able to capture the lightning in a bottle and help craft the holy grail of '80s hard rock guitar sounds.

This also speaks to the importance of having the right people witness and recognize greatness at the right moment. A year earlier, Gene Simmons had seen the same thing (by accident, as he was actually there to catch a set by George Lynch's band the Boyz), and had been captivated by the same magic. Gene, ever the businessman and looking to delve into other areas of the business, took Van Halen to New York to record a series of demos that are now widely available for perusal on the internet. And while they definitely capture the ability and charm of the young Van

Halen, these demos are not the fully formed band that would emerge a year later through the guidance of Templeman and Landee.

But back to that kid from Burbank . . . the petite, chiselled cheek boned, feathered hair wonder that was Randy Rhoads. He of long-suffering but high-drawing club band Quiet Riot, who had managed through hard grift and bullish tenacity to secure themselves a recording contract (albeit for the territory of Japan only, with CBS Records). On two albums of highly questionable subpar material (I can say this with a fair bit of authority . . . I was hired to write "sound alikes" for an excellent documentary called *Randy Rhoads — The Quiet Riot Years* and was shocked that the majesty that would reveal itself in the writing and playing of just a few years later was barely to be found in these first two feeble attempts), the electricity that Rhoads brought to Hollywood stages was simply not captured on vinyl. At least not until 1980.

It's interesting to look at the role Van Halen played in creating the opportunity for Randy to finally find his own voice and ultimate place in rock history.

In 1978, Black Sabbath was decidedly a fading proposition. Hard living, bad business, and substance abuse had taken a toll on the heavy metal innovators, and despite managing to record a reasonably solid effort with *Technical Ecstasy*, this was a band running on fumes. Still, they were doing business at the gates, and since they recorded for Warner Bros., it made sense to look to a young, unknown band on the label roster to serve as support . . . a band who could fill time on the ticket bill without drawing too much attention from the headliner. The choice of new labelmates Van Halen as that opening act would prove to be a dramatic "changing of the guard" event, and perhaps the moment when the performance bar for the '80s was set. While Sabbath will always be considered the undeniable architects of heavy metal, all reports suggest that the young, hungry lions of the Van Halen camp positively devoured the wounded, exhausted Sabbath, night after night. Thanks for the riffs, Tony Iommi . . . we'll take it from here.

To be fair, there are reports that the Sabs still held their own with their impermeable legacy of great songs, but there was no doubt rot had set in. A final gasp with 1979's *Never Say Die!* ultimately signaled the end for Ozzy's tenure with Sabbath. On a ship full of drug addicts and alcoholics, Ozzy managed to somehow pull rank as the worst of the bunch and was dismissed for his failure to even show up for songwriting sessions for a new album.

Effectively, two major events occur out of this change. Sharon Osbourne, under the employ of her father and Black Sabbath manager, Don Arden, takes it upon herself to save a drugged out and disillusioned Ozzy and resurrect his career. This would entail putting together a team of crack musicians, mainly U.K. veterans who could work with Ozzy and understand him in that particular way that English musicians understand each other. Enter bassist Bob Daisley from Rainbow and, later, drummer Lee Kerslake from Uriah Heep. After attempts at securing topflight guitarists like Gary Moore and Michael Schenker failed to yield results, the net was cast in Los Angeles to find a guitarist who could provide the golden riffs that would lift Ozzy out of his artistic stupor.

Randy Rhoads's decision to audition for, and ultimately accept, a position in the Ozzy Osbourne band marked two things for the young Burbank prodigy: a heartbreaking end to his partnership with Kevin DuBrow in Quiet Riot after two albums that failed to set the Japanese market on fire, and the start of pop metal. The release of 1980's Max Norman–produced *Blizzard of Ozz* was a showcase for Randy Rhoads's razor-sharp guitar sound and riffs that could convey upbeat positivity and menacing metal (often within the context of the same song). It is also important to note the contributions of Daisley and Kerslake on this record (and the even more powerful and developed *Diary of a Madman* album). These albums were written under the auspice that *Blizzard of Ozz* was to be a *band* effort and, in fact, the name of the band as well (early 8x10 promotional photos corroborate this story). As such, Daisley and Kerslake served as much more than the hired-gun session players that history and Sharon Osbourne have cast them to be. Daisley was a key melodic and lyrical architect, and Kerslake's unique grooves and power fills were arguably a major inspiration for the rhythmic inventiveness that Rhoads brought to the magical riffs of these two albums.

Rudy Sarzo: You could see Randy's potential playing with Quiet Riot, but if you listen to the last recording Randy ever did with Quiet Riot, I would say . . . I was there, "One in a Million," it was one of the last recordings. And you listen to his work on *Blizzard of Ozz*, and we're talking like months apart from each other, one was '79, and then he started recording with Ozzy in '80 . . . It's so different. It's like two different people, right? It's not because Randy was different, no. It was because [of] the music industry. There was no sense of him coming into a Quiet Riot rehearsal and say, "Hey, I've got this idea for a song, 'Revelation (Mother Earth)'." It could have been made up by anything else, but musically, "Revelation (Mother Earth)," we could have never done that. Impossible. There are bits and pieces of a song that used to be called "Teenage Anthem," and then it got rerecorded as "Winners Take All" on the *Condition Critical* record.

I was not aware that Randy Rhoads was a classical guitar player until I started teaching at Musonia, and in between students he would pick up the acoustic guitar and start playing classical, and I'd go, "Wow. I didn't know you could play like that."

With Quiet Riot, we had to get up there and be electric and be rock'n'roll, whereas when he was recording with Ozzy there was no question about bringing [his classical influence] out because at that moment he did not have to please the record companies anymore. He's playing with a recording artist named Ozzy Osbourne, so he asked Ozzy, "What do you want me to write?" And Ozzy said, "Be yourself." That's it. He did not have that opportunity, while he was a member of Quiet Riot, to be himself, to be Randy Rhoads. He was a little bit of Randy Rhoads, a part of Randy Rhoads, that he thought that the record company allowed him to be, but he wasn't the full Randy.

The chemistry of this union of musicians worked in tandem with Ozzy's melodic voice to create a unique combination of metal and melody. Love or hate Ozzy's nasal vocal tone, the man is blessed with a purity of intonation that floats beautifully above heavy guitar riffs, revealing an accessibility and human vulnerability that often evades more technically gifted singers, who try to take on the power of the electric guitar head and pounding drums with warbling vibrato and Valkyrie-esque screams.

Now, if there ever was a singer who *could* match or better the power of his ensemble, it was the great Ronnie James Dio, who had taken Ritchie Blackmore's Rainbow to the top of the silver mountain with three albums: *Ritchie Blackmore's Rainbow* (in case you forgot who was running the show); '70s metal's most epic stand, *Rising*; and the slightly less epic but still solid *Long Live Rock'n'Roll*. If you ever hear a wizard, dungeon, or dragon reference connected to a minor-key metal guitar riff, you can often find its genesis at the beginning, middle, or end of the Rainbow.

1980's *Heaven and Hell* takes all of the values of '70s-era Black Sabbath and refines them into a tighter, cleaner, and more focused package. The choice to replace Ozzy with the physically diminutive, but giant of presence, Dio was inspired and inspiring. Iommi's guitar riffs took on broader anthemic qualities, cleanly picked arpeggio passages leading into ominous and highly developed power chord themes, Dio rising to the challenge with tales in "Neon Knights" and "Children of the Sea" providing both-sides-of-the-coin commentary on all of life's allures and pitfalls. Has there ever been a singer so committed to warning his audience of the traps awaiting us out there in the real world? "Look Out!" It was heaven and hell out there, but somehow we could all be safe together as we traversed evil spaces both mythical and real in the grooves of the vinyl.

Heaven and Hell was custom made for a dark arena jam packed with sweaty 15-year-old males swathed in denim, leather, and cheap weed. When I hear this new, emerging metal sound from 1980, it's hard not to have a composite image of an older teenager come to mind, threatening and exciting at the same time . . . just the kind of dude Dio would warn you about.

Any kid who ever dared to enter the sliding glass doors of a darkened arcade knows the thrill and danger that emanated from these

Jordache-sporting creeps, plugged into the pinball and video games that "bleeped" and "blooped "around us. Their scrawny backs would often be covered with tobacco smoke–polluted jean jackets sporting logos of the bands that were creating the soundtrack for their thinly mustachioed, oily skinned, testosterone-fueled existence. These logos, sometimes hand drawn, sometimes in the form of bootleg patches from various head shops, indie record stores, or the back pages of a rock magazine, could be considered indicative of the musical crossover that was occurring . . . first wave bands like Zeppelin, Purple, and Sabbath were now being joined by solo Ozzy, Van Halen, and a swathe of new bands, many emerging out of England, who were marrying DIY values gleaned from punk and new wave with the frustration of trying economic times and the hard rock of their forefathers.

The "new wave of British heavy metal" was a term coined by journalists from *Sounds* magazine in the U.K. (that would ultimately spawn *Kerrang!*), as a means of identifying a movement of musicians who were rejecting the punk and new wave music being foisted upon them in favor of riff-based, first wave heavy metal that was played with more speed and ferocity. Bands like Iron Maiden, Def Leppard, Saxon, Venom, Samson, Girlschool, Vardis, Girl, Angel Witch, Tygers of Pan Tang, Blitzkrieg, and Diamond Head were staring down the barrel of economic austerity and a grim choice between dangerous factory work or long lineups collecting dole. The movement become so strong that eventually the major labels took notice, and, as we will see in the next chapter, many of these bands were offered major label recording contracts . . . with a precious few managing to grab a hold of the brass ring and move into the upper echelons of rock stardom. A proliferation of indie labels such as Neat, Ebony, and Bronze, built out of small recording studios and aided and abetted by a variety of distributors, ensured that bands of high quality (well, varying quality) who fell outside the tastes of a broader mainstream audience could still enjoy the thrill of having their sonic vibrations captured on black wax, slipped into a paper sleeve, and placed on the shelf of their local record shops alongside their heroes and DIY contemporaries.

What is truly refreshing about the NWOBHM was that bands could merge any collection of their past influences and still be accepted as long as they were loud and fast. Iron Maiden's Steve Harris took elements of

Genesis and Jethro Tull and mixed them with the melodic twin guitars of Thin Lizzy and a punk rock admiring singer (Paul Di'Anno) who could actually sing. Bands like Venom turned a fascination with Kiss and their own inability to play their instruments well (or even tune them properly) into a major plus, compensating for a lack of musicianship with crushing volume and copious amounts of echo, throwing in a dash of satan and a lot of speed to help invent what would become black metal. Motörhead took their inspiration from a combination of Little Richard, big band swing courtesy of the double kick drum fury of Philthy Animal Taylor, inhuman doses of methamphetamines and whisky, and a simple motto . . . everything louder than everything else. They would ultimately become the godfathers of thrash metal.

Music provided both an escape from reality and a hope for a more colorful future. Veteran acts Judas Priest, Whitesnake, and Gillan (the latter two projects built around Deep Purple vocalist alumni David Coverdale and Ian Gillan) were reinventing their songwriting in fresh new ways that allowed them to cross the divide from first- to second-wave hard rockers and guarantee their respective logos a place on the back of any good headbanger's jean jacket. NWOBHM-hungry rockers would congregate at clubs like the Heavy Metal Soundhouse on nights hosted by radio DJ Neal Kay to be introduced to the freshest hard rock sounds from around the world, all the while inventing a new move called "head-banging" and throwing shapes with cardboard guitars, fueled by ample supplies of volume, lager, and cider.

In this environment, the power of the collective musical identity was amplified and taken to heart. A commitment to being a denim-and-leather rocker was something to be taken seriously, and the reward for loyalty was belonging, and a music to call your own.

Man, what a time to be a rock'n'roller, fan or musician. The first wave of heavy metal–heads had showed the faithful what was possible with the hard-edged sounds pioneered in the '60s and developed further in the '70s, and a second wave of rockers latched on to a faster, harder aesthetic, with dreams fueled by the now established knowledge that there were people all over the world who wanted to hear hard and heavy music.

So many templates for the hard rock to come were established in the short years between 1978 and 1980, but the real fun was about to start in the years covered in our next chapter . . . as appetites for hard rock increase, so, too, do the variations on the theme of drums, guitars, bass. In 1980 alone, we have landmark albums by AC/DC, Loverboy, Judas Priest, Ozzy, Motörhead, Black Sabbath, Rush, and Scorpions, all helping drive the hard rock juggernaut into the future.

Even though 1981 through '82 preceded my own meaningful introduction to hard rock, I can experience the passion of discovery that I imagine existed within the hearts of the fans who came before me as I write. Through the magic of recorded media, I am able to go back in time to place myself in attendance at those gigs captured on the famous live albums we talked about earlier. I can imagine shaking off the cold of an industrial work week with a pint and a headbang in the heyday of the NWOBHM. I can even become that loathsome teenager playing *Tron* in the arcade who would spit on me for standing too close.

I also feel the anticipation of writing about (and falling in love all over again with) the music the artists that introduced this glorious music in my life in chapters to come, this time with a greater understanding of where it all came from. Kinda like I when fell in love with Van Halen in 1986 with *5150* . . . and then went back and heard *Van Halen I*.

In 1981, Saxon reminded us that denim and leather brought us all together . . . but let's see if they will keep us together as all of these disparate influences work their way through musicians and the record industry on their way to the fans.

Denim, leather . . . and spandex. The future's so bright, you'll have to wear mirrored shades.

CHAPTER 5
1981 TO 1982

HOT, YOUNG, RUNNING FREE . . .
A LITTLE BIT BETTER THAN (IT) USED TO BE?

To my ears, 1981 was the year when hard rock bands started sharpening their blades, carving out prime slices of metal from the bountiful carcasses of the '70s rock mammoths that roamed the earth in the last decade. Refinements in songcraft and production, and an exciting move (well, for a guitar player at least!) to expound upon the virtues brought to light by the work of Eddie Van Halen and Randy Rhoads created a *"Shock of the New"* excitement. Even in the midst of changing tastes in the mainstream and movement toward new wave synthesizers and skinny ties, new mixtures of heavy metal thunder, punk attitude, hot-rodded guitars, and pop sensibility were finding footing with a young audience.

It's pretty startling to hear the progression in polish and heaviness that exists between Ozzy Osbourne's *Blizzard of Ozz* and 1981's *Diary of a Madman*, despite being recorded mere months apart. From the opening drum salvo of Lee Kerslake's thunder toms to its Sabbath-with-a-facelift opening guitar riff, "Over the Mountain" is a statement of heavy metal intent bathed in gothic occult darkness that somehow sounds energized, modern, and uplifting. Rhoads's great legacy as a player lies in his ability to take standard rock guitar conventions and apply rhythmic and harmonic variations borrowed from classical music that don't ever make you *think* they are coming from classical music. He may have been borrowing *very* liberally from Leo Brouwer's "Etude No. 6" in his classical guitar intro to *Diary*'s title track, but its dark beauty offers a haunting premonition of the heaviness to follow. Randy is feeding us the classics, but we feel like we're munching on metal.

> **Rudy Sarzo:** I wasn't there during the making of *Blizzard* or *Diary*, that was Lee Kerslake and Bob Daisley, but I was there when we used to write songs in Quiet Riot, which was only a few months before he was working with Ozzy. So I can tell you about Randy's way of writing. He was very giving. You know, Randy was a teacher, so if you come up with something, he would take it and make it more musical. He would just expand on it — he would just make it better. That was his natural nature until he thought it was musically correct because he had all of this knowledge, theory, composition to back it up.

In fact, Randy's greatest gift to Ozzy was his ability to translate the tritone-inspired heavy metal riffs of Sabbath and apply a sonic modernity and accessibility to them. A tritone is a musical interval, also known as the diabolus in musica for its clashing sonority that in the late 18th century was purportedly evil enough to conjure the devil himself. By mixing a little California sunshine with the grimy industrial din of Sabbath's Birmingham roots, Rhoads and the lineup that conceived the first two Ozzy albums are highly responsible for setting up metal's crossover to a mainstream American rock audience.

Ozzy really only entered my radar in 1982, with the release of *Speak of the Devil* (*Talk of the Devil* in the U.K.), a live recording of Black Sabbath classics recorded to fulfill contractual obligations. The album was recorded by Ozzy's solo lineup at the time, which tragically did not feature Randy Rhoads. Released in November of 1982, *Speak of the Devil* was recorded in September of that year, just six months after Rhoads was killed in a bizarre plane crash involving the driver of the band's tour bus, Andrew Aycock, an amateur pilot with an expired license, and the band's wardrobe person and cook, Rachel Youngblood. While on the *Diary* tour, the bus driver had decided to stay the night at a friend's home in Leesburg, Florida, en route to a stadium show. Parking the bus on Jerry Calhoun's property, which also served as a private plane hangar, Aycock went and commandeered one of Calhoun's planes without permission.

This led to an invitation for a joyride, which was strangely accepted by the usually flight-reticent Rhoads. In what is generally accepted as a prank gone wrong, Aycock took to flying very close to the grounds, "buzzing" the house on the property. On the third of these passes, the wing of the small plane clipped the tour bus, violently shaking the band and crew inside from their slumber, and more devastatingly, sending the small aircraft into a fiery crash that resulted in the loss of three lives.

Rumors and speculation have long spun around this strange accident (Why was the pilot buzzing the tour bus? Was he high? Suicidal?), but the end result was the loss of one of the world's great guitarists. While the entourage (which included drummer Tommy Aldridge, bassist Rudy Sarzo, keyboardist Don Airey, and manager Sharon Osbourne) were still deeply in grief, they applied a decidedly British stiff-upper-lipped ethos to an old adage: the show must go on. Ozzy and team quickly bounced back to fulfilling their touring obligations, frantically trying to find a replacement who could survive the baptism by fire that awaited. The first person to step up was Irish guitar virtuoso and fellow Jet Records recording artist Bernie Tormé, who made his brave and terrifying debut with the band at Madison Square Garden. Tormé was just about to release his own album, however, and he made it clear that his stint in the band was not to be a full-time solution, thus opening the door to a young Bay Area guitarist by the name of Brad Gillis. Gillis would take a break from his band, Ranger — later to become the highly successful Night Ranger upon Gillis's return to the fold — to join the Ozzy tour. Night Ranger would go on to secure their own major label contact and release their debut album *Dawn Patrol* in 1982, an album which merged an early '80s AOR (album-oriented rock) sound with a flashy twin guitar attack that would help to shape the sound of mid-'80s commercial pop metal.

The *Speak of the Devil* live album proved Gillis to be a player of distinctive tone and formidable chops and foreshadowed what audiences would come to hear in the decidedly more commercial fare that Night Ranger would offer. His whammy bar work and quick-fingered facility hinted at the new type of guitar playing pioneered by Van Halen and Rhoads, a decidedly American approach.

The first time I saw and heard *Speak of the Devil*, I was at my cousin's cottage, a 10-minute walk through the woods from my own, for a summer night's game of Monopoly. Growing up in the North, it was nothing to take a flashlight and walk unattended at night, even though the remoteness from the nearest town with electricity led to pitch black past 9 p.m. But after being exposed to Ozzy's grim visage on the cover, adorned with costume store–level vampire teeth and congealed blood dripping from his mouth (which, admittedly, looks more like Smucker's strawberry jam to my adult eyes), and the demonic riffs and threats of fairies wearing boots, hand-grabbing Lucifers, and warring pigs, I was completely freaked out. I'm sure I missed collecting my $200 a few times as I passed GO, as all I could focus on was the deliciously evil tuneage cranking from the boom box on my uncle and aunt's red-and-white-checkerboard card table.

When it was time to make that walk home by myself, my mind raced with the sinister howl of Ozzy's voice and satanic exhortations as my heart pounded in 6/8 time to the gothic blues shuffle gallop that brings the song "Black Sabbath" to its grim conclusion. The silhouettes of the massive pine trees that lined the well-worn path to my cottage took on ghastly and horrible dimensions, terrifying and taunting me into a state of total mental anguish, a heavy metal *Symphonie fantastique* of a fever dream. When I finally made it home, my eyes were wet with tears and my body was covered in a lather. I would never look at those woods in the same way again at night, a true moment of innocence lost as I feared for my soul and safety. And yet, I couldn't wait to return the next day to hear those riffs and see that album cover all over again. Like Dangerous Toys would sing on their 1989 debut in a paean to Alice Cooper, another artist known to put a little shock in his rock: *I think I like being scared!*

Randy Rhoads would come to deeply influence me years later, with the posthumous release of 1987's *Tribute*. As we discussed previously, the beauty of the live album to the budget-conscious teenager is that we get the best of the collected works and hear them in a spirited energy exchange between audience and artist. Along with the incredible cover image of

Ozzy hoisting Randy up in the air, toward his rightful place among the heavy metal gods, the gatefold album art included a heartfelt letter explaining why Ozzy had decided to release this album and what the guitarist had meant to him as a musician and a friend. I had no cynical concept of marketing ploys then, and the sentiment of the letter struck an authentic chord with me. *Tribute* felt important, and I felt like I was being introduced to something and someone very special. Around this time, guitar magazines were writing floridly about the album and Randy's innovative playing, and in doing so they introduced him to young players like me who may have missed him when he first made his mark. I was so moved by Randy's dedication to his art, and in particular his strong desire to continue his studies in traditional classical guitar, that I was inspired to study classical guitar myself. This inspiration also dovetailed with my budding awareness of neo-classicist Yngwie Malmsteen, whom I first discovered with 1986's *Trilogy* album. I found the notion and the imagery of musicians taking the power and energy of hard rock and melding it with the sophistication and technical mastery of classical music to be incredibly romantic. It felt like a connection to the past, yet framed in an utterly modern and exciting context. Man, if I could play like *that*, I'd be *special*. Of course, a few thousand other guitar players had the same idea . . . but I didn't see too many people doing it in North Bay, so maybe I'd have a shot!

Years later, I was offered the opportunity to record an album of famous classical guitar pieces as part of a series of instrument- and genre-specific titles, all featuring the greatest hits of classical music. *The #1 Classical Guitar Album* would feature pieces by Bach, Albéniz, Dowland, and . . . Rhoads. I can remember the look of concern as I broached the idea with my label up at the offices of Universal Music Canada, but I was steadfast in my belief that Randy's classical guitar piece "Dee" should be included on the album. "Dee" was a solo guitar piece that Randy had written for his mother, and it had been included on *Blizzard of Ozz*. It is a simple piece, with innocent nods to Bach and lute music of the Renaissance, but putting it on a heavy metal album was a bold and inspired choice. It was my contention that Randy had influenced just as many people to play classical guitar as any of the other composers that were to be featured on the album. I'm proud to say it was included in *#1 Classical Guitar Album*, and, for all that the *Tribute* album gave me in terms of inspiration, it was wonderful to pay tribute to Randy in this way. I hope I did the piece justice.

As great as Randy's musicianship was, I have to say that his striking image also resonated with me in a meaningful way. Randy possessed the beautiful physical appearance of a rock god, so small and thin that he was often mistaken for a girl, but he was also larger than life when striking a power stance with his custom Flying V or cream-white Gibson Les Paul Custom. He was blessed with cheekbones you could cut diamonds with, and a head of hair that took Mick Ronson's feathered blond shag cut and extended it down even further past the shoulders.

I later recognized just how much inspiration Randy took from David Bowie's six string foil in the shapes he would throw across the Hollywood stages he'd rock with Quiet Riot, and later on in stadiums with Ozzy. These moves added a decidedly testosterone-fueled energy to his stagecraft, creating a gender fluid yin and yang that would go on to define much of the look and feel of rock performance in the '80s. He also employed a number of the sonic techniques that Ronson had perfected, like using the toggle switch between a neck pickup with the volume rolled off and the fully engaged bridge pickup, creating a stuttering effect that sounded like an evil Morse code. There were also the scraping glissandi pick slides that sounded like an airplane taking off, and the deep bending of the guitar's neck and strings to create otherworldly howls. When you add these visual aspects and sonic tactics with Rhoads's impressive mastery of modal theory, classical harmony, rapid-fire right-hand picking, smooth left-hand legato technique, *and* his universally acknowledged humility, you have a rock guitar inspiration for the ages.

Randy's marriage of '70s glam rock–pop sensibility and classical inspired heaviness also gave wings to Ozzy's sonic identity. That sound that would forever be tied to the persona built upon by his wife and manager Sharon's carefully orchestrated publicity stunts as well as Ozzy's own penchant for chemically fueled misadventure. Let's face it, if you are biting the head off a dove in a record company boardroom, there has to be some semblance of preparation going on, and you need someone crazy enough to do it.

Stunts like this are straight out of Sex Pistols impresario Malcolm McLaren's school of manipulation . . . create a combustible scenario, egg on a drug and/or drink-addled protagonist to be the spark that starts the fire, sit back, and collect the press clippings and increased revenue generated as a result. However, in Ozzy's case, there is an authenticity to the behavior that actually comes across in his vocal delivery. It's a plaintive, almost pleading melodic timbre that speaks to his humanity. We want Ozzy to do these outrageous things, but we also want everything to work out for the guy, and when we hear him, we feel that he wants the best for us as well. It's not too late to learn how to love and forget how to hate . . . we come for the freakshow, but we stay for the hope in the music.

In 1981, Iron Maiden came along and upped the ante on their second album, *Killers*, doubling down on both the progressive rock elements of their style as well as the heaviness. There was an improved clarity in the overall sound over the debut, largely attributed to producer Martin Birch, who had made his name on landmark albums by Rainbow and Black Sabbath. On *Killers*, guitarist Dennis Stratton was replaced with Adrian Smith, which speaks to the power of human chemistry within a band. In combination and in contrast to coguitarist Dave Murray's rolling legato flurries, Smith's highly developed melodic chops helped to create one of the most identifiable traits of the Iron Maiden sound: two guitarists who could sync up in twin guitar harmony, but also soar as individual soloists.

Much of what we have come to know as quintessential Maiden comes from the sound of the drums and the bass guitar. In the case of the first three Maiden albums, the drumming of Clive Burr is pitted against one of the most personalized bass sounds in rock history, the metallic clang of Steve Harris.

In 2018, I had the opportunity to tour with Steve Harris's British Lion as a guitarist for the support band, Coney Hatch (who themselves had been touringmates of Iron Maiden in 1983 on the World Piece Tour). British Lion is a band Harris takes on the road or into the studio whenever there is downtime in the Iron Maiden schedule. (Harris will sometimes take British Lion on tour with Maiden, not as support, but so that the band can play on Maiden's days off . . . there's that British work ethic!)

At the first soundcheck, I marveled at two things (well, I marveled at lots of things, not the least of which was when Steve Harris walked up to me to hand me my pass for the tour . . . turns out he's also a pretty great tour manager!). As Harris and his tech dialed in his bass tone, I was taken aback by how much treble (or "high end") and midrange frequencies there were in his sound. As Harris attacked the strings, there was an audible "clank" that at times overtook, to my ears, the melodic content of what he was playing. In combination with his fleet-fingered and aggressive right-hand technique, it was thunderously loud and seemingly totally domineering.

However, when the rest of the band fell into their respective roles in the songs, it became clear that what Harris was actually achieving was something definitive and majestic . . . a sound that would work in conjunction with the other instruments while cutting through with the signature lines that drive the music. It was *his* signature sound, borne of a deeper vision. This served as a lesson to me that in the greatest bands and their recordings, the roles and sounds of the individual players are always best utilized in service to the collective big picture and should not only be heard as stand-alone entities. A close listen to Motörhead's classic 1981 live offering *No Sleep 'til Hammersmith* highlights the same point. Lemmy's bass sound on that recording has more in common with razor blades than it does with the warm, low-end supporting tones we often associate with bass guitar, but the space left for the pointed, foot-fueled flurry of Philthy Animal Taylor's double kick drum assault allows the drummer's best traits to shine through and forces guitarist "Fast" Eddie Clarke to find his own sonic space and approach to playing. Were you to isolate Clarke's guitar parts in any given mix, you would hear an incredibly resourceful player whose Chuck-Berry-on-amphetamines style would place him miles apart from his power chord–wielding peers.

Speaking of individual identity and its role in a group, there is no move riskier in a band's career than the changing of the lead vocalist guard, and in '82 Maiden would roll those dice in the name of artistic vision. Where Paul Di'Anno embodied a true punk rock ethos in his devil-may-care lifestyle choices, Maiden was a machine driven just as much by the work ethic of bassist and band leader Steve Harris and manager Rod Smallwood as it was by the music. By all accounts, a good time was never discouraged in the Iron Maiden camp *after* the work was done, so long as it didn't affect the next day's efforts. The seeds of discontent were also sown in the field of artistic differences, with Di'Anno growing increasingly dissatisfied with Maiden's progressive rock leanings. Enter Bruce Bruce, a.k.a. Bruce Dickinson, then vocalist for NWOBHM contenders Samson. Dickinson would prove himself, throughout his life, a man of prodigious talent, a world-class fencing champion, a pilot, a successful author. All of this ambition, ability, and achievement represented in a voice so expansive, expressive, and powerful, that the man has been dubbed "The Human Air Raid Siren." With the release of 1982's *The Number of the Beast*, Iron Maiden as the world at large would come to know it was truly born, with the influences of its punk rock past eclipsed by the galloping strides and stratospheric vocal melodies that would set the course for Maiden's ultimate world domination. Their epic tracks ("Hallowed Be Thy Name," "Children of the Damned") took on a broader shape, and their sing-along anthems became more strident and elated. Major key melodies like the ones found on the title track and the galloping "Run to The Hills" could have come straight out of a Handel oratorio. Mind you, idiosyncratic stage props, mascots ('ello Eddie!), and theatrics that are hallmarks of a Maiden concert might have made for a better opera than oratorio . . . but that's nitpicking, innit?

Maiden made it feel safe to exhort the number of the beast (for it *is* a human number), so full of sunshine was its ringing refrain and hummable and strum-able bass guitar hook. It's not a stretch to say that an entire school of influence was born with the marriage of Dickinson to Maiden, and the results would be seen in examples of power metal (Helloween, Iced Earth) and progressive rock of the '80s and early '90s (Savatage, Queensrÿche, Dream Theater).

One of my biggest pet peeves about the critical dismissal of 1980s hard rock is that it all sounds the same . . . lifeless, generic, processed, artificial, lacking warmth. To my ears, the '80s are defined in the early part of the decade by three components: the refined American corporate rock of AOR radio, the punk and early British hard rock influence on the burgeoning NWOBHM, and the distinctly German approach of Scorpions and Accept. In the case of the latter, there is one man in particular who would come to hold as much sway over the sound of '80s hard rock as anyone who came before or after.

Michael Wagener started Accept in the 1960s with his friend, vocalist Udo Dirkschneider. Michael fell under the spell of the electric guitar, but he was also interested in the electronic engineering side of music, ultimately earning a degree and going on to build his own 16-track recording studio in Hamburg in 1979. (A mandatory stint in the German military made remaining a member of Accept too difficult to accommodate, but Wagener would remain a friend and professional ally.) In charge of all aspects technical and financial that are key to running a studio, Michael developed the ears, knowledge, and personal skill sets that would later serve him as a producer and mixer.

It's strange to think how many millions of dollars were made and albums sold as a result of a fortuitous meeting, but it's not a stretch to say that when American singer Don Dokken met Michael while touring in Germany, the course of the recording industry for the upcoming decade was set. What started as a friendship between two musicians led to an invitation to visit Dokken in his hometown of Los Angeles. His visit in L.A. was long enough for him to establish that this was where he could find the talent and opportunity to make his mark, and he returned in 1980 to permanently set up shop. Sharing a house with Dokken, Alan Niven (noted record producer and music executive, and manager for Great White and Guns N' Roses), and Ratt drummer Bobby Blotzer, Wagener found himself surrounded by a veritable Who's Who of the L.A. music scene, although at that time the meager accommodations they shared mirrored the struggle they were all going through. An offer from his old pal Udo Dirkschneider to come tour Europe with Accept (who were now picking up steam as a touring act) as a live sound engineer ultimately led to Wagener finding himself in the studio with Accept as a recording engineer. The result would be 1981's *Breaker*, the first of a string of albums that would see Accept eschew attempts at commercial acceptance in their pursuit of a heavier signature sound.

During this period, Don Dokken, frustrated by his lack of progress in America, returned to Germany to record some demos to try and secure a recording contract, believing that the acceptance of a heavier style of music and production was more in alignment with his own aesthetic. Together with Wagener (and with L.A. musicians George Lynch, "Wild" Mick Brown, and Juan Croucier), Dokken was able to attract the interest of French label Carrere Records (home to Saxon), who released *Breaking the*

Chains . . . an album that would eventually find a U.S. home in a revamped version on Elektra Records . . . thanks to the legwork of one Alan Niven.

Alan Niven: This guy (Don Dokken) came into Greenworld and walked into my office, put his feet on my desk, hadn't even said hello, threw me an album, said, "I want you to do for me what you did for Mötley Crüe."

And, of course, I got Mötley onto Elektra through my relationship with Tom Zutaut: Tom got an A&R [artists and repertoire] gig, and Mötley got onto Elektra. But, you know, Don had made this record in Germany, and he said, "I want you to do for me what you did for Mötley," and I lived with the record for a week. I called him back in, and I said, "I can't sign you." And the look on his face, and he said, "You fucking signed Mötley Crüe, and you won't sign me? My record's far better produced, I write better songs than they do." I said, "Well, I think that's part of the point, Don. How old are you?" And he said, "Oh, I'm 30." I said, "Right, if I sign you to this little fucking company [Greenworld] here now, I'll be doing you the biggest disservice of your life. You need to be on a major label right now. Let me see what I can do." So I went chasing Zutaut and said, "Here's your second signing."

And Tom brushed me off for about a month or so, and I said, "Well, then I'm going to send it to some other people," and I sent a copy to Cliff Burnstein. Cliff Burnstein and Peter Mensch had a company called Q Prime, a management company, and were just starting to do well with a band called Def Leppard. So I sent this record to Cliff and didn't get much of a response, and then one day I'm sitting in my office and the receptionist says, "Cliff Burnstein on line one for you." So I pick it up, and I go, "Hi Cliff, what are you doing?" He said, "I'm standing in a record store. I'm up in Boston, and there's a record playing." And he said, "I thought to myself, I know that record. How do I know that record?" And I said, "Well, what are you listening to, Cliff?" He said, "I'm listening to the same record that you sent me, and it sounds great in this store. Have Don call me." So that's how Don got signed by Cliff and Peter. Once Cliff and Peter signed him, Tom Zutaut came back into the picture and went, "Okay, you're on Elektra." So out of that, Don and I formed a friendship. . . .

Don and I shared a house, which was entertaining, but living with Don made me even more in a position where I knew what was going on and what wasn't going on. Bobby Blotzer lived next door. He played Ratt. It was Don who told me to go and see a band called Dante Fox. I went to see them three times — they sucked. They were terrible, and I think after the second time I went to see them, I'm driving all the way from Sunset down Palos Verdes, over Palos Verdes and around to the tiny little cottage I had overlooking Catalina Island. It was idyllic, it was fabulous, it was beautiful. But at four o'clock in the fucking morning, and I have to be back in the office at nine, I'm going, "Why the hell am I even going and seeing this band?" And again, one of those rare moments of intelligence, I sat there and I went, "Analyze Don's record. He's a very sound songwriter, and he's obviously got production chops. If he's telling you to look at something, maybe you're missing it and you need to go and look again." So I went a third time and they were terrible until the encore. And they came out and played "I Don't Need No Doctor." And [Mark] Kendall took the fucking roof off the place. I was like, Oh my God, that fucker can play. He's got skill.

A career in rock'n'roll is ultimately predicated on relationships, and in the case of an amiable and talented fellow like Michael Wagener, it wasn't long before his work in Germany and his frequent trips back to Los Angeles would see him capitalize on his reputation. From traditional German heavy metal (Victory, Accept) to NWOBHM (Raven) and first wave L.A. metal (Malice) to AOR (White Sister) and punk and new wave (X, 45 Grave, the Plasmatics), Wagener proved himself as a mixer who could bring out the sonic elements that best served the song, regardless of genre. His ability to find authentic energy in a production and song could give commercially accessible music an underground edge and make edgier music more accessible. In terms of the American scene, there are three early '80s albums that place Michael Wagener at the forefront as a pioneering mixer, engineer, and producer. The aforementioned *Breaking the Chains*, Great White's *Out of the Night*, and Mötley Crüe's *Too Fast for Love*, an album that saw Wagener brought on to mix what the band themselves have referred to as a sonic mess. Wagener would make his biggest mark in the mid- to late '80s as the producer of bands such as White Lion, Extreme, and Skid Row, among others, but his earlier forays are a link between European and American heavy metal and hard rock.

> **Alan Niven:** Okay, so Don says, "Fly Michael over, he'll be perfect." And I'm like, "Well, if you say so, Don." I mean, you know, it does cross my mind, no engineers in L.A.? We've got to have Michael Wagener? So I fly Michael over, and we do the first Great White EP, and then I subsequently find out that Michael had worked on Don's first record and Don needed Michael to be here to work on his new stuff and I was paying for him to cover, and I went, "Oh, very interesting. Got it." You know, Wags went on to an extraordinary career himself, and believe it or not, there was a time when the three of us were living in the same house. I swear to God, the only thing I saw Michael eat was macaroni and cheese. I mean, we did not have a pot to piss in. Don would buy an old Cadillac, would get some black lacquer paint and redo the finish of the Cadillac and add 300 bucks to it and put it back on the market, and that's how the rent got paid. We were scuffling, all of us were scuffling, but, you know, Bobby Blotzer lived next door, Mick Mars was down the street . . . I think you can almost see the case that the last cool major rock'n'roll wave that went through Los Angeles actually rose up out of the South Bay. Hermosa Beach, Redondo

Beach, and then flowed up Sunset, because basically we were all living in the South Bay in Hermosa Beach, and the beautiful thing then was because we could afford the rents. When people ask me why there's no good rock'n'roll in L.A. anymore, I have a simple two word answer: real estate.

Mötley Crüe's story of four misfits coming together from disparate backgrounds to create the world's most decadent rock'n'roll lifestyle brand has been documented to great effect, largely by the band themselves. The band was formed under the watch of bassist Nikki Sixx, who took years of childhood neglect and abuse and channeled his rage through an escape into the glam, punk, and hard rock music of the '70s. After attempts with bands like Sister (featuring W.A.S.P. frontman Blackie Lawless) and London (a band that would become far more famous as a stepping stone for L.A. musicians who went on to greater things rather than for its own creative output), Sixx assembled a ragtag team of musicians in the name of vision, desperation, and an ability to eschew societal consequence in the interest of immediate self-satisfaction. Groupies, mountains of cocaine, overdoses . . . to paraphrase Sixx, the Crüe were a reflection of the basic desires of American youth . . . all they wanted was sex, drugs, pizza, and more sex. As a good Catholic boy turned on to 1983's *Shout at the Devil*, that statement both bothered and titillated me. Surely, I could enjoy this music without forsaking the values that had been instilled within me by parents, the Church, and the Nippissing Catholic District School Board! I swore never to do the sex (until after marriage) or the drugs (ever), but I could at least enjoy a slice of pizza on the biweekly occasions when Dad would order a pie in on payday, and I could listen to some Crüe in my bedroom, an innocent indulgence in the only vice available at the time.

Being a young, practicing Catholic heavy metal fan, and later a musician, proved to be an exercise in sometimes futile negotiations with God. I'd find out years later on the road, vices are like potato chips . . . it's really hard to stop at just one.

The group of musicians Sixx chose speaks more to human intuition than it does to any obvious indicators that these misfits would actually make it to rehearsal, much less take it to the top. Mick Mars, the aging, impoverished, and health-challenged journeyman musician, high on skill but low on luck. Vince Neil, the bleach-blond surfer dude whose ability (or inability) to sing is made irrelevant in light of his more important skill: a knack for shaking his hips and igniting lust in young girls. Tommy Lee, the skin bashing, cymbal thrashing, teenage circus of a man-child whose enthusiasm bordered on the cartoonish. And then there was Sixx himself, a musician of modest technical ability, but with a lyrical flair for capturing the rage of youth and an ear for stealing the parts of '70s rock that made you want to throw a brick through a window just for the hell of it. This was Mötley Crüe, coming together to fulfill a combination of ambitions, a feverish Hollywood dream borne out of selfishness, childhood hurt, financial ambition (as in making enough to eat or to support a child), lust . . . and somewhere in that mix, a deep love of music.

The independently financed *Too Fast for Love* is a fucking mess, if you look at it elementally. Out-of-tune vocals (and the odd guitar), weird disco bass lines, and an egregious use of cowbell are just some of the sins of commission that infect the grooves of this album. The arrangements are sometimes angular and obtuse. It was made on a very thin budget, and it sounds cheap and amateurish.

It's also one of the greatest rock'n'roll albums ever made — even if the guy who actually helped bring it into the world doesn't quite hold it in the same regard.

Alan Niven: No, no. Mötley Crüe are nothing like a visionary. For one thing, they are a knock-off of old Alice Cooper. Them and Blackie Lawless. They're Alice Cooper knock-offs, both of them. All right? The thing that impressed me about the band was that, despite the fact he couldn't play bass, Nikki was very smart, very street aware, very image aware, and if you actually look at the Mötley Crüe catalog, there aren't that great songs in it, but Nikki knew how to work it. He was a very smart guy. He's a marketing guy; he's not a bass player. And the thing that got me — and everything for me is always personal — there's got to be something that ignites something within me, to connect with it, and I'm listening to "Piece of Your Action," and I'm going, "Fuck. That's a really good Cheap Trick song . . ." And it is . . . and it was really good, and I loved early Cheap Trick. I thought their first two albums were fucking brilliant. I adored those first two albums. So, when I'm listening to "Piece of Your Action," I'm going, "Oh, I recognize this. This is rock'n'roll. My God, we can have rock'n'roll at Greenworld? I'm in. I am going to be a driving force behind this. I want this. This makes me feel I want to get out of bed in the morning." You know?

As stated above, I wouldn't come to know *Too Fast for Love* until three years after its release, having fallen under the spell of 1983's *Shout at the Devil* (It even took me until 1984 to get to that record, if memory serves me correctly). But when I finally heard the debut (the reissued major label version, with a heavier but ultimately worse mix courtesy of Roy Thomas Baker), I can distinctly remember feeling even more conflicted than I did listening to *Shout*. While that album made me feel like I was doing something bad, when I listened to *Too Fast for Love*, I felt like *these guys* were doing something bad — not just morally, but musically and visually. It all looked and sounded wrong . . . but it felt fucking right. So right. I could sing every chorus back after the first listen. Listening to *TFFL* gave me the same feeling I got when I would take my paper route collection money and spend it on a pack of cigarettes at the local corner store. Sick to my stomach, guilty, and excited beyond my wildest expectations. Cheap euphoria, who says you can't buy a thrill?

Stylistically it's a mix of '70s bubble gum–pop songwriting and punk instrumental spraying and praying, peppered with moments of actual virtuosity in the drums and guitar department. Kiss, Cheap Trick, the Sweet, the Raspberries, the Sex Pistols . . . and plenty of heavy in Mars's thick distorted guitar tone and Lee's double kick throttles. "Live Wire" is as driving a metal anthem as anything that came before it, and its distorted eighth-note guitar riffing feels like an American refinement of what was happening in England with the NWOBHM. "Public Enemy #1" sounds like the Bay City Rollers on blow, "Merry Go Round" is an evil take on trademark Beatles' descending chromaticism. There's an added dash of creepy L.A. quaalude vibes and some Hitchcock-ian *Psycho* stabs thrown into Mars's vomiting guitar solo. The title track steals a Cheap Trick riff, inverts it, and glues it onto a four on the floor, shout-along one note chorus. Actually, most of the chorus melodies rarely go beyond a four-note range, but they are the *right* notes. And when the melodies do become more adventurous, the effect is quite glorious. Melodies like the ones found in "Starry Eyes" could easily have found a home on a Cheap Trick or Big Star album. There is a fair amount of musical ambition on here too. I'd love for someone to tell me what genre of music you could easily classify a song like "Come on and Dance" as. I guess it's kinda power pop in the verses, but that chorus is what . . . disco punk? Actually, that's exactly what it is. Problem solved.

At the time of this album, Mötley Crüe is clearly a highly codependent ecosystem that only these four human beings could create or exist within. Nikki Sixx was and is the Crüe's principal songwriter, but it is the collective offerings of the group that create the sound we associate with the band. Mick's guitar tone is an unholy mix of Be Bop Deluxe, Duane Allman (the dude plays a mean slide), Mick Ronson, and the sicker elements of Jeff Beck. More importantly, he had an impressive arsenal of licks and hooks at his disposal, a rich guitar vocabulary well-honed on the Top 40 circuit. On "Piece of Your Action," he marries "Statesboro Blues"–inspired slide licks to a metal-disco groove, and one of the heaviest chorus riffs of the era. Vince's nasal whine and rasp are as annoying as they are addictive, and his instinct for melodious vocal phrasing and delivery create a delicious tension as he fights the limitations of his instrument to intonate the notes properly. This sounds like a slam, but it is a thing of true rock'n'roll beauty. Vince does not get the credit he deserves as a unique vocalist in a sea of singers who may eclipse him technically but fail to make the same emotional connection to what they are singing. Tommy's high school marching band drumline rudiments and assimilation of the influence of Tommy Aldridge and Mick Tucker created a new sound and drum-feel, swinging and stomping. It is a uniquely Hollywood feel that many have emulated and desecrated, but few have replicated.

If you take one of these elements away, everything dies on the Hollywood and Vine. I often wonder what would have happened with

Mötley's sound had the mainstream metal boom of '83 never happened. Would they have continued making music that was this ragged, jagged, and avant-garde? Would we have had the wake of Los Angeles hard rock groups that tried to emulate their success by taking random elements of the sound and style (sans artistic vision) in order to "get signed" or "make it"? If not, maybe we'd all be remembering anew how stupid Flock of Seagulls' hair was, and we'd be calling new wave "hair pop" or "butt synth." Music critics always need somewhere to direct their ire, after all.

As Mötley Crüe were doing their part to create a new rock amalgam on the West Coast, a band of New York rock survivors were establishing dominance in the clubs of the Tri-State area, having begun their mission in the mid-'70s, albeit with a sound and attitude that reflected the colder, harder, and arguably tougher aspects of their environment.

Twisted Sister took the imagery of the New York Dolls and Kiss but delivered it with a healthy dose of Long Island attitude and aggression in their stage show. They may have been wearing mascara, rouge, and women's clothes, but when stretched over their linebacker frames, the look became as imposing and ominous as the threatening-cum-humorous banter coming from lead singer Dee Snider and guitarist and acting band manager Jay Jay French.

Twisted Sister worked the cover band angle for years, eventually moving from Lou Reed, Alice, and Dolls covers into the burgeoning heavy metal that was making its way from England. Considering the timeframe, and that bassist Mark "The Animal" Mendoza was a member of the Dictators, it's hard to say whether Twisted Sister were influenced by punk, or if they were in some way a part of the New York punk scene themselves, but the songwriting style that would inform their first two independently produced singles "I'll Never Grow Up, Now!" and "Bad Boys (of Rock'n'Roll)" would not have been out of place on a Ramones album. These were anthems that spoke to youthful disenfranchisement, but somehow purer of heart, more chaste. If there was anger there, it felt like righteous anger, and the major key melodies offset by legitimate heavy metal power chord punch would create the template for a song that in 1984 would elevate hard rock and heavy metal to a new, mainstream status. I am fighting every urge to tell you right now how that song went on to change the course of my life, and ultimately bring me to work with its creator some 30 years after it was released . . . but let's keep it in context, baby.

The independent singles would eventually make their way overseas and grab the attention of a small English label called Secret Records. The band would take a leap of faith, supported by the impressive fan base that allowed them to fill venues with thousands of people, sans major label support, and make the trek to the U.K. to record. Twisted Sister would be connected with UFO bassist Pete Way, who would produce (in the loosest sense of the term) their first full-length album, *Under the Blade*. Released in 1982, the album was a musical combination of Judas Priest, AC/DC, and Alice Cooper–inspired anthems composed and delivered with authority by vocalist Dee Snider. It's an important record that captures the sound of a band who are fighting against time and the ravages of a disco-corrupted scene that had threatened Twisted Sister's financial life-support system in the clubs. *Under the Blade* shoves a knuckle-dustered fist under the noses of the pretentious new wave that is taking away the dollars and interest of major labels.

Under the Blade is the sound of Twisted Sister standing tall in makeup and platform heels in front of the thousands of NWOBHM fans that they were determined to win over during festival opening slots in rainy, muddy English fields, staring down the bottles of piss and indifference with a violent defiance. In connecting with the heavy metal and glam sounds of the U.K., and adding an American classic rock melodic sensibility and shockingly theatrical yet tough performance flair, Twisted Sister built a legacy that I would only come to truly appreciate after their mainstream success had long passed.

Def Leppard's *High 'n' Dry* and Foreigner's *4* were both released in July of 1981. On the surface, these records don't have much in common. What links them is a producer: the person who would help them best serve the songs.

Def Leppard, coming off the modest success of 1980's youthful *On Through the Night*, were still in their early twenties (with one member in his late teens). That first album had some cool riffs and some catchy hooks . . . diehards might even consider songs like "Wasted," "Rock Brigade," and "Hello America" to be canon classics. But truthfully, the album only hinted at the talent, potential, and ambition that the young Leps possessed. The decision was made to procure the services of Robert John "Mutt" Lange, fresh off the monumental success of AC/DC's genre-defining opus *Back in Black*, to produce *High 'n' Dry*. Closer to the truth is that it was Mutt who chose them.

Def Leppard had already separated themselves from the NWOBHM hopefuls, but with the addition of Mutt as an essential sixth band member, they were paired with someone who had the talent and vision to match their ambition and raw potential. Where some bands might have balked at the strong, critical influence that Mutt would exert on their songwriting and performance, Def Leppard were more than willing to be vessels of Mutt's talent and knowledge. And that's not to suggest that they were empty vessels — far from it. Each member of Leppard was in possession of wonderful instincts, distinctive characteristics, and the tireless work ethic and shared vision that are crucial to massive success. Mutt Lange, to his credit, was wise enough to recognize their individual strengths.

Years later, as my band Trapper were on tour supporting Def Leppard on a string of Canadian dates, guitarist Phil Collen (not yet a member of the band during the recording of *High 'n' Dry*, but soon to join for the recording of 1983's breakthrough *Pyromania*) would intimate just how crucial Mutt's influence was on Def Leppard. I asked Phil about his time as lead guitarist for Girl, a wonderful glam rock–meets–Van Halen cocktail that also featured future L.A. Guns vocalist Phil Lewis. He suggested that had that band worked under the direction of a producer as talented as Mutt Lange, they might have gone much farther.

High 'n' Dry grafts pieces of AC/DC riffage and high intensity vocals (Elliott is pushed far beyond the range he demonstrates on their debut album) to Queen and Sweet–inspired harmonies. In "Bringin' On the Heartbreak," an early (and arguably the greatest) example of the hard rock power ballad, we hear traits that would later come to define Leppard as a band that were miles beyond their peers. Clean, classically inspired arpeggiated guitar figures build to majestic power chord gallops. Lead vocals are infused with a high level of articulation, elocution, and attitude. It actually didn't really matter what Joe Elliott was singing about, he is one of those singers who proves that the *way* you sing a lyric is actually just as important as the lyric's literal meaning. I'd make the case that it's *more* important in the context of intended emotional impact, especially in hard rock. That may be because if I actually internalized what so many of these bands were singing about, I may not be able to justify listening to it . . . but we'll save that suggestion for later, because that is definitely not the case with Def Leppard.

Take the song "High 'n' Dry (Saturday Night)," for example. I mean, we can all see what the topline message is in the words of the song. It's party time, there's booze and a woman. But why is he high and *dry*? He has both whisky and wine, he's let us know that he's not one who enjoys being alone, nor is he foolish enough not to have made plans for the week-end. He's going to turn out the lights, and, presumably, he and his woman will engage in some adult activity. Suggesting that he is *high* makes sense, sure . . . but dry? Not so much.

Okay first of all, you would be absolutely justified if you wanted to smack me in the mouth for that smug assessment of the lyrical content. Clearly, the actual message just doesn't *matter*, and critics who choose to jump on this sort of thing are missing a greater artistic point.

What matters is how the words sound, or, more importantly, how they *sing*. The emotion they generate is more important than the construction of a cogent narrative. The internal rhyme of "high" and "dry" makes you want to sing it over and over again, as does the interstitial incantation of "Sa-tur-day night!" It's about finding the rhythm of the words, the right accent on the right syllable, the attitude and the enunciation. The decisions of where to push the voice into rasp or let it return to a softer vocal timbre. Mutt Lange is a master of making such decisions, vocally and instrumentally. *High 'n' Dry* is the album where we hear the Def Leppard–orchestrated guitar sound start to take shape as well. Where we might see only two guitar players in the music videos, what we are hearing on the record is actually layers of carefully selected guitar tracks, overdubbed and played on different guitars that accentuate certain frequencies in the equalization spectrum.

While a giant step forward, *High 'n' Dry* still weighs more heavily on the side of raw, organic, and unpolished in terms of performance and over-all tonality (a reason why many fans feel this is Lep's strongest album). I tend to see it as a perfect snapshot of where the band were in terms of their musical abilities and where they were hoping to go on future releases.

Foreigner, however, were a different case altogether. Already three albums deep into a multiplatinum career, the band was looking to correct a slight dip in their commercial fortunes. *Head Games* was a little slower out of the gate than its predecessor *Double Vision*, which had sold seven million units. *Head Games* would only manage a measly five million when all was said and done.

Bringing Mutt Lange on to update their sound bought Foreigner back the couple of million albums they had lost previously (that must have been *so* hard on them), and it was achieved through 10 months of laborious effort and innovation. Lange brought the digital elements that had previously been the domain of new wave and pop artists into the Foreigner sound, and this would go on to have a massive influence on commercial hard rock of the '80s, ultimately helping it translate to Top 40 radio.

The LinnDrum machine was an electronic unit that could be manipulated and programmed to create a wide variety of percussive textures. At the time, many drummers saw it as a threat that might replace the physical role of the drummer with "perfect" (a.k.a. metronomically precise) time-keeping. Music that incorporates electronic drums can rankle drummers and analog purists alike and is often criticized for its synthetic or stiff feel; however, to some ears it removed a barrier to achieving a sustained and consistent energy, helping to enhance the euphoric feeling that is often associated with '80s music. In the '70s, the metronomic stability and four on the floor rhythmic sensibility of the musicians in bands like Chic was highly coveted as it kept people on the dance floor — this being the case, it stands to reason that a consistent programmable option (that didn't talk back or take up precious studio time setting up a drum kit) would be appealing.

A second technological strategy Mutt incorporated on 4 was bringing U.K. new wave phenomenon Thomas Dolby into the studio to blind the masses with the science of his synthesizer programming. Dolby helped Foreigner and Lange create textures and dreamlike atmospherics that would support Lou Gramm's radio-ready crooning on "Waiting for a Girl Like You," and the pumping, pulsing bass lines in anthems like "Juke Box Hero" and "Urgent." While keyboards and synthesizer hogged a fair share of the sonic spectrum, there was still room for the roar of Mick Jones's Les Paul on tracks like "Nightlife" and "Break It Up." Both Thomas and the LinnDrum machine, along with the Fairlight emulator, would make their presence felt and heard on the next Def Leppard album. The results would be game-changing for '80s hard rock.

This amalgam of '70s electric guitar playing, straight-ahead rock grooves, dreamy keyboards, and anthemic tenor voices (or mezzo-soprano, in the case of Pat Benatar) were all over FM radio, and starting to cross over in a big way into Top 40 thanks to artists like Foreigner, Billy Squier (an early example of how to truncate and refine the Led Zeppelin sound for cross-over appeal), Journey (whose fortunes changed for the commercial-better with the addition of the Babys' keyboardist and composer Jonathan Cain), and a Canadian band who would go on to prove crucial to the crossover success of hard rock in the mid- to late '80s, Loverboy.

Loverboy came out strong in 1980 with their self-titled debut, produced and engineered by a crack team from Vancouver, BC. Bruce Fairbairn, Bob Rock, and a young assistant engineer by the name of Mike Fraser. With the members having experienced Canadian success with bands like Streetheart and Moxy, there was a focus on taking the lessons learned in their collective pasts and crafting tight, concise, and powerful bursts of melodic rock energy. Mission accomplished on classic tracks like "The Kid Is Hot Tonite" and "Turn Me Loose," the latter retaining a whiff of the disco-funk that had reigned so supreme just a year prior, but with the distinctive crunch of Paul Dean's electric guitars and the unabashed vocal wailing of Mike Reno.

Marc Lafrance is a Vancouver-based musician who has lent his stellar vocals to multi-platinum recordings by Mötley Crüe, Bon Jovi, Loverboy, The Cult and many more.

> **Marc LaFrance:** Bob Rock and Mike Fraser, all these guys, during that early part of time, they were [engineers] in train-ing. They were a part of these sessions, and this is where they honed their skills. They were under the control of Roger Monk, who was the main engineer at Little Mountain Sound at that time . . . pretty much trained Bob Rock and

Mike Fraser. I mean, Mike Fraser, when he first worked at Little Mountain Sound, he was like the janitor. He eventually would be sitting in on the sessions and he started being the tape jockey. So when I came in around 1980, these guys were well under way. They'd learned their skills from the jingles, and then the recording acts started coming in, which was kicked off by essentially Loverboy. *Loverboy* was kind of the first big record that Fairbairn did with Bob Rock as engineer. The Bon Jovi guys heard the *Loverboy* record, and that went huge, right? When Bon Jovi came, it opened the floodgates for other bands to come. Bon Jovi had the *Slippery When Wet* album recorded there, and a lot of other bands came because of the great producers, plus the infrastructure was now in place to be able to create the sounds needed to have a great sounding album.

1981's *Get Lucky* took that formula, threw it in a skin-tight pair of red leather pants and a headband, and brought it to the next level. "Working for the Weekend" was the ubiquitous paean to the good life that took this album to four times platinum in the U.S. alone. The song will forever be tied in my memory to the sunscreen slicked, bronzed bodies of bikini clad women and their Speedo-wearing suitors cruising the shores of Lake Temiskaming. This was definitive party music, the sound of the ultimate good time. Canadians were pretty damn good at creating this sound, as a year later Aldo Nova would take his song "Fantasy" to the Billboard Top 10 album charts, racking up double platinum sales in the process.

Mike Fraser: The first Loverboy record had good success down in the States, so we came back [to Little Mountain], and when we were doing the second record, Paul Dean was driving us nuts because in between [the two Loverboy records] I think *Foreigner 4* had come out. Paul wanted their record to sound like [4]. He just drives Bob and Bruce nuts. Always A/B-ing things, "No, no. We need to have this kind of drum sound. This kind of guitar sound . . ." Every day it was just something else. So we finally got through that record, and off they went. Paul was down in L.A., and I guess Foreigner were in some studio, so he went in there and the band hadn't been in there yet, but he was looking around and all these microphones everywhere and he's checking out everything. And that was one of the things, too, in our session, he always said, "No, no, they had these microphones up in the corner, 10 feet away from the drums, and . . ." Just driving us nuts. So anyways, fast forward, and I think it was Bruce Fairbairn was down there maybe for a Grammy thing or something like that, and he ran into Mick Jones from Foreigner and tells him about this. He says, "Oh man, Paul used to drive us nuts, he wanted their records to sound like you guys and this and that." And Mick's like, "Holy shit," he says, "We were referencing the first Loverboy record, we wanted to sound like *that!*"

So Bruce says, "That's too funny." He says, "Well, Paul had come down, and told us you guys were recording and he even tape-measured microphone distances and all that." He goes, "What mic? . . . we didn't have any room mics on the drums. Those mics were just sitting there, they weren't even plugged in." So here's Paul, driving us nuts, he's got all the dimensions. I thought it was so funny, them trying to steal off each other.

Both Loverboy and Aldo Nova would be a huge influence on a young New Jersey artist who would record a song a year that would meld the sensibilities of both acts into a surprise independent radio hit. John Bongiovi had been pounding the Jersey club scene, inspired by local heroes like Bruce Springsteen and Southside Johnny. With a name change and an eye and ear for musical combinations, Jon Bon Jovi would go on to merge working-class American Dream parables with the aforementioned successful Canadian take on AOR music to kick down the doors and create arena rock that leaned as heavy on musical hooks as it did his own good looks.

But a few bands would reach platinum heights before young Jon, and it is the next part of the story where this music comes fully alive for me. It's a beautiful thing to go back and connect with music that came before your time, or at least before your awareness of its existence. It is another to express your feelings about the music that dovetailed with your coming of age, the music that ignited a passion and charted a life course. This is where we're at in this story, and this is where life becomes electric for a young boy from the North . . . and for many millions of rock'n'roll fans around the world.

Hold on . . . hold tight . . . we're gonna rock tonight!

CHAPTER 6
1983 TO 1984

METAL ENTERS THE CHARTS AND HEARTS OF NORTH AMERICA

I t wasn't exactly a straight path that brought me to Metal Mountain. There were arguably dubious musical stops along the way, a few key moments of musical connection to decidedly un-metal songs and genres that would elementally influence my musical tastes. But these seemingly disparate early influences would help set the hook for the lifelong love affair I would come to have with commercial hard rock and heavy metal, and might provide insight, clarity, and hopefully fodder for discussion into how metal and hard rock moved from the underground to the top of the charts.

It was the year 1983 that I recall music becoming fully alive inside of me. Looking back as a 50-year-old man, it seems strange to think that I could experience such acute awareness of existential purpose so early in life, and even more strange that I am still moved in almost the same way by that same music to this day. In many ways, I'm sure much of this will read like the story of any other sixth grade student hanging out somewhere on the fringes of elementary school social circles in the 1982–83 calendar year, shivering in anticipation of all the changes that awaited. But, to paraphrase a Steely Dan lyric, it was through an introduction to two of the biggest hard rock albums of all time that I knew all at once who I was.

Music often opens gateways to social acceptance, and our preferences can serve as a concert ticket, maybe even a backstage pass, that provides access to the experience of friendship, or maybe even romance. No guarantees, of course. Is that a cassette copy of *Thriller* in your pocket, or are you just glad to see me?

Yes, *Thriller*. That all-time bestselling, ubiquitous piece of R&B, pop, and, by virtue of a barrier smashing solo courtesy of one Edward Van Halen, rock that was de rigeur listening amongst my French-immersion classmates. Through constant, active listening, I developed a love for the incessant grooves of "Billie Jean," the epic funk of "Thriller," and, most crucially, the electric guitar riffs and licks of "Beat It." Of all those amazing tracks, "Beat It" was the *one*. The other songs, all wonderful compositions, moved me, but "Beat It" *grabbed* me. I loved the adrenaline rush I received from the four on the floor beat, and the consistent pulsing dynamic thrust of the music. Just like when I'd hear Van Halen's "Jump" the following year, the music got me up and I didn't want anything to bring me down.

Steve Lukather's lockstep rhythm guitar hooks and bass playing did the heavy lifting and set the table for King Eddie Van Halen to deliver a 16 bar master class on how a guitar solo can elevate a song.

As far as I recall, before *Thriller*, I got my music from the AM radio . . . like water from the tap, I didn't really think about it, it was just always there. Well, sort of. You had to put in the time to hear the songs you really loved, waiting for the DJ to announce your faves so that you could hurry round the radio to soak in the goodness. Two songs in particular stoked an early fire in my heart, songs whose elemental qualities completely aligned with those I would feverishly seek out when listening to and searching for hard rock in the years to come.

Joan Jett's "I Love Rock'n'Roll," a cover of a 1976 song by the Arrows, is as perfect a hard rock confection as one could ask for. It possesses a nasty riff-based, three-chord guitar progression and a caveman drum beat that even the most rhythmically challenged among us can grasp onto. It's so simple, you might not notice the not-so-caveman addition of two extra beats before the broken-down pre-chorus. (Time signature changes? What is this prog rock?) And that chorus . . . what an exultation of the teenage experience! A sweet and sour mix of major and minor blues–scale melody that smears like peanut butter and jelly on Wonder Bread. There is so much wonderful imagery in the song, and Lord, how that imagery rolled off the tongue . . . a record machine, being 17, a smile so hard it makes you wanna get up and ask for a name. All wrapped up in the glorious, dismissive nonchalance of realizing that none of it matters . . . *'cause it's all the same*. I guess we might as well just *rock* for two minutes and 45 seconds. God, the power of not caring seemed so liberating . . . not caring if you were cool, if you got shot down by a girl, if you flunked a test. I could barely comprehend the concept. Still can't.

Forgive me here while I take my old records off the shelf, but today's kids will never know how good it feels to put another dime in the jukebox, baby. With access to all the world's music on a touchscreen device you carry in your pocket, the valuation of the music is lost somewhere in a negligible charge on a parent's credit card, and with it I suspect so, too, is some of the excitement. I still connect the thrill of the music with the *loss* of my hard-earned money as it slid into the slot and the magic of watching the intention of your purchase physically manifest itself into transcendent electric bliss. Speaking of access, "I Love Rock'n'Roll" was the first song that had me sitting by the radio, waiting for it to come on so I could fumble with my Radio Shack boom box and record it. A budding bootlegger could only pray for clear AM reception to permeate the walls of our little cottage through the wooded wilds, hoping that some longwinded DJ wouldn't sputter verbal nonsense over top of the song.

While the songwriting credit goes to two men, Alan Merrill and Jake Hooker, it was its delivery by a woman that transformed a great, but typically bloke-ish, English pub rock song into a masterpiece. Jett is one of the world's great rhythm guitar players and a rock'n'roll emotive force. Her double-tracked vocal timbre and flipping of the gender script makes the track sound tougher and meaner. The raspy break in her voice is a timbral quality I would come to covet and a major contributor to the goosebump experience I would chase for years to follow. Of course, I wouldn't connect Joan Jett with her street cred pioneering punk rock'n'roll past in the Runaways until years later. I wouldn't even associate her pummeling power chords or shouted vocals with any specific subgenre. It was only rock'n'roll, and I didn't just *like* it. I loved it.

Lee Aaron is a multiplatinum Canadian artist who made her international mark with 1984's *Metal Queen*, one of the great anthems of female empowerment. She has gone on to enjoy a career that has touched on metal, rock'n'roll, jazz, blues, soul, and even opera. Some of her early inspiration came from the Runaways and their pioneering presence as trailblazers for women in rock.

> **Lee Aaron:** I discovered the Runaways in a pile of LPs my dad brought home when the radio station at the college where he worked replaced their vinyl collection with eight-track. I remember the covers of *Queens of Noise* and *Waitin' for the Night* (both released in '77) and being astounded at how incredibly badass they all looked. There was nothing sexual about those covers, just pure attitude and head-to-toe leather, all of them snarling at the camera from behind barbed wire and bars. It was the antithesis of my mother's music — Olivia Newton-John and Anne Murray, who were all over the radio at the time. They were singing about real-girl issues like equality, sexuality, and being in a rock band in such a visceral, in-your-face way, it *totally* spoke to my teenage heart. It managed to be hard rock, glam, pop, punk, and metal all at once. I knew that I wanted to make music like that.

A second song that gave me that euphoric feeling, resonating with me as if it were mine and mine alone, was Laura Branigan's 1982 smash "Gloria." I actually owe my first live radio performance to this tune. Dialing into North Bay's 600 CFCH to request the song (because clearly, hearing it seven times a day in regular rotation was not enough), a cunning DJ had me state my full name and sing a timid, dreadfully out of tune version of the chorus into the receiver of the rotary phone attached to the wall of my kitchen, in order to "prompt his memory." Of course, he recorded it, and my "performance" was repeated on air as an intro to the song over the course of the week. For this performative sin, I was mercilessly mocked by my fellow students and altar servers at the Pro-Cathedral of the Assumption parish, as well as my minor league hockey teammates. It wasn't the last time I'd get screwed around by the music industry, nor was it the last time I'd sing out of tune on the radio. Despite my embarrassment, I recognized that having the balls to reach out makes shit happen.

"Gloria" is a marvel of a composition, upon analysis. The song is really just a rolling series of hooks, with a strange pseudo refrain–type payoff that puts as much emphasis on its main musical figure as it does the repetition of the name Gloria over said part. Once again, the song is a cover of a male singer's performance (Italian artist Umberto Tozzi), but Branigan's version is far more upbeat. Tozzi's romantic lyrics are rewritten here as a weird chastisement of a delusional woman, her self-aggrandizing perspective putting her in desperate peril of losing her "innocence" to the lures of marrying for money and afternoon delights. Men really covet a woman's innocence, it would seem, and for a long time it was a male's perspective on women's choices that permeated the airwaves and grooves on our records. Lee Aaron was a pioneer in changing this when in 1984 she released the iconic "Metal Queen," arguably the first feminist anthem in heavy metal history.

> **Lee Aaron:** No secret, I stumbled through some very sexist and embarrassing marketing strategies — clearly designed to attract a male audience — in my rookie years. It was both enlightening and disheartening for someone who got into this industry to create music. I experienced firsthand how women within the hard rock world were marginalized as either "sexy babes" or novelty acts. If you tried to "own" your sexuality — like the male acts — perception was, you were a slut or a vixen. It was an incredibly unfair double standard.
>
> "Metal Queen" was my artistic attempt to put women — especially women within the metal or hard [rock] genre — on equal footing with the guys . . . as it should be, and as it is today. It was a push back against all the objectification. It was a statement about taking back our power.
>
> Today, I have had both men and women alike fist-pumping in front of the stage, and so many tell me that song has empowered them and given them strength during challenges in their life; so, truthfully, it has evolved into more

of a genderless anthem. Its motivation was feminist, but it's pretty cool that it's morphed into something bigger than that.

I have the honor of playing "Metal Queen" beside Lee as her current guitarist, and the song still retains all the strength it had for me when I first heard it in my youth. But before Lee's vocals entered my life, it was Laura Branigan that was showing me the power of the female voice in a male-dominated industry. The lyrics to "Gloria" seem wholly incongruous to Branigan's powerful, anthemic vocal delivery. Her tone is bell-like, but there is a hairline crack in that bell that helps Branigan achieve a perfect vocal rasp when she pushes the top of her range. It almost makes me wonder, in retrospect, if Branigan were flipping the gender script in her own way, taking a typical sexist male interpretation of a woman's romantic life and owning the sexual liberation criticized therein through her vocal performance. I still feel her power when she sings this song.

Mind you, none of this mattered to me then, just as the meaning of lyrics often don't matter very much to me now. I was chasing that adrenaline rush, best discovered in one part of the song in particular. The "lift" (or what would be the pre-chorus if the song actually had a chorus) contains a three-note electric guitar riff that follows the lyric "you don't need to answer" that I would hotly anticipate. This was followed by a power chord move on the guitar that comes after Gloria keeps 'em "hanging on the li-ine," landing directly on the "uh-oh" that never fails to accelerate my heartrate. That electric guitar motif only comes in once, but the muscle memory of its effect stays with you physically throughout the song. The high is sustained through the electro-disco goodness of the four on the floor beat and the numerous synth brass and string pad flourishes that elevate the song as it progresses. The only adrenal respite in the whole song comes from the very effective syncopated bass line that dances in and around the line "Well you really don't remember, was it something that they said, all the voices in your head, calling Gloria!" It's a brief moment of melancholic empathy for old Gloria, and it really sets you up for the musical plunge from the top-of-the-rollercoaster feeling that follows.

That's a lot of pop talk. But there's the rub. Because 1983 was the year metal went pop, straight to the top of the charts.

Quiet Riot, that struggling California bar band that just wouldn't let go of its faded glitter rock aspirations in the face of new wave, power pop, and punk, somehow transcended their plight as has-beens and foreign curios in the Japanese marketplace to rise to number one on the Billboard album charts with their *Metal Health* album. Ironically, it's an old chestnut from the '70s glam rock era that was responsible for an incredible change in fortunes, courtesy of the vision of one Spencer Proffer.

In Tom Beaujour and Richard Bienstock's revelatory oral history of the '80s scene, *Nöthin' But a Good Time*, Proffer, a record producer whose Pasha label imprint was funded and distributed by CBS Records, reveals how he was ultimately looking for a band to record the song "Cum on Feel the Noize." In the case of Quiet Riot, it was the belief in the power of the song, classified by Proffer as "participatory rock," that fueled his interest in the band. Proffer needed a vehicle to deliver the song, and he found it when prompted to check out DuBrow (an act operating under lead singer Kevin DuBrow's name after the departure of Randy Rhoads and bassist Rudy Sarzo to Ozzy's band, featuring Frankie Banali on drums) at the Country Club venue in Reseda, California.

A deal was struck. If DuBrow and band were willing to record "Cum on Feel the Noize," Proffer agreed to record some of their original songs that he felt fit in with the "participatory rock" angle that he hoped would entice the executives at CBS records to stand up and take notice of him. Dubrow added Snow guitarist Carlos Cavazo to the lineup and cut the first four songs of what would become the *Metal Health* album (with bassist Chuck Wright appearing on two cuts, "Metal Health" and "Don't Wanna Let You Go"). Bassist Sarzo returned to the fold initially as a guest to perform on a track called "Thunderbird," a song Rudy had worked on with DuBrow prior to leaving to play with Ozzy that would become a tribute to the late Randy Rhoads. He laid his parts down so quickly that he was asked if he could play on three more cuts in order to maximize usage of the block of precious studio time that still remained. The tragic plane crash that claimed Randy Rhoads's life had made the idea of carrying on with Ozzy untenable for Rudy, and the rekindled chemistry from these sessions planted the seed that he just might be able to rediscover the joy in playing music that he'd lost after the death of his friend.

Judas Priest's twin guitar attack and soaring vocals have been an influence on a wide variety of metal bands.

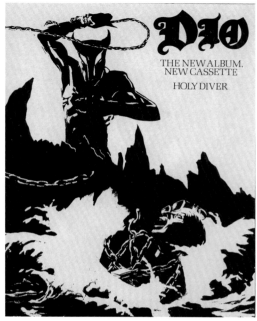

The power vocals of Ronnie James Dio and the raw, youthful aggression of Vivian Campbell's guitar playing made Holy Diver an instant classic.

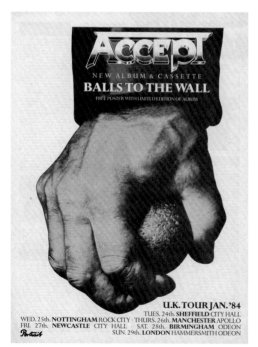

Accept's sound is a deft blend of concise songwriting and teutonic metal power.

While many '80s bands copied the look of Hanoi Rocks, few could capture their strut, swagger, and spirit.

Whitesnake pumping out the video product just prior to their big visual and sonic 1987 makeover.

Great White played classic and classy hard rock that was low on frills, but high on thrills.

Def Leppard and the song that many consider to be the greatest example of the pop/hard rock hybrid.

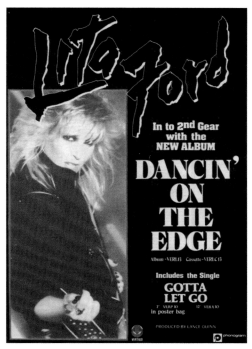

Former Runaways guitarist Lita Ford's succesful solo career was largely fueled by her incredible guitar playing.

Twisted Sister found massive success after years in the trenches of the Tri-State club scene thanks to a combination of killer hooks, stunning visuals, and a sense of humor.

Mötley Crüe took the influence of Kiss, punk rock, power pop, and heavy metal and created a sound and a look that kept parents awake at night.

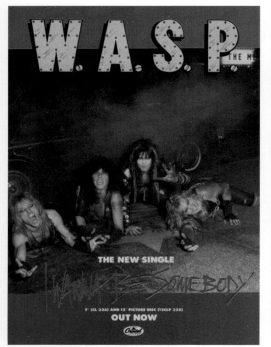

W.A.S.P. took rock'n'roll theater to extremes, backing up the shock with high-quality hard rock.

Quiet Riot, hot on the heels of platinum success with one Slade cover, hoped lightning would strike twice with "Mama Weer All Crazee Now."

Iron Maiden found success in the face of poular trends by sticking to their musical integrity, a trait that carries on to this day.

Collectors frothed at the mouth for rare, limited edition picture discs like this one from Mötley Crüe.

Bon Jovi peddling their wares just prior to the massive commercial breakout that awaited them in 1986.

Dio's third album carried on in the tradition of anthemic hard rock tinged with Dungeons & Dragons–esque morality.

Dokken was the successful melodic rock vehicle for vocalist Don Dokken and virtuoso guitarist George Lynch.

Ozzy tried his hand at big hair, big fashion, and big booming '80s production with Ultimate Sin, which featured the stunning guitar work of Jake E. Lee.

Ozzy showed off his crack band and flashy new wardrobe and hair style on this stellar live concert performance video.

Kix ultimately found platinum success in 1988, but only after doggedly working the U.S. club circuit with their unique and sometimes quirky take on hard rock.

Ratt found platinum success once again with Dancing Undercover, *thanks in great part to the tandem guitar work of Warren DeMartini and Robbin Crosby.*

Poison's debut album attracted many record buyers with its highly stylized look and spirited hard rock hooks.

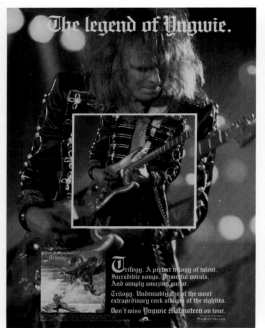

Yngwie Malmsteen brought a more commerical
edge to his groundbreaking new-classical guitar
work on Trilogy. His influence would be heard
on many recordings throughout the '80s.

Tesla came across as the workingman's
hard rock band with a down-to-earth
image and a rootsy, hard rock sound
heavy on sing-along melody.

Kix worked with producer Beau Hill on this
1985 album who applied many of the sonic
traits he applied to his succesful work with
Ratt and others.

Cinderella's early adaptation of a
classic hair metal look at times betrayed
the blues-based depth of the hard rock
contained on their debut album.

Ads like this one for guitar hero Paul Gilbert were commonplace in music publications, selling the high performance, virtuosic rock'n'roll dream.

Bon Jovi took melodic hard rock to the top of the commercial mountain with Slippery When Wet, and brought attention to Vancouver's Little Mountain Sound studio as the place to go for bands looking to cross over to a wider audience.

Frehley's Comet was the solo vehicle for Kiss guitarist Ace Frehley, and saw the guitarist exploring a more commercial hard rock sound.

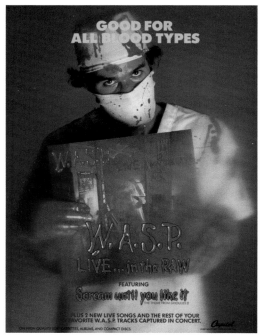

W.A.S.P. delivered the best of their catalog on this brash and boomy live album.

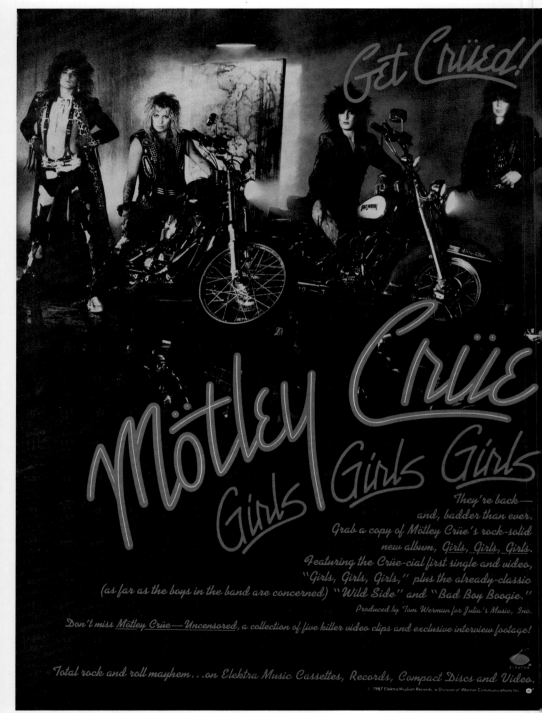

Mötley Crüe adopted a grittier "leather and mortorcycle" look and sound for Girls, Girls, Girls, foreshadowing a move away from the spandex and pastels of the first half of the '80s.

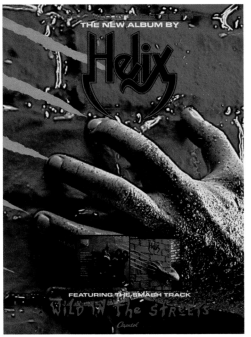

Helix applied modern hard rock production to their well-honed classic hard rock style on Wild in the Streets, *a gold-selling album in their native Canada.*

Def Leppard's Hysteria *stands as a high-water mark for state-of-the-art '80s rock production, courtesy of master producer Mutt Lange.*

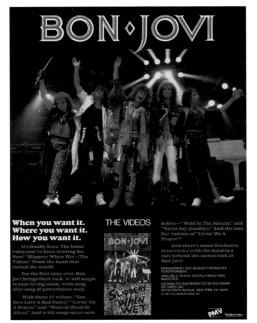

Video played a huge part in Bon Jovi's success, bringing their photogenic good looks and arena-ready performance chops to the living rooms of fans around the world.

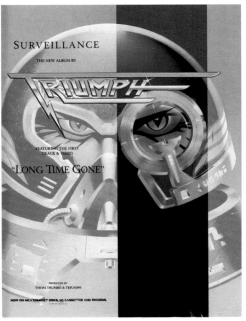

Triumph's Surveillance *blended the band's highly developed musicianship and progressive rock leanings with a glossy production that was au courant at the time of release.*

Christian rock band Stryper may have been spreading the Good News in their lyrics, but their album productions sounded very much in line with their Sunset Strip–sinning contemporaries.

Decline of Western Civilization *was a documentary that shed light on the desire, desperation, and often the delusion of aspiring Sunset Strip musicians.*

Europe took The Final Countdown's *iconic keyboard riff to soaring levels of success, and followed up with 1988's* Out of this World.

Van Halen were one of a very few bands who succesfully managed to navigate the changing of a lead singer. Sammy Hagar's second album with the band continued the multiplatinum streak of 1986's 5150.

Randy Rhoads, along with Edward Van Halen, ushered in the era of the '80s rock guitar virtuoso with his unparalled performance acumen and classically informed musicianship.

DONALD GADZIOLA

Paul Gilbert is a shining example of an artist who found acclaim in the 1980s but continued to grow and develop as an artist, making high-quality music to this day.

MICHAEL MECHNIG

Warren DeMartini, who with Dokken's George Lynch and Ozzy Osbourne guitarist Jake E. Lee made up the trinity of Californian guitar heroes that would carry the torch passed to them by Eddie Van Halen and Randy Rhoads.

Warren DeMartini lays it down live in concert.   ROBERT BURSEY

With these recordings, created on off-hour "spec time" due to a non-existent budget, Proffer was able to solicit just enough support from his relationship with CBS to complete the album.

Against all odds, Quiet Riot became the band that cut a path through Billboard charts dominated by all manner of synth pop, new wave, and post-punk bands like the Police, Men at Work, Lionel Richie, Soft Cell, Duran Duran, and Michael Jackson to claim the number one spot on November 23, 1983, fueled by one man's belief in this "participatory rock" concept, and the chemistry of the four musicians that would ultimately reclaim the name Quiet Riot.

It is participation that is key to the entire '80s hard rock concept. By making the audience feel like a part of the music, rather than an empty receptor for any given artist's musical genius, Quiet Riot were able to connect in an intrinsic way. It actually goes beyond emotional response and moves into a more kinesthetic realm. DuBrow has stated that the title track of *Metal Health*'s call to arms refrain ("Bang your head! Metal health will drive you mad!"), was inspired by an overseas conversation with Rhoads during the guitarist's time with Ozzy. Rhoads explained the phenomenon of young NWOBHM fans responding to the music they were experiencing in concert by literally banging their heads in unison in front of the stage. This choreographed response took on a literal audience, and soon the metal-loving youth of Europe were identifying as "headbangers." DuBrow took the phrase and glued it onto a song that Cavazo had brought to the band from his former outfit Snow, and suddenly "No More Booze," a song that at one point seemed destined for the scrap heap of late '70s L.A. metal, was transformed into the classic that kicks off metal's first Billboard chart-topper.

Easy to shout along with (it's only one note, albeit supported with expertly fashioned "football harmonies," carefully crafted to provide a melodic glue that helps the shouting stick to the brain), the lyrics deliver explicit instructions on what to do with your body while listening to the song. Nothing new in the realm of dance music, but fairly unique to heavy rock. Dancing was often a challenge for awkward adolescent boys (it certainly was for me), the clear audience for this music. "Metal Health" came with its own user's manual, and an excuse for the pseudo-violent behavior you were compelled to exhibit. C'mon, Mom . . . it's not my fault! Metal health *will* drive you mad!"

AC/DC is the high-water mark for hard rock rhythm guitar, and "Metal Health" applies the simple principles of open position power chords played on Gibson guitars through dimed Marshall stacks with an almost reverential perfection. Carlos Cavazo's guitar sound in both rhythm and lead capacities is incredible on this album, and his melodic sensibilities and violin-like solo tones elevate every one of the selections. On "Cum on Feel the Noize," his elegant lines are as triumphant as a Handel trumpet concerto, yet still retain the snaggle-toothed snarl of Angus Young. His very literal interstitial guitar lines and sound effects on "Slick Black Cadillac" bring to mind Ritchie Blackmore's "Highway Star" turn on *Machine Head*, as he combines melodic motifs with all manner of vehicular sound effects on his six-string laser. His solo guitar showcase piece "Battle Axe" is a highly engaging and enjoyable composition, with Baroque-inspired arpeggios locking horns with diminished scale runs and wailing string bends. "Battle Axe" was the first solo guitar piece I ever heard on a record, and at first I was perplexed by it . . . why was Carlos playing by himself? Why didn't they put another song with lyrics on? Of course, this was all prior to my exposure to Edward Van Halen's instrumental solo showcase "Eruption," or even Randy Rhoads's work with Ozzy, so perhaps this was a case of Carlos trying to stake a claim to his own guitar hero identity. Or maybe it just sounded cool.

The rhythm section approach of Frankie Banali and Rudy Sarzo (and, lest we forget, the deep pocket, heavily chorus–effected bass grooves of Chuck Wright on his two appearances) is noteworthy for its maturity . . . yeah, that's right. The record rocks hard into the new pop metal frontier with big gang vocal shout-alongs and blazing guitars, but it grooves like a '70s record in many ways. Banali's heavily Bonham-inspired kick drum and open, ringing tom fills set up transitions in exciting yet supportive ways. While there are no overt displays of technical virtuosity in his playing, the *authority* behind the grooves suggest to the listener that what we are hearing is just a smattering of his capability. Frankie plays for the song, crafting parts that the kids can air drum along with. The perfect example is his iconic intro to "Cum on Feel the Noize." There are few approaches quite as effective or exciting as starting with a bare bones drum beat and a solitary, impassioned, lead vocal (as we'll see, Dee Snider and Twisted Sister certainly agreed). In this case, Banali and Sarzo start at the absolute top of their dynamic range, fortissimo or bust right from the get-go. We are spared any waiting time before getting into that glorious chorus, as DuBrow jumps all over it a mere two bars into the song. At that point, it doesn't really matter what comes after lyrically, we've already bought in. Fortunately, what does follow is hook after hook, and even though the song was written by Slade members Noddy Holder and Jim Lea, there couldn't have been a better song to highlight Quiet Riot's underdog status. So you think his singing's out of time? So you think he's got a funny face (or a receding hairline)? . . . DuBrow ain't got no worries, and he sings the song with the power of conviction that comes of years of rocking for rock's sake alone. And to be fair, he was still fluffing up enough curl on top to make a passable appearance at hair metal's debutante ball, such as this album was. Girls would rock boys, and we'd all feel the noise.

The other major hard rock release that bothered the upper reaches of the Billboard chart in '83 was Def Leppard's *Pyromania*. With producer Mutt Lange applying the elec-trickery conjured on Foreigner's 4 to Leppard's developing sense of classic songwriting and AC/DC's approved guitar and vocal approach, a 10-million-selling (in the U.S. alone!) monster was created. It was a transitional album that in many ways split the difference between the heavy metal riffs of yesterday and the sounds that were currently dominating radio airwaves. This is best demonstrated on the songs that would become *Pyromania*'s defining singles. "Photograph" starts with one of the catchiest guitar hooks ever conceived, but its voicing in the upper-mid register of the guitar has more to do with Keith Richards or Mick Ronson than Tony Iommi.

Mutt's elemental rearranging of the sonic priorities of the components of a classic rock song (guitars, bass, drums, vocals, keyboards) is striking. Where traditionally a hard rock band would support a chorus with big, open, crashing guitars painted with double coats of distortion, the guitars of Steve Clark, a soon-to-be-jettisoned Pete Willis, and his successor Phil Collen, take on a more developed sense of melodic and harmonic purpose. This is perhaps most evident in the fact that the chorus of "Photograph" doesn't actually utilize distorted power chords. Leppard offer delicately picked guitar arpeggios by contrast, with electronically time-locked drums and multilayered background vocals providing the propulsion and timbral thickness. Joe Elliott's "I don't want your (photograph) . . . I don't need your (photograph) . . . All I got is a photograph" are given ample room to become the listener's main focus as they are pulled into this surprisingly gentle but ultimately euphoric fantasy of a chorus. But the rock of ages is never too far away, always coming back around to pump out eighth-note guitar grooves that reinstate the vigor of Leppard the *hard rock* band. This is *not* Foreigner, this is still a band of youthful, energized, wild young men, and we feel their energy through every "WO-OAH" or "F-F-F-FOOLIN'!" Often layered background vocals can sound too soft and pillowy, a sonic cotton candy that can take the edge off a rockin' tune. But Leppard's dense background vocal arrangements are sung with a punk rock energy and the conviction of a lead vocal, albeit with every vowel, breath, and nuance executed with a knowing discipline.

> **Lee Aaron:** Def Leppard's *Pyromania* changed everything. After it was released in '83, it pretty much defined the '80s heavy rock sound. We *all* wanted *that* sound, and we spent hours in the studio trying to emulate that monstrous snare vibe on *Metal Queen*, ha, ha! It was also a time when a lot of new technologies were being experimented with, like gated reverbs, drum machines, and synthesizers. So that said, my '80s albums definitely have an '80s "sound," which locks those albums into an "era" of music which doesn't necessarily transcend time the way the Beatles or Rolling Stones or Bowie records do. My nostalgic side embraces the sound of those albums, but my artistic side feels they could have benefited from more classic production values.

The thwack of the synthetic snare drum and the pump of the mechanical kick provide a very specific kind of energy. Surely, these must have been challenging times for drummers weaned on the freedom and expansiveness of being able to organically respond to the music happening around them. The drum parts on *Pyromania* and albums that came after almost seem to follow a didactic demand from the producer, and we feel the accountability of each kick drum pattern and tom fill. Regardless of how the sonics of these programmed percussion parts sound in retrospect, they felt like a delineating factor between New and Old at the time of *Pyromania*'s release. It seemed to place Def Leppard on a separate path even from contemporaries like Quiet Riot and Mötley Crüe. Sonically, *Pyromania* felt like it had as much in common with Duran Duran and the Police as it did with heavy metal.

Oddly enough, where the sounds on *Pyromania* seemed to align with contemporary new wave artists, the look of Def Leppard was remarkably lowkey. While each member of the band was surely blessed with photogenic good looks and all manner of fantastic rock star coifs, they didn't adopt the androgyny or sartorial derring-do of bands like Culture Club or Duran Duran. Sure, there were the odd studded bracelet, the leather strides, a bit of eyeliner to bring out Elliott's already striking peepers, some questionable Union Jack "short" shorts. But really, they looked like regular blokes, rock'n'roll Cub Scouts who'd been allotted a few quid to grab some "rock clothes" at the Camden Market.

And here is where the real dangers and thrills come into play. It wasn't all that threatening to play loud, rude, and aggressive rock'n'roll with distorted guitars while still adhering to traditionally ascribed gender perceptions in the early '80s, nor was it that scary to play around with gender while making music that is just as likely to be piped into your dentist's office as it is to be playing on MTV. But somehow, the combination of heavy rock music with an over-the-top, gender-bending visual presentation struck fear into the hearts of parents and societal leaders in equal measure to the excitement it generated in the hearts and loins of the intended audience. We'd been there before with Kiss and Alice Cooper, and, no doubt, eyebrows were raised as high as the picket signs warning of eternal damnation at their concerts. But prior to the ubiquitous reach of MTV, these shock rock shenanigans seemed to fall more into the realm of the abstract cartoon, a troubling absurdity more than an actual threat to the established conservative Christian mores that formed the basis of American (and by extension, Canadian) life for so many.

Mötley Crüe had already begun making a mark with their hedonistic debut, but on their 1983 album *Shout at the Devil*, they intensified their attack on the music market by amping up the sex, satanism, and violence with a visual concept that was equal parts *Mad Max*, Sunset Strip, Kiss, and *The Exorcist*.

With custom outfits by designer Fleur Thiemeyer (a major styler of artists like Olivia Newton-John, Rod Stewart, and a veritable Who's Who of '80s hard rock and metal artists) and promo photos taken by Barry Levine on a set that looked like the Hell that had been described to us by our priests and teachers, *Shout at the Devil* was youth rebellion on stun. Musically, a case could be made that their debut album *Too Fast for Love* is far richer in terms of innovation and dangerous spirit, but the songs on *Shout at the Devil* took on a more refined and simplified arrangement approach that helped mainline the anti-establishment message into the ears of an impressionable youth market. In much the same way *Destroyer*'s slick production would come to define Kiss to a mass market, *Shout at the Devil* is the ultimate musical and visual crystallization of what Mötley Crüe would come to represent to their fanbase and society at large.

Musically, *Shout at the Devil* is a darker exploration of the bombast of anthemic simplicity of Kiss, an embrace of German and U.K. metal plod and pump à la Accept, punk rock's shout-along choruses, and a state-of-the-art take on classic American rock like Ted Nugent and Aerosmith, where the signature guitar riff is almost as important as the vocal hook, a credo expounded by producer Tom Werman.

The album begins with a post-apocalyptic, spooky synthesizer and sound effects–laden spoken-word preamble called "In the Beginning." The piece is delivered by someone named "Allister Fiend" (the voice actually belongs to the album's British engineer, Geoff Workman). Allister Fiend serves as a mascot on selected pieces of Mötley merch, but as far as mascots go, he didn't really capture the imagination in the same way Iron Maiden's Eddie did. Then again, when the artist is more visually colorful, scary, and striking than the mascot, it kinda defeats the purpose of even having a mascot in the first place.

"In the Beginning" is a rip-off of David Bowie's 1974 "Future Legend" intro to *Diamond Dogs*, certainly, but it's an *inspired* rip-off nonetheless. And let's face it, how many kids in the American Midwest or in small-town Northern Ontario had ever heard that Bowie intro, anyway?

Where Bowie did what Bowie does, waxing all abstract, detailed, and poetic, Nikki Sixx cut to the chase, setting up a scenario of cities fallen into slums where evil stands strong, decimated by the power of all man's sins. Quickly and efficiently, we the "youth" are placed as protagonists in this passion play of good versus evil, our preconceived notions of those designations challenged by the flush of new rebellion. We are given the role of Children of the Beast, which sure feels a whole lot like Satanism, but wait . . . the "beast" is actually a composite of every parent, priest, teacher, or cop that ever kept us down! In a mere 1:14, we are called to a dark pep rally, preparing us to shout at the devil (not *with* the devil, as an earlier iteration of the album was purported to do. This was before Sixx freaked himself out and abandoned his real-life flirtation with Satanism due to supernatural events involving flying forks and spoons . . . I'm thinking one of those was a coke spoon). It's a brilliant concept, this empowerment of the listener. It makes the rest of the album feel like a life event, a statement of personal intent . . . a choice. As far as I remember, I didn't have a lot of choice in 1983, and listening to *Shout at the Devil* felt like a doozy.

And into the music we go, riding the synthesizer and English accent-inflected monologue crescendo of "In the Beginning" into the title track's sickly, warbling, vibrato-laced power chord riff that sounds almost supernatural. Mick Mars's guitar tone on the entire album connects to the look, concept, and artistic intention. It drips with a midrange distortion that is nowhere near the gloriously thick harmonic crunch of their debut, but that's not to say the tone has been thinned out either. More like sharpened to a deadly point. The metallic sheen of the NWOBHM seems to be a sonic influence here, updated takes on Saxon and Judas Priest tones delivered by a player informed by '60s and '70s influences like Mike Bloomfield, Bill Nelson of Be Bop Deluxe, the Allman Brothers, and Ritchie Blackmore. The lead lines are tortured and slippery, like souls trying to ascend out of the depths of hell only to be smacked back down by the hand of the very devil we're supposed to be shouting at (or is that *with*? So confusing!). But they are also memorable, just as his rhythm guitar parts elevate the chord structures with hooks and attitude. Mars also gets an instrumental showcase on "Shout at the Devil," but rather than a display of technical virtuosity, Mars delivers a delicate, pseudo-Spanish arpeggiated minor key acoustic piece with a harmonized electric guitar melody. "God Bless the Children of the Beast" scared the shit out of me more than any piece on *Shout at the Devil*, like a satanic "Malagueña."

The title track gives us a taste of some of the isolated elements of Tommy Lee's drum kit. The pillowy thud of his kick drum landing on the two and four backbeat accentuating the repeated tribal chants of "Shout . . . Shout . . . Shout," the splashy trash of his hi-hat cymbals marking the quarter-note pulses, the machine gun "rat-tat-tat" snare drum fills that bring in the song's Godzilla-like groove. The entire band lopes and throbs along demonically on the back of Nikki Sixx's bass tone and approach. Sixx attaches his lines to the simple chordal moves of the album's compositions, not so much generating harmonic or melodic content as creating a sludgy, quaalude-affected low range quagmire. It's a druggy and dark sound, but highly effective. Even when Sixx is chugging along with the idiosyncratic eighth-note grooves that heavy metal is known for, it never sounds jubilant . . . more like a strung out horseman of the apocalypse hanging on to the reins of his steed with one hand, a bottle of Jack Daniel's in the other. Having had the opportunity to listen to the isolated bass tracks from this album, it's clear to me that any other bass player would have taken away from the magic of this album . . . it *had* to be Sixx, punching and sliding off the notes, his artistic intention miles above his technical ability. The fact that he was playing his parts in utter pain with a pin in his shoulder (the result of having crashed his car in a drunk driving accident) just adds to the struggle. On *Shout at the Devil*, we hear the sound of the room, we hear the drugs, and we hear the personalities that went into its creation. Later iterations of this style of rock'n'roll would forget just how important personality is in making iconic rock'n'roll, choosing formulaic repetition over inspired creation.

As much as any singer before or after, Vince Neil should be credited for making the case that sometimes the best singer for a band may not be a very good singer at all. For whatever technical or tonal shortcomings are on display, Neil's vocals have just the right amount of cutting clarity and sinister snarl to bring home the messages on this album . . . just as with

Ozzy, we believe him. It's actually a wholly different heavy metal experience than listening to say, Ronnie James Dio.

While Dio's 1983 solo debut *Holy Diver* would most likely share album rack space alongside *Shout at the Devil* in most '80s hard rock fans' record collections, I believe they satisfy, not necessarily by design, different musical cravings. The Dio band was made up of three veteran musicians (Dio, drummer Vinny Appice, and bassist Jimmy Bain) and one fiery virtuoso in newcomer Vivian Campbell. In combination, they created an album that has urgency and immediacy but also features performances highlighting virtuosity and technical skill. I asked Vivian to walk us through the process of creation for *Holy Diver*.

Vivian Campbell: I really think it was organic. We literally went into a room and just played. Jimmy Bain was a great riff guy . . . I had some ideas, some riffs, and even when we had something that was very pedestrian, just like a couple of chords or whatever, what Vinny played behind it, what Vinny Appice played as a drummer really brought impact to it. Even if Vinny just gets in a room and starts playing, Vinny has the same attitude toward drumming that I have toward guitar playing . . . He fucking brings it, man. He plays, he's just laying it down. He's slamming it. He's such a great, dynamic drummer, and such an inventive drummer, too, a creative drummer within the hard rock mold, and so even sometimes when we'd go in and it's like, "Anyone got anything?" "I'm not really feeling anything." "Jimmy, you got something?" "No, not really." Vinny would start playing a beat, and Jimmy and I would go, "Oh yeah, okay. We can . . ." And we'd come up with something.

And so the songs . . . Ronnie came into that album having already written the "Holy Diver" song itself, the title track, and he had somewhat of an idea for "Don't Talk to Strangers," but other than that, I mean we had to come up with the rest of the album, and so we went in and played and it has that feel to it. I think that's part of what makes the album so great is because it has this from-the-ground-up, organic feel to it, and it's also got this mad, mad energy that came from Vinny's drumming, from my approach to guitar playing, from Jimmy's . . . Vinny and I always say about Jimmy, may he rest in peace, that Jimmy could plug into a toaster and get a great tone. He just, he was a very simple, very fundamental bass player. He didn't do anything of the fancy slapping or whatever, didn't try to overcomplicate parts, just play what was needed and his groove was impeccable and his timing . . . It was just these great elements that we had. And then, of course, Ronnie, who was the best of his genre, just had this golden voice to lay on top of it, and Ronnie would come in every night in rehearsals after Vinny and Jimmy and I had been there for several hours, kicking around ideas, and Ronnie would come in and he'd have these books of lyrics, these spiral books, and he'd listen to what we laid down that day, and he'd open his books and he'd look through and then when he'd find something, you could see the cogs turning in his mind and he'd be penciling away. And then he'd just step up to the mic and that was it. By 10 o'clock at night, we'd have a song. Just like from three in the afternoon when we'd start riffing. Ronnie would come in about seven and by 10, 11 that night, it was pretty much there or thereabouts. So it just happened very naturally and very organically and there was no pressure, because we were a new band, nobody was expecting anything really. We were just laboring away in some nondescript rehearsal room in Van Nuys, California.

As much fun as it is to sing along with classics like "Rainbow in the Dark," "Stand Up and Shout," or "Holy Diver," let's face it . . . most of us could never actually *sound* like that. I'm going to bet that more people have lip synced to "Rainbow in the Dark" than actually tried singing along.

Rather, we are enriched by the noble efforts of music from players who spent time in iconic bands like Black Sabbath and Rainbow, astounded by the majesty of RJD's tone, vibrato, and range. We can air guitar along with Viv, but any aspiring six-stringer actually trying to match the intensity and technical prowess of the guitar playing on that album would be putting their newly calloused fingers through quite a test. That's why it was surprising to hear Vivian's perspective on his own playing in relation to what was happening in the American guitar scene at the time.

Vivian Campbell: I am a really aggressive guitar player. It's very physical to me when I play the instrument, and when I first landed in L.A., and I came across all these GIT guitar players, they just had so, so much incredible technique, playing 32nd, 64th notes with great clarity, and this alternate picking and stuff, but they were barely playing the instrument physically compared to how I played it. You know, there's no way I could play like that, and it was a great source of frustration for me for many, many years in the '80s because I was thinking, Why can't I play like that? It is so obvious now, with the benefit of all this hindsight, that I'm too physically ham-fisted with the guitar to ever play like that, you know?

While the Crüe sport two arguably great musicians in Lee and Mars, the strength and appeal for the audience is in the ability to sing (or shout, or chant, or grunt) along with the choruses. "Too Young to Fall in Love," "Red Hot," "Knock 'em Dead, Kid," "Ten Seconds to Love" bring the listener into the concept of participatory rock championed by Spencer Proffer with Quiet Riot. Maybe this created a shorter path to connection that allowed Mötley to sell more albums. And perhaps this is part of the reason we see an artist like Vivian Campbell begin a path toward exploration of music in more diverse bands like Whitesnake, Riverdogs, and ultimately Def Leppard, bands that were not averse to the musical influence of other bands in their hard rock.

Vivian Campbell: That's where I kind of started to butt heads with Ronnie a little bit because Ronnie definitely wanted to keep this . . . a very, very classical metal band. I mean, the guard rails were pretty close. We were following a pretty narrow path, whereas, personally, I was 20 at the time, I was open. I was a sponge. I was taking in all these different influences, and not just within hard rock, but for me, my musical development, I was starting to get into singers and soul music and Elvis Presley and Aretha Franklin and all sorts. I had all these different influences that I wasn't necessarily bringing into Dio . . . but it was going into me personally and I'm kind of, in whatever way, trying to push beyond these guard rails that Ronnie wanted to keep us in, but I totally understand why he did it. I mean, that's where he came from — Sabbath, Rainbow, the 1970s metal thing. It was a very well defined roadmap that he was wanting to follow, and that's actually what did set us apart a little bit from a lot of other bands who were happening at the time. Plus you know bands like Mötley Crüe were coming up and they were very image-driven, it was very sexual and stuff. We weren't like . . . Dio was not a sexy band, we were like . . . There was no smiling in photographs or anything like that . . . It was serious metal, you know what I mean? So that's kind of where it was, whereas with me I was thinking, Well you know maybe there's something to what these other guys are doing as well, but with Ronnie, no. He wanted none of that, we were following the straight and narrow. But it worked, it worked for the band. I totally get why he was wanting to do that.

The more mystical, mythical musings of bands like Dio, Iron Maiden, or Queensrÿche are better suited to displays of musical virtuosity, as they create a cinematic experience for the listener that very clearly lies outside of the normal suburban teen's life, and most likely outside of their ability to recreate musically. Perhaps this is why young musicians of that era (and today, judging by the thousands of YouTube videos on offer) were so inspired by these bands and the host of shredding guitar players to push their own technical boundaries.

As an aspiring guitar player, the thought of being one of a select few who could play technically demanding heavy metal guitar à la Van Halen, Rhoads, and Malmsteen was incredibly appealing. An identity that didn't involve prodigious athletic or academic gifts. Something I could work on alone, in the privacy of my bedroom, away from the imagined slights and mockery of the jocks, or the popular girls I was in love with. I wouldn't touch a guitar until Christmas of 1985, but the seeds were planted around 1983 through '84.

In 1983 a young Yngwie Malmsteen made his international recording debut with American band Steeler. At the invitation of Mike Varney, founder of independent shred guitar record label Shrapnel Records and writer of a column that championed upcoming guitar heroes in *Guitar Player* magazine, Malmsteen flew from his home in Sweden to join meat-and-potatoes metallers Steeler. Steeler featured Nashville–raised vocalist Ron Keel, who would go on to form his own eponymously named band, Keel, a perennial opening act for major label artists that, despite a series of reasonably strong major label recordings, never quite scaled the heights of the bands they supported.

Yngwie went on to become an instant sensation in Los Angeles, long lines forming outside any club that Steeler happened to be playing. Yngwie's playing was easily the most thrilling aspect of Steeler's solid if unspectacular debut, and it wasn't long before he began hunting out opportunities more in line with his abilities and ambitions. Ultimately ending up in former Rainbow frontman Graham Bonnet's Alcatrazz, Yngwie elevated their strange take on AOR-inspired pomp rock to impressive heights with his combination of Bach and Paganini–inspired harmonic and melodic sensibility and a technical command of the instrument that appropriated the attitude, showmanship, and sonic adventurousness of Jimi Hendrix, Ritchie Blackmore, and Eddie Van Halen. A trip to Japan would help cement Yngwie's legendary status, and it wasn't long before he was jumping ship once more . . . this time to lead his own band, Rising Force, his ultimate goal of having total artistic control of his music and recorded output achieved in record time.

Yngwie's rapid ascent would inspire legions of like-minded players to push the limits of technical ability on the instrument, and Varney's Shrapnel Records label was there to collect the best of those players and forge an independent community that would have a massive underground effect, creating an artistic instrumental subculture within heavy metal that embodied its look and image, but with an intense focus on musical excellence, delivered with a marketing attitude and low-budget aesthetic that drew parallels with the NWOBHM and punk movements that came before it. Interestingly enough, as the decade progressed, some of these bands (Gilbert's Racer X, Jason Becker and Marty Friedman's Cacophony, Tony MacAlpine) would receive high-profile exposure and big-budget marketing dollars from guitar companies who were selling record numbers of pointy six-stringed planks to the inspired and prodigious youth of the world who gobbled up information and insight found in pages of glossy guitar magazines. Speaking for myself, I always had more guitar magazines than albums, as they were a cheaper alternative to access the sounds of these artists . . . import indie records were an expensive proposition in Northern Ontario, but with a little elbow grease, some detailed guitar tablature and interviews, and the inspiring advertising images of these big haired, neon colored guitar gods, I could get a taste of what they were all about with much less financial (but much more physical!) pain. The Shrapnel Records roster would go on to serve as a career launching pad for players such as Marty Friedman (Megadeth), Jason Becker (David Lee Roth), Greg Howe (Michael Jackson), Paul Gilbert (Mr. Big) and many others.

Yngwie posed the first real threat to Van Halen's throne . . . not that Eddie likely noticed. Operating on an entirely different plane as the first-to-market, prototypical American superstar hard rock band, Van Halen had spent the first part of the '80s going from strength to strength, even correcting a slight dip in popularity in 1981's *Fair Warning* (considered by many to be Eddie's greatest artistic statement) with 1982's cover heavy–content light *Diver Down*. At the behest of producer Ted Templeman and singer David Lee Roth, VH fired up Roy Orbison's "Pretty Woman" as a stopgap single and took it zooming up the charts, only to have to come up with a full-length release post-haste to satisfy demand.

Frustrated by the fact that his own compositions were given short shrift in order to make room for more cover tunes (he even had to sacrifice an original buoyant, bubbling synthesizer riff in order to make it the bedrock of a cover of Martha and the Vandellas' "Dancing in the Street"), Eddie vowed to never lose control of his music making again. He ended up building a studio in his home that he would dub 5150, and with the help of engineer and sonic coconspirator Donn Landee, they'd make a place to sweat and create the music that would define '80s commercial hard rock.

The release of 1984 dovetailed beautifully with MTV's expansion into the homes of suburban America. The ragtag, spontaneously euphoric performance video highlighted every personality in the Van Halen band . . . Roth's multicolored martial arts moves, Eddie's iconic striped guitar mastery and impish grin, Michael Anthony's jovial and glassy-eyed supporting role, and Alex's total command of his cartoonishly large drum kit. In fact, every video from the 1984 album seems like it's straight out of *Looney Tunes*, replete with corny jokes, fast cars, stripping teachers, big stages, bigger hair. It all seems a product of cocaine and confidence, politically incorrect to the max, but not a whiff of aggression or anger to be found. A Van Halen video was what we all hoped partying would be like when we got older. Of course, it wasn't . . . but, for a few precious teenage years, there was hope. It was a spirit and an image that were aped by numerous bands over the years, but all too often fell short. An air of seriousness and self-importance ruined the party, an idea that moving like Roth or finger tapping like Eddie could somehow benefit you in a material way if isolated and co-opted, a formula that was employed to move product, get sex and drugs, to achieve power and success.

Van Halen enjoyed all of those trappings, of course, but as a by-product of purity of intention. Van Halen was the result of two iconoclasts, one a musical genius, the other a student of diverse philosophies and disciplines . . . and, just as key, two members with subtly prodigious gifts (Michael Anthony's harmony vocals, Alex Van Halen's swing and progressive classic rock drumming) and the grace to realize that their role was to frame the picture painted by the visionaries, while still adding a dash of color.

The musical performance and content on 1984 exists on a higher plane than that of other hard rock releases of the time, and this is something that would remain consistent for the majority of Van Halen's performing and recording career. Despite the trends that may have been popular during any given Van Halen release, the band remained unfazed and untouched . . . they simply created the music that they were meant to create. Older fans may have balked at Eddie's use of keyboards on "Jump" and "I'll Wait" at the time, but these songs reflect the exploratory innocence and innovative spirit of his guitar playing, virtuosic and driven by a sonic searching and yearning. His AC/DC-inspired rave ups on "Panama" and "Drop Dead Legs" go so far beyond the initial inspiration, they are only really recognizable upon Eddie's revelation of their roots. The same can be said of the Allan Holdsworth–inspired lead playing on songs like "House of Pain" and "Girl Gone Bad" and peppered throughout the album. It's definitely there, but in fragments that almost immediately become his as he reacts to his own phrasing and muse. The tones, the articulation of ideas from all players, the *joy* of this music are at once the standard that other hair metal hopefuls hoped to achieve and the holy grail they were simply never destined to find. Even when acts went on to marginally greater success than Van Halen, they simply could not meet the artistic triumph that Van Halen themselves seemed to have stumbled upon.

Of all the guitar players that attempted to capture the spirit of EVH's playing, Warren DeMartini of Ratt may have come closest. This is not to discount George Lynch and Jake E. Lee, the other two players I have noted as part of the post–Van Halen hair metal guitar trilogy. To their credit, they always seemed to be on a different path. Lynch's work on Dokken's 1984 release *Tooth and Nail* may have had sprinklings of Van Halen's influence, but the aggression, and the melodic and harmonic intricacy of his playing come from a unique artistic vision, that of a contemporary staking out his own space. Unfortunately, the strained interpersonal chemistry in Dokken may have created a dissonance that impacted the compositional strength of the band. Dokken had good, sometimes great, songs in "Alone Again," "Into the Fire," and "When Heaven Comes Down," but if you ask most guitar playing fans of Dokken, there was a tendency to lift the needle and memorize the exact location of those magical Lynch solos on the grooves of a vinyl record.

Jake E. Lee's work on Ozzy Osbourne's *Bark at the Moon* was conceived under what must have been an inordinate amount of pressure. *BATM* was the first new music recorded by Ozzy since the passing of Randy Rhoads, and the eyes and ears of the music community were on Jake. Fittingly, he'd make his first major appearance with Ozzy on Heavy Metal Day at the 1983 U.S. Festival, and he handled it with confidence and aplomb to the delight of the 300,000-plus strong crowd. To many, this was the day that heavy metal overtook new wave music as the "kids' choice," and truly became a mainstream music market contender. With a lineup that boasted Mötley Crüe, Quiet Riot, Triumph, Judas Priest, Ozzy, Scorpions, and headliner Van Halen, the event represented a wonderful microcosm of everything heavy metal had been previously, and what it would be in the future . . . North American, British, and German influences all on display, with the mighty Van Halen standing head and shoulders above all comers — even if, on that day, a combination of alcohol and other party favors enjoyed during a long day in the California sun certainly seemed to affect their performance. But once again, much of the beauty of Van Halen lies in the fact that they could fall apart at any time, but rarely did. And in the end, the band reigned triumphant. Even when Dave forgot the fucking words.

But back to Jake, who should be given credit for trying to forge his own sonic identity with a cleaner, brighter Stratocaster-based guitar tone and sound that in the hands of a lesser player could be unforgiving. The naked clarity of his sound and attack brought riffs like the one found in *BATM*'s title track, front and center in the recording, its only adornment being a touch of delay and some gooey, chewy phasing. Jake, a child of the '70s and a student of progressive rock like Mahavishnu Orchestra and Cactus, eschewed a higher gain sound for the organic warmth and purity of players like Jimi Hendrix but still delivered technically advanced goods with monster left hand intervallic stretches, a highly developed "circular" picking style, and an aggressive approach to high-speed scalar sequences. The fact that Jake was one of the few players who did not employ a whammy bar did not stop him from torturing the necks, headstocks, and tuning machines in his efforts to achieve dramatic dive-bomb effects. If anything, this violent hands-on approach created even more sinister soundscapes.

Before landing the gig with Ozzy, Jake had made the move to Los Angeles along with fellow San Diego transplant Stephen Pearcy, hoping that their band Mickey Ratt could get a piece of the action taking place in the late '70s Hollywood scene. Joined by towering blond guitarist Robbin "King" Crosby (yet another San Diego native) and some interchangeable rhythm section members, the band moniker was eventually shortened to the catchier Ratt. Jake was soon fielding other offers, including one from Ronnie James Dio, but ultimately landed the gig with Ozzy, edging out competitors that included George Lynch (who had already been passed over initially for Randy Rhoads). Warren DeMartini had been building a solid reputation as a hot player in San Diego and ended up moving to Los Angeles the day after he graduated high school to replace Lee in Ratt. DeMartini moved into Lee's apartment, and Warren and Jake would go on to inspire each other to push the limits of their guitar technique and musical imagination, often sharing the riffs that would end up on *Bark at the Moon*, and Ratt's massively successful full-length major label LP *Out of the Cellar*.

Ratt's sound is an updated take on Aerosmith's *Rocks* album mixed with Van Halen's debut, Judas Priest's twin guitar propulsion, and a hint of vintage Alice Cooper in the vocal department . . . maximum impact utilizing minimal melodic range that always somehow finds the perfect note to land on.

With a look inspired by the fashion-forward New Romantic era, Ratt moved away from leather and chains and adopted a brighter scarf-and-spandex look that combined Duran Duran with Van Halen and Aerosmith. The combination of Pearcy, DeMartini, Crosby, bassist Juan Croucier (who jumped ship from Dokken's rocky relationship boat), and drummer Bobby Blotzer created a sound that matched the look. There were plenty of sing-along hooks that married Pearcy's "Ratt"-ish rasp with Croucier's smoother, more traditional vocals (more "lead support" than background, especially in the anthemic choruses) and roving bass lines. Blotzer was a technically gifted drummer with a unique and highly musical approach to fills that energized transitions between parts of the songs. But the heart of Ratt'n'Roll, as the band would come to define their sound, was the guitar interplay between Warren and Crosby, with DeMartini's lead and rhythm guitar approach becoming one of the most recognizable of the '80s.

The opening riffs that propel "Round and Round," "Wanted Man," and "Back for More" are hook-laden dances between major and minor tonalities, evocative of a poppier take on Van Halen's "Unchained," the shimmering arpeggios and slippery power chords of "Panama," the dynamic and two note–power chord guitar approach of VH's verse breakdowns in "Running with the Devil" or "Beautiful Girls." But they are by no means strictly imitative. Unique melodies and hooks poke their heads out of DeMartini's power chord crunch and aggressive right-hand picking attack (an approach shared with both Lynch and Lee), making his guitar parts sonically definable, and often as easy to sing along with as the vocals. When it comes to solos, DeMartini's use of wide intervallic stretches, smooth as silk legato left-hand slurs, and flurries of alternate picked notes (a combination evocative of Uli Jon Roth) are delivered with a highly syncopated phrasing style that never feels forced. Interestingly enough, there is a noted similarity of the left-hand vibrato of DeMartini and George Lynch. They both employ a specific violin-esque technique that involves rapidly oscillating between a note one fret above and below the targeted pitch by sliding up and down in a quick, aggressive manner, rather than the more traditional approach of bending and releasing the string. I have heard this approach unfortunately referred to as the "whack off" vibrato technique (and now we can all never unhear it). DeMartini, Lynch, and Lee all take the "tried and true" idiomatic blues scale moves and blend them with more exotic sounds and extreme levels of technical proficiency. Unfortunately, in years to come, many would apply the techniques and licks of these fine players but would miss out on the phrasing and dynamics that lie at the heart of true music conversation.

While DeMartini is often singled out for his playing, the contributions of Robbin "King" Crosby might be easy to overlook. But it was he who was considered the de facto leader, an imposing, statuesque Adonis with a heart of gold, a gifted songwriter, and a rock-solid rhythm *and* lead guitarist. In any other band, Crosby would have been more often credited for his command of traditional classic rock licks, facility, and taste on the instrument. Sadly, his diminishing role of importance and perceived value in the band would dovetail with a burgeoning heroin habit. Depression, dependency, and a loss of self-worth would see Crosby take on a lesser creative role in the band, and ultimately would lead to his tragic demise. But in this book, and in the hearts of millions of fans, he will be celebrated for his offerings. After watching a young Ratt tear up the stage at Perkins Palace on a pro-shot 1984 video on YouTube recently, I was reminded that in any other situation, Crosby would be the *lead* guitarist, his great phrasing, touch, and ample firepower on full display. Just as importantly, Crosby possessed the undeniable "it" factor that all rock gods demonstrate onstage, his shock of blond hair contrasting Pearcy's Prince-esque stylized cut, Croucier's mop of Bolan-esque curls, and DeMartini's effortlessly cool Keef crop. Blotzer's perfunctory rock mullet fit the times as well, but he always looked like a jock who was playing the part to "make it."

One of my favorite moments in the interplay between DeMartini and Crosby comes in the "Wanted Man" solo. DeMartini comes out guns a-blazing with an elegant attack, giving us a virtuosic eight bar clinic on the hallmarks of his style. When Crosby steps into the ring to respond to this tough act to follow, he delivers what is arguably the most powerful finale to *any* Ratt guitar solo. With a smear of licks in the vein of Jimmy Page that deftly slur and stumble their way across bar lines, Crosby lands on some lower register phrases that would make Billy Gibbons proud, and ultimately leaps back up to culminate the phrase with a staccato two-pitch eighth-note motif before sending us back into the chorus with a soaring vibrato. I think what I love about this performance is that it sounds like he is a former champ, up against the ropes, having been dealt a series of high-performance blows from a younger, stronger fighter. Inevitably, in another fight or challenge, he will be bested . . . but in this moment, he finds it deep within himself to come back and play at the absolute best of his abilities. Speaking personally, DeMartini is a much bigger influence on me, especially for his work on later releases. But the emotional high point of the "Wanted Man" guitar solo duel comes from King Crosby.

I wish I saw more of this type of interplay in the Ratt guitar partnership. But even when he wasn't physically playing the parts himself, Crosby was an encouraging presence to DeMartini in the studio, the sign of a true partner.

Like Vince Neil, Stephen Pearcy's vocal gifts are not necessarily demonstrated in his range, intonation, or elocution. What he has is a *tone*, and when his vocals are doubled in the recording studio, the result drips with attitude and character. Often it is bassist Juan Croucier who is left to do the melodic heavy lifting in the vocal department, and the mix of Pearcy's vocal rasp with Croucier's cleaner singing tone is a wonderful combination. But it is Pearcy who possesses the irresistible and intangible quality that made kids like me want to spend hard-earned paper route money on Ratt headbands at the local record store.

I've come to recognize in myself a knack for blurring timelines to suit my narrative. Perhaps, as my dad would always jokingly say, "I've already told you more than I know!" I can't honestly remember which I discovered first, Mötley Crüe or Twisted Sister, but I do know that my love of Mötley intensified because of my love of Twisted Sister.

It was Dee Snider and crew that set the hook deep in my mouth with the release of their 1984 *Stay Hungry* album. And thank God for the standard industry practice of including B-sides from previous albums on 45 RPM singles, because it was through my purchase of the *We're Not Gonna Take It* and *I Wanna Rock* singles that I discovered two of my favorite songs from their previous album: the title track to 1983's *You Can't Stop Rock'n'Roll* and "The Kids Are Back." In my nascent musical mind, I could tell there was something different about the sounds and feels of the recording sessions represented on the A- and B-sides of these singles. It was not as dramatic as discovering *Too Fast for Love*'s aural sickness after having ensconced myself in the much more slick, yet not quite as sick, sounds of *Shout at the Devil*. But the B-side cuts on those Sister singles did reveal themselves to be heavier, the guitars more hairy with overdrive, the drums more aggressive. What remains constant, however, is Dee Snider's voice. The intensity, the belief, the commitment, and the anger come through no matter what is happening behind him musically.

If "Cum on Feel the Noize" rode Spencer Proffer's concept of participatory rock to the top of the charts, "We're Not Gonna Take It" took the concept even further and put it explicitly in the title of the track. No surprise since Twisted Sister had built their reputation through dragging their audiences (willing or not) directly into the performance, using their rabid energy to rage even harder, or their apathy to fuel their own internal fires, with Snider pointing out any audience member not fully engaged in the Twisted Sister concert experience and eviscerating them with all manner of threat and put down. *We* were in this *together*, and if the band were not going to put themselves above their audience, you better believe that any hipster with arms folded and a bored look on their face was going to come under some serious verbal fire from Twisted Sister's imposing frontman.

That concept of *we*, that feeling of belonging to something bigger, was, and is still, so intoxicating to me . . . A.J. Pero's triplet-laced drum-and-cowbell intro set the tempo (following Quiet Riot's lead of kicking off with an iconic drum part) and thus steeled our nerves for the a capella (see QR again) chorus that kicks off the song. There are great similarities to the melody of the Christmas carol "O Come, All Ye Faithful," perhaps lingering in Snider's songwriting brain from his days as an award-winning chorister (Dee may have been a foul-mouthed heavy singer, but he was a classically trained one). The descending major scale power chords that led us into the verse could have come right off of *Never Mind the Bollocks, Here's the Sex Pistols* — direct, powerful, and hooky. It reads as authentic, maybe because there is genuine punk legacy inherent in the band, thanks to the time Mark Mendoza spent in the Dictators.

There's a reason why children's songs employ similar melodic motifs — they're easy to remember and the perfect soundtrack to playing and having fun. Adults and kids play with different things, but the concept in their music is the same.

The spirit of inclusion in the lyrics is relentless. "We've got the right to choose," "This is *our* life, this is *our* song," "We're right, we're free, we'll fight, you'll see" . . . So many rallying cries, delivered on a surprisingly sparse and simple sonic foundation . . . two chugging palm-muted eighth-note rhythm guitars courtesy of Eddie "Fingers" Ojeda and Jay Jay French, Mark Mendoza's highly melodic and aggressive bass style providing much of the motion. Much has been written about some of the members' disdain for the production delivered by Tom Werman on the *Stay Hungry* album. It certainly doesn't come anywhere close to representing the ferocity of the band's live performances, or the powerful *You Can't Stop Rock'n'Roll* album that preceded it. However, as a delivery mechanism for the power of Dee Snider's voice and message, I would argue that the production is a great success. Its midrange "honk" and slightly muted guitar and clanging drum sound translate very well on radio and TV. As a band with a garish, colorful, and powerful image perfectly suited for the video zeitgeist that was '80s music culture, this was crucial. That snare drum hit you square between the eyes on the two and four, and Dee's voice was loud and clear on a bed of plucky eighth-note guitars. Those driving eighths were the sound of the '80s, just ask the Cars, Rick Springfield, 38 Special, or a host of other guitar driven pop phenoms.

This sound, coupled with the *Looney Tunes*–meets–*Animal House* inspired hilarity of their videos, made anthems like "We're Not Gonna Take It" and "I Wanna Rock" (lest we forget that even in participatory rock, the power lies fundamentally in the choices of individuals) digestible for mass consumption. But in no way is this a sell-out situation, or any less *metal*. I actually don't believe there is anybody more heavy metal than Dee Snider. If anything, these sonic accommodations were important factors in the development of free thought that Dee Snider was offering. The sound was accessible, which in turn allowed young, timid people access to the empowering message that Dee was laying down. He was standing up for us, but more importantly giving us the strength and tools to stand up for ourselves. It didn't hurt that he had one of the most lyrical and naturally gifted guitarists at his side; Eddie Ojeda's solo in the ballad "The Price" evokes the lyricism of Leslie West of Mountain, his singing vibrato and perfect string bends mournfully echoing Snider's story of the numerous personal costs associated in a life spent in search and service of the rock'n'roll dream. His playing, along with the two-fisted, Fillmore East–influenced classic rock riffing of Jay Jay French served as my earliest guitar inspirations. The thematic solo in "We're Not Gonna Take It" was the first guitar solo I ever got under my fingers, that magical descending riff the first I could actually play along with as the record spun. Magic.

And I'm not just talking out of my ass when I say Dee Snider is metal incarnate. I can bear personal witness to this, having had the opportunity to spend months working with him.

On a Christmas musical. And yes, it was a *metal* experience.

And yeah, everything he does, whether it's singing, acting, working out, writing a screenplay, or even eating a doughnut hole is *metal*.

When I heard that Dee Snider was bringing the musical he had written, *Dee Snider's Rock & Roll Christmas Tale* to Toronto for a run, I immediately contacted my good friend (and manager of the band I was playing in at the time) in New York, Danny Stanton. Danny was Twisted Sister's agent, and my band Four By Fate had recently played a festival with Twisted Sister, Marilyn Manson, W.A.S.P. and others in Belgium. I was hoping to get a chance to maybe audition for a guitar slot in the pit orchestra.

I was then informed that the band in the musical were expected to perform onstage . . . as actors. Having recently seen a production of *Rock of Ages*, where the band engages in the story in a minimal way, I figured I could bluff along. All worth it for the chance to work with the man who wrote the song that inspired me to play guitar. Danny managed to arrange the opportunity for me to audition and then sent me the score . . . and the script. To my shock, and admittedly a small degree of horror, there was a sizeable speaking role for the "character" I'd be auditioning for, Johnny B. Greate. There would also be singing. And dancing.

Oh shit.

After consideration, I figured even the chance to be in the same room with one of my heroes and get to play my Eddie Ojeda red-and-black-target graphic Kramer guitar alongside him was worth the almost certain humiliation I was going to face. Having played a gig in Northern Ontario with Canadian art-rock pioneers Rough Trade the evening before the audition, I got up early to make the six-hour drive back to Toronto. This was a good thing, as a person can't help but feel bolstered in their own rock star esteem when sharing the stage with Rough Trade's iconic vocalist Carole Pope. Still basking in her reflected cool, I was tired but fairly relaxed. I had committed my audition lines to memory, and I was willing to accept my fate.

Driving straight to Toronto's Winter Garden Theatre, I entered through the backstage door and walked up the stairs. It was a veritable sea of *real* actors. The vibe of the room was as frosty as any I've ever walked into, cut-eyed intimidation and chest-puffing tactics on full display. Squeezing into a chair with my guitar cradled between my legs, I was immediately grilled by various people . . . the fresh meat being tossed to the lions. "Who is your agent?" "What have you done before this?" As I glanced around the room at the perfectly manicured, beautiful people, all delivering their lines to themselves, I started to get infected with the tension. Watching people go in and out, I envied their confidence and poise . . . but I was bolstered by what I was hearing coming out of the room. The role of Johnny B. Greate required a *lot* of onstage guitar playing, much of it in a technically challenging '80s shred style. And how can I put this gently . . .

For the most part, none of the guys auditioning for my part could play very well.

When it was my turn to be called in, I was disappointed to see that instead of Dee Snider seated in front of me, I was faced by seven unimpressed, and unknown to me, individuals looking back at me. As they introduced themselves, it became a sea of titles: director, choreographer, music director, wardrobe, sound design, blah, blah, blah. Because this had been arranged by an outsider, I was assigned an agent who looked less than thrilled to see this acting neophyte sullying the audition room. She sat alongside the others, who, much to my horror, had me start with the lines. Standing in that big space, staring into the eyes of an actual human actor who was delivering their part of the dramatic exchange in such an accomplished way made me realize how truly unprepared for this I was. I stumbled through about half of my prepared dialogue before being politely but swiftly cut off. They had heard enough of that from me.

Fortunately, I was still invited to take the stage, where the music director immediately seemed to latch onto the fact that I was a musician. While I didn't immediately make the connection, Doug Katsaros has worked with Bon Jovi, Paul Stanley, Rod Stewart, and Elton John, to name but a few. The minute he dug into the piano, I felt that kinship and the power of his musicianship, the thing that goes unspoken when you've spent a lifetime pursuing music. Every awkward moment of my pathetic "acting" display was gone, and I instinctively did what I do in response to music that moves me . . . I cranked the backline-supplied Marshall amp and played my ass off. That sounds egoed out, but it is much more a testament to the supporting power of a great musician. The score comprised variations of themes from Twisted Sister classics . . . I already knew every word, every riff, every melody, and I could read a chart down.

When we finished, I looked up at the faces that minutes before had been buried in their notes and were now looking back at me with interest.

Even at the age of 42, I had been blessed with a good mop of curls to toss around that had fortuitously decided to stay attached to my scalp, and the summer's touring had kept me looking pretty lean. I was rocking a pair of motorcycle boots, so teetering on high heels looked like a possibility, and I sang the parts with the requisite attitude, not like it was a Sunday matinee showing of *School of Rock*. For the first time since walking in that room, I saw smiles.

But I wasn't there yet.

The agent walked toward me and pulled me aside. I was told (not to be confused with being asked) that an acting coach would be at my house later that day. Dee would be coming to callbacks tomorrow. Learn to act by then.

So back home I went, shortly to be joined by an amazing acting coach whose name escapes me, but to whom I'll always be grateful. By drawing comparisons with acting to performance practices that I was already familiar with as a musician, he coached me to a point where I could envision myself speaking lines to thousands of people, feet planted, embodying my character. Sorta.

Returning the next day, the herd was thinned, but the air was even thicker with competition. As I walked into the room, everything disappeared but the massive presence of Dee Snider. Standing six miles high and two miles wide, he looked at me in that way that Long Islanders can do so effortlessly . . . like they are impermeable to any bullshit whatsoever.

"You're Danny's friend, right? Cool, nice to meetcha. Danny told me about you."

This time I was to act out my lines in an actual scene mock-up, with other potential cast members. Doing my best to remember the valuable lessons I had learned, umm, the day before, I dove in. After a blur of exchanges, I was asked to go again, with a few suggestions. Applying the changes to the best of my ability we hit the scene one more time. This time, I heard a few chuckles from the creative team . . . had I just delivered a joke? Adrenaline shot through me . . . this is addictive shit.

Finally, I was asked to hit the stage one more time. Here it was. I was going to sing and play the song that inspired me to be a musician . . . in front of the man who wrote it. Whatever else happened in my life, I knew that this was a moment to cherish. The nerves were gone, replaced by gratitude. I would savor this, and even if it ended here, I'd be a happy man.

When it was all said and done, I was asked to stay in the room. Three more actors came in to audition with me. Then another three. Then a new combination. Holy shit.

Finally, when it was time to leave for the day, I was told that the team would deliberate and let me know the decision. The vibe was much warmer, and as Dee approached me to shake hands, he said something that I will never forget.

"You rose to the occasion."

I thanked him and turned to leave, my face flushed with pride. Whatever was to happen was to happen, but I at least had those words to take with me. But before I hit the door, I heard a woman's voice calling behind me.

"*Hey?* What size shoes do you wear?"

It was the voice of Dee's wife, the amazingly talented and inspirational designer Suzette Snider, who had designed all of the most iconic Twisted Sister outfits over the years and was doing the same for this production. With the rest of the team looking slightly wide-eyed, Suzette went on to say something to the effect of, "C'mon, he's the one! He's got the gig!" and started to take measurements. My admiration for Dee and his work ethic applies equally to Suzette, who would go on to mentor me through everything from proper accessorizing of rock clothes to application of stage makeup and removal of unwanted body hair . . . going so far as to take an electric razor to me with a Long Island–inflected cry of "Oh *hell* no, this shit is coming off *now*." Paul Stanley's chest hair has *nothing* on my shoulders!

She also wasn't afraid to remind me that in the few months off between the audition and preproduction that I had packed on a few extra pounds . . . fairly obvious when sliding into the carefully measured wardrobe and skin-tight spandex pants! Fortunately, a month of intense choreography helped to correct that little issue.

Throughout the run of *Dee Snider's Rock & Roll Christmas Tale*, Dee, Suzette, and the rest of the incredibly talented cast and crew would change my life in ways previously unimaginable. I was challenged and encouraged to see beyond perceived limitations, and the result was the greatest professional experience of my life.

It was my '80s dream come true. I got to put on makeup, candy-cane spandex, (it was a Christmas show after all!), leopard print jackets, and glitter in my hair. But most importantly to me, I got to stand to the left of the greatest heavy metal frontman in the world and play a pointy electric guitar.

And it all started in 1984.

Before we're done with this year, though, I have to address one band that had as big an influence on the L.A. bands that rose to prominence in the mid- to late '80s as Van Halen did on bands of the early part of the decade. A band whose "theater of the mind" performances involved raw meat being hurled at their audiences, the drinking of blood from skulls, live worms being consumed onstage, and naked women tortured on racks — a sadomasochistic circus taking place under a flaming stage logo that spelled out W.A.S.P.

Speaking strictly in terms of the music, the self-titled debut album by W.A.S.P. resembles a teenage boy's perception of what sex must sound like. This is an admittedly gross and disturbing thought, but it goes beyond the carnal thrills and table-leg humping desires of the pubescent male . . . it speaks to danger and freedom, the shock and awe of physical discovery via testosterone. Perhaps the fact that Twisted Sister went out as massive headliners and pop culture icons while W.A.S.P. has enjoyed a considerably lesser profile speaks to the intensity of their art. Or maybe Twisted Sister just had better songs.

To witness a W.A.S.P. concert in a small, 500-seat-maximum capacity venue like the Troubadour, to feel the heat of the flames from their onstage burning logo backdrop blasting your face as they licked the very flammable wooden roof of the esteemed venue, was an impactful and mind-altering experience.

Coupled with the physically ominous presence of frontman Blackie Lawless and guitarist Chris Holmes (and really, the whole band once you place them all in stack-heeled, thigh-high leather boots!), W.A.S.P. in concert was a full contact sport, with audience members often feeling the band's sting literally as Lawless put his training as professional baseball pitcher to use, hurling raw meat at high velocity into the stunned gathering. In one instance, a girl's arm actually became impaled on a hook that had been fashioned to one of Chris Holmes's stage outfits. Seeing her as a cloying fan and potential threat to the band's safety, a security guard pulled her off of Chris, thus tearing a huge gash in her arm, the real blood mixing with the fake prop stuff coming off the stage. *This* was truly dangerous rock'n'roll.

It's interesting to note that Mötley Crüe's Nikki Sixx did a short stint in Lawless's band Sister, which also featured guitarist Randy Piper. Sixx surely picked up more than a little inspiration for Mötley's own chainsaw-and-fire-infused live shows . . . and also directly lifted the symbolic use of the pentagram as part of the stage show and, ultimately, album art.

Musically, W.A.S.P. had the songs and sound to back up their shocking visuals, a combination of heavy metal riffage and glitter rock anthemic qualities. Not dissimilar to what Great White were doing at the time, and not surprising since both bands had interchangeable members at various points in their earliest incarnations.

The song "Animal (Fuck Like a Beast)" was supposed to be the first track on W.A.S.P.'s debut album. It turns out that Capitol Records, the major label that (at the behest of Iron Maiden manager Rod Smallwood, who was at the time handling W.A.S.P.'s business affairs) signed the band to a lucrative multi-album contract, was not about to endanger the band's commercial chances by issuing a track that would surely get them banned from mass market retail. This was 1984 after all, and while we weren't quite living the totalitarian nightmare foretold by George Orwell, this was still an America under the sway of right-wing Christian values. Yes, sex sells; but while there seems to be no greater sign of God's love for his American people than free-market capitalism, there are limits to such things. Jesus saves, but parallels with bestial copulation just weren't going to fly with the parents of the corn-fed children of the Midwest and Southern states.

And yet, if ever a song was to define what W.A.S.P. stood for sonically and visually, surely it was "Animal." "Animal" was ultimately issued as a single via U.K. label Music For Nations, which turned out to be a brilliant marketing move. Before we North American kids ever heard the song, we would learn about its twisted and perverse charms through imported metal magazines like *Kerrang!* or excerpts of forbidden lyrical reprints in rags like *Hit Parader* or *Circus*. Ultimately, the song was returned to its place as track number one of this album in a 1998 reissue, so in the name of the original intent of the art, we'll start there . . . even if it causes us to come to a challenging moral and ethical crossroads.

"Animal" kicks off with a thundering, descending riff that has anchored everything from Bach's "Bourée in E minor" to Ozzy's "Mr. Crowley." From there on in, it's a pulsating, throbbing thrill ride throughout, all chorus-effected power chords and a pumping single bass note figure that seldom deviates from its eighth-note thrill-kill mission. At only eight bars into the album, the tone, feel, sonic identity, and moral decrepitude of this classic piece of '80s metal is firmly established. And yet, nothing prepares for the banshee howl that spits out the song's first lyrics: "I've got pictures of naked ladies, / lying on their beds / I whiff that smell and sweet convulsion / Starts a-swellin' inside my head."

The vocal timbre that emanates from Lawless's six-foot-four frame is demonic, shrill, and cursed (or blessed) with a braying vibrato that sprays melodies like blood from shredded vocal cords. It is a raw and pain-inflected sound, yet highly infectious and addictive. It matches the psycho-drama of the fantasy-drenched sexual violence of the lyrics, rantings of a sex-crazed loner, frustrated and thwarted as he stares at a pornographic magazine "making artificial lovers for free" (pathetic frustration amplified by being too broke to afford to pay for sex?). And as the song's relentless riffs and rhythms play out, so does an increasingly violent scenario of sexual domination . . . he's gonna do whatever he wants to (to ya), he'll nail her ass to the sheets. He's a fucking predator, licking his chops, a wolf in sheep's clothing. He's gonna steal and feel her love . . . like an animal. As much as we want to get lost in the hooks and power of the music, the way the words sound and feel coming off the tongue, we encounter the great dilemma that faces so much of the music from this era.

It's a theme that pops up a lot with W.A.S.P. . . . "On Your Knees," "L.O.V.E. Machine" . . . women objectified — things to be coveted and taken at will. The extension of this comes in "I Wanna Be Somebody," a celebration of a decidedly male desire to take as much as you can of *every-thing*: shiny cars, dirty money . . . lots of rock'n'roll.

Much of W.A.S.P.'s early lyrical content represents an attitude toward women that I can never condone. It's a celebration of fulfilling one's own base desires regardless of the cost to others. Free speech and rock'n'roll defenders often argue that these ideas were healthy expressions of fantasy that actually dissuade violent action, but how can this be true if it is void of female voice? It's one thing for a woman to express a consensual sexual preference for sadomasochistic behavior, it's another for a man to foist it upon an audience under the auspice of "free speech." Especially if that audience is young, impressionable, and at a critical age where the formation of how they will relate to the world is occurring. It has been argued that it is actually the job of parents to monitor and control, and in my case, they did. (Oh God, how they did. Record smashing was a real thing in the Kelly household.) But how many angry, sexually searching, impressionable young males who didn't have parental guidance developed a negative attitude regarding woman due to these misogynistic exultations? W.A.S.P. surely weren't the only ones who perpetuated these attitudes, but they were the only stage act featuring a naked woman strung up on a rack, with a bag over her head.

Maybe an "artistic license" case could be made for this type of performance art if women were treated as equals in our world, or shown in other roles in the heavy metal genre. Alas.

Ironically, the video for Lee Aaron's female empowerment anthem "Metal Queen" was banned on a number of video channels for "violence" and "inappropriate content" (in other words, a woman wielding a sword and refusing to be dominated).

> **Lee Aaron:** The whole hard rock genre [and] record industry was policed by men back then, so you can't really point a finger at one particular band. The antics of those bands, however, certainly didn't help. Their audience was my audience, and it influenced the way I was viewed. In a weird way, it was confusing for them and for me. They may have bought a ticket to my show because they had the album and really dug the songs, but [some] also felt they had license to shout sexist comments my way. And worse, actually thinking that I might appreciate them. I became very good at deflecting sexist hecklers.
>
> Being treated as an equal and with respect among my peers was the biggest challenge. There was this pervasive

idea within that genre that women were props to be molded, dressed, and displayed in ways to please men and elevate their virility factor. Your value was viewed as higher if you were a "babe," but having your voice heard — I mean *really* heard — in the boardroom or the studio was much tougher. I remember being on my sixth album, which went platinum, and most industry folks still didn't know I wrote my own material. It was an uphill battle for respect.

The intrinsically predatory, degrading, and selfish lyrics of many W.A.S.P. songs put them in a rare category for me: music that I love to listen to but sometimes feel bad for listening to. And it's something I recognize that I increasingly have to account for as I continue to enjoy this music as an adult. In a lesser way, I also have to account for the fact that I have not mentioned "Heaven's on Fire," perhaps the greatest hard rock song ever written, in a chapter about hard rock music in 1984 . . .

But here we are, loud and proud and on the charts, heavy metal now the preferred iteration of rock'n'roll for millions of kids. Time to send in the (record industry) clowns and sell more of it. It's a weird transitional year, 1985, lots of awkward things to hear and look at for sure. But there were still people turning hard rock music into gold, and I'd love to help you pan for some of the best of what was out there musically. Ultimately, it's all a big setup for 1986, when things started to really go off, commercially, for hard rock and heavy metal.

CHAPTER 7
1985 TO 1986

SNAP, CRACKLE, AND POP METAL

atholic guilt? It's real. And I'm feeling some of it over my omission of a number of albums in the last chapter.

The Germans really get short shrift. Accept's *Balls to the Wall*, the only heavy metal album that I know with lyrics written by a female band manager, Gaby Hoffmann (a.k.a. "Deaffy"), that openly celebrate gay sex (I guess the lyrics on some classic Judas Priest cuts were fairly thinly veiled, in retrospect), and Scorpions' *Love at First Sting* both made stylistically influential and commercial dents in the American musical landscape. "Rock You Like a Hurricane" is probably worthy of a chapter in and of itself.

Former Deep Purple frontman David Coverdale, at the behest of American A&R guru and visionary John Kalodner, reimagined his solo outfit Whitesnake as a hot American hard rock commodity in 1984's *Slide It In*. As far as transitional albums go, *Slide It In* is an interesting case, in that it existed in two formats with different mixes. The version of the album released in Europe and mixed by Martin Birch has a toe in the sonic warmth waters of the '70s, while the much shinier "Americanized" version remixed for FM airplay in the U.S. by Keith Olsen foreshadowed the self-titled follow-up album that would appear in 1987 and come to be seen by many as hair metal's defining moment.

Kiss scored a non-makeup era victory with *Animalize*, in particular with the cut "Heaven's on Fire," co-penned by Paul Stanley with Desmond Child. Child is a New York–based songwriter and song doctor who had helped Kiss navigate the choppy waters of disco with his composition assistance on "I Was Made for Lovin' You," and kept Kiss similarly au courant with the wide open verses, campy, play-tanic innuendo of the lyrics, and the bone simple guitar and vocal hooks of "Heaven's on Fire."

Bon Jovi successfully appropriated foundational work laid by Aldo Nova and Billy Squier on their self-titled debut, with the hit single "Runaway" serving as a hint of what would come when they themselves would bring Child into their songwriting fold on the 1986 blockbuster *Slippery When Wet*.

I didn't talk about Autograph's *Sign In Please*, an album I bought on cassette on the same trip to Records on Wheels that saw me purchase Nena's *99 Luftballons*. The joy I received from discovering that Autograph were much more than their one massive hit "Turn up the Radio" balanced out the disappointment in discovering that Nena's album was also much more than her one massive North American hit . . . but half of it was in German.

Side note: I had the opportunity to play on the finale of Germany's version of the popular TV series *The Voice* with Nelly Furtado back in 2012 . . . and Nena was one of the judges. While I should have probably been concentrating on the performance with the show's orchestra, all I could do was stare at Nena (the song started with acoustic guitar, and I was seated at the very front of the stage) . . . I swear that a very particular chemical smell from those days back on Lake Temiskaming was in the air in that German television studio, the scent from those CBS cassettes when you first peeled off the cellophane wrap and cracked the lid of the case. I can only assume that Nena herself smelled much nicer.

I also feel a degree of shame for not having talked about Canadian legend Helix's first two major label albums, *No Rest for the Wicked* and *Walkin' the Razor's Edge*, especially in light of the fact that they, along with Honeymoon Suite, were the first band I ever saw in concert. Never mind that I would one day join the band as a member and continue to write and record with them long after my departure. If we are talking about participatory rock, Helix's breakthrough single "Rock You" literally spells it out. Gimme an R, indeed. Along with Regina, Saskatchewan's Kick Axe (part of

Spencer Proffer's stable of artists at Pasha Records along with Quiet Riot and W.A.S.P.), Helix were transforming their experience as veterans of the grueling Canadian bar circuit in the '70s into some highly compelling and competitive melodic hard rock in the 1980s.

To assuage the guilt of some of these sins of omission, I tell myself that I did write a book called *Metal on Ice: Tales from Canada's Hard Rock and Heavy Metal Heroes* that makes the case that Canadian hard rock bands were delivering at a level equally high as (or higher than) their more commercially successful counterparts. The mid-'80s saw bands like Helix, Kick Axe, Lee Aaron, Honeymoon Suite, Anvil, and more create some amazing albums, and in doing so helped to extend Canada's reach into the worldwide market.

Alas, as I learned in writing *Metal on Ice*, writing is a tortured game of word and time constraints. Factor in my nonchronological consumption of these albums and a bit of ADD, and I'm afraid it all adds up to making me a pretty piss-poor historian. Then again, this book isn't so much about history as it is a reflection on the evolution of and artistic intention behind a sound, and some insight from the people who were there making it.

I might just have to let go and let God, in His many mysterious forms, lead the way as we dip back and forth through time to discover and reflect. You see, I may have been livin' for givin' the devil his due with my metal dalliances, but one of my more profound moments of hard rock conversion happened in church. You gotta sin to be saved. Or do you have to be saved to really appreciate how much fun it is to sin? I'm sure the answers lie on side one of Stryper's *Soldiers Under Command* . . . they managed to win (without sin) the hearts (and presumably souls) of thousands of headbangers by rocking for the one who is the rock with Priest-style (yeah I went there) twin guitars.

When I think of 1985, I visualize it as much as I hear it. A palette of purple and pink pastels, band portraits framed by various geometrical shapes, a softening of the edges that still leaves just enough of a point to draw a little blood. The look of a lot of the design aesthetic of the time seems to play up a sense of the overblown, but not in the sharp contrast of the blacks, reds, and oranges of the albums that came before. The album designs on second efforts by Ratt and Mötley Crüe have a feeling of commercial refinement about them that still generates excitement and energy, just a little softer. Less about gonzo machismo and testosterone, a nod to the more inclusionary appeal that commercial hard rock was starting to take.

Before we take a look at musical nuts and bolts, I thought it would be fun to share some quotes from one of the best reviews I have ever read. Written in 1985 by Tim Holmes for the September 12th, 1985 issue of *Rolling Stone* magazine, it references a host of records from that year while providing a hysterical and fairly balanced portrayal of how '80s hard rock was critically and commercially perceived. As a diehard lover of a big chunk of the hard rock music of the '80s, Holmes's tone does, at times, cause me to bristle. But it also serves as a nice reminder, smack dab in the middle of the era, of what defenders of the heavy metal and hard rock faith were up against in terms of critical validation:

> Heavy metal is the idiot-bastard spawn of rock, the eternal embarrassment that will not die. It's music that doesn't care what you think. Like some mythical beast that's part tyrannosaur — slow-moving and pea brained — and part Hydra — multiheaded and malevolent — heavy metal just keeps forging on, flattening everything in its path.
>
> Radio, by and large, won't play it, but so what? These bands sell millions of records and fill stadiums. Critics scratch their flaccid quills against the hide of the beast, but even if a head should fall, there are ninety more ready to spring up in its place. Punk seemed to offer the kids an alternative in terms of grunge, incompetence and snotty, nosethumbing attitudes. After all, what was punk rock but a revved-up morass of heavy-metal chords? But punk remains a cult taste; what went wrong?
>
> The key to the whole shebang is the Guitar Solo. Punk rock is just too damn smart for its own good, whereas heavy metal, by virtue of its undeniable stupidity, has a built-in survival mechanism that guarantees its astounding regenerative capacity. How else do you explain the ongoing commercial

impact of all these groups that possess the exact same idea of what makes a band? The Guitar Solo — the stupider, the better. (Though a screeching, ultrasonic lead singer helps, too.) *This Is Spinal Tap* was homage, not parody.

One of the points I try to make in defense of the heavy metal and hard rock of the '80s is the innovation and musicianship that was inherent in the guitar playing. At the end of the day, the guitar heroes of the '80s were what would go on to define the decade in musical terms, inspiring metal to rise to ever-increasing heights in terms of development of playing technique and instrument refinement. In 2022, you can't walk into a musical instrument store without hearing some aspiring teenage shredder applying techniques like "tapping," "sweep picking," or "string skipping," which were developed and brought to the lexicon of guitar playing in the '80s. Here it is being described as "dumb." Is "dumb" another way of saying emotionally vacant? Void of soul? Tasteless with no sense of direction or greater artistic purpose? If that's what Holmes means, I don't buy it.

Then again, this could be overaction clouding my judgment, a result of years of dodging the critical slings and arrows of critics and contemporaries alike. Who knows, maybe we who defend this music shouldn't be so afraid of dumb. One person's "dumb" could be another person's "direct and powerful." Or maybe dumb is just a way for the joyless to describe fun.

Like so many other young burgeoning metal fans, I didn't realize that Spinal Tap were a fictious band of characters created for a 1984 "mockumentary." I wouldn't see the actual film until years later, but all of the ads that were so brilliantly created and placed alongside the heavy metal hopefuls in the day made it appear that Spinal Tap were a real band . . . the only thing looking slightly fishy being some absurd song titles ("Sex Farm"? "Big Bottoms"?) and maybe Derek Smalls's Saxon-esque moustache. I just thought they were another umlaut sporting, leather pant stuffing, pointy guitar wielding band that seemed dubiously old. When I actually did see the movie, I saw how the hilarious scenes of overblown excess, displays of stunted intellect, and sundry clichés could have rankled the heavy metal artists this movie was clearly making fun of. In my life as a musician, I've experienced more than my fair share of "Spinal Tap" moments. It's inevitable . . . so much of what we do as touring artists is ridiculous, and our reality as "traveling circus people" is vastly different than those who observe us.

It's easy to believe that there are rules that don't apply to you as you go from town to town, staving off hours of boredom with all sorts of distractions that vary from harmless to harmful. Much of this behavior takes place in the hopes of sustaining the addictive rush of performing, that all too small amount of time you are paid to do ridiculous things onstage for the entertainment of the people who get to go back to their homes when the show is done. Back to a life the performer has chosen to leave behind.

Whoa. That hit a bit close to home . . . kinda like Spinal Tap does, but not quite as funny. Maybe Spinal Tap is a gift of levity for hard rock musicians to help them survive a vicious cycle.

Darn it if the look, feel, and, yes, the smells of this movie don't illicit an excitement inside me akin to watching a genuine rock concert. Christopher Guest, Harry Shearer, and Michael McKean kinda nailed the musical vibe too. The soundtrack to the movie may consist of parody songs played in a watered-down heavy metal style, but they sure are catchy, effectively re-creating the sound of a band whose former glories lay in the '60s and '70s, and who are now trying to contend with this new heavy metal aesthete. An aesthete that, as Holmes suggests below, relies heavily on testosterone-fueled pseudo heroism.

> Heavy metal is boys' music, using the electric guitar as a desperate and obvious symbol of adolescent hormonal hysteria. Heavy metal may not be high (or any sort of) art, but it is heroic, and its heroes assume one of several poses: sexual athletics (AC/DC); the ascendancy to manhood via a pulp-fiction variant on knife-wielding juvenile delinquency (Twisted Sister); insane instrumental "virtuosity" (Yngwie Malmsteen); the good old transcendent rock & roll PAR-TY! ethic (Scorpions, Ratt); or any combination thereof (Mötley Crüe).

Ah yes. Guitar as phallic symbol, that's an easy one . . . funny how something that means so much to one person can be so easily compartmentalized into something so meaningless to someone else. But even if Holmes's base reduction of heavy metal's use of the electric guitar were true, it doesn't necessarily negate the importance of the instrument or the role it plays. If our drive for sex is second only to our drive to feed ourselves, surely this totemistic representation offers something more than sheer affectation or compensation for inadequacy. I mean, if we are choosing to be blind to the fact that electric guitar is perhaps the world's greatest expressionistic musical tool, able to conjure tones and colors that reflect the entire spectrum of human emotions, then I guess I can live with the presumption that my chosen instrument represents virility in its ultimate form. Well strung equals well hung, all things considered.

It's tough to have the words of someone with a much more developed command of language lay down such a damning edict, making a case for the intellectual vacancy of this music I want to defend. Surprisingly, I find Holmes's writing quite liberating, edifying, and even uplifting. It's a bit of a blessing to find this review at this point. It speaks to the insecurity I feel when I hear people whom I perceive to be cooler, more hip, or more refined in their musical tastes denigrate music that has inspired me in so many of my life choices. In essence, when I face the pain of being ridiculed for listening to the music that was a shelter from other forms of ridicule in life, I am forced to confront my own insecurities. And the sting isn't quite as bad as I feared.

If I'm saying I'm into this for the adrenaline rush of it all, the visceral sound of the music, the thrill of thwarting the danger to my mortal soul as I drink in the images and sounds, maybe that's enough. The truth is, I know that a lot of the lyrics and posturing in hard rock music is barbaric, sexist, and, ultimately, pretty stupid. Tim Holmes is right. But even in his castigation of the intellectual content inherent in the music, the undeniable spirit of heavy metal is celebrated in his review. Maybe for the first time, I can exercise true duality of mind . . . some of this thrilling, important music has elements that are inherently stupid, and I can still love it. And it can still be art. Art doesn't have to hinge on satisfying a checklist of intellectual or moral requirements.

1985 will always be connected to my first pangs of musical anticipation, particularly in the case of Mötley Crüe, Ratt, and Twisted Sister. I had devoured and fully digested blockbuster breakthrough records by each of these bands and was now aware that there was a process at play . . . these guys were going to make *more* of the stuff that I loved, but it was going to be *different*. And, I hoped and believed, it was going to be *better*.

So many fans of hard rock and metal expect their favorite bands to keep regurgitating the same formulae that they have relied on in the past. I mean, if AC/DC is indeed the standard for guitar-based hard rock, you could make a case for the success of brand consistency (even if on their '85 release *Fly on the Wall* they make a few sonic and lyrical concessions to the processed drums and randy rantings of their current contemporaries). But this isn't Coca-Cola, this is rock'n'roll . . . this is art. Artists by their very nature want to change and grow. People who make their money off of artists know that trends in the arts can change, and that there is a balancing act between knowing when to ride the wave of a trend, and when to back a change in the game.

For better or for worse, Mötley Crüe have been leaders and game-changers in their career more often than they have been followers. *Shout at the Devil* had created a ravenous fan base who were ready to take a walk on the dark side, or at least live a life of vicarious pseudo-Satanism as they devoured those tasty Mars riffs and Sixx licks. *Shout at the Devil* was a marvelous sonic confection, a heavy metal record with enough hooks and sing-along power to warrant repeated plays, and a representation of successfully mounted teenage rebellion. Surely, the next album was going to be a sequel: *Shout II — Satanic Boogaloo*?

Instead, we got *Theatre of Pain*, described here by Tim Holmes in his acerbic review of the album:

> Moving up the ladder of civility, we find Mötley Crüe waxing philosophic on *Theatre of Pain* — their third and most techni-cally proficient album — which owes a lot, if you can believe the press bio, to sixteenth-century Italian commedia dell'arte. The cover photo of the Mötleys gussied up like postapocalyp-tic Botticellian angels further supports the claim. Sandwiched betwixt the rock anthems ("Louder Than Hell" and "Raise Your Hands to Rock") and the hard-boys-on-the-road laments ("City Boy Blues" and "Tonight [We Need a Lover]") are some

plaintive ballads ("Home Sweet Home"), salutes to roots (a chartbound remake of Brownsville Station's "Smokin' in the Boys Room") and a martial call to brotherhood called "Fight for Your Rights."

The comedy and tragedy masks that adorn *Theatre of Pain* couldn't be more apt, in light of the circumstances in which Mötley Crüe created their third album. Considered an "abortion" of an album by principal song-writer Nikki Sixx and the rest of the band, it was partially created during the fallout from the car accident involving lead vocalist Vince Neil and Nicholas "Razzle" Dingley, the drummer for highly influential Finnish rock band Hanoi Rocks.

Hanoi Rocks were a band on the brink of world domination, with a new album produced by Bob Ezrin that had successfully refined the raw, Stones-Dolls-Mott The Hoople–inspired sound of brilliant earlier inde-pendent albums like *Bangkok Shocks, Saigon Shakes, Hanoi Rocks* and *Back to Mystery City* for American consumption. *Two Steps from the Move* was released in August of 1984 on Epic Records and was chock-full of highly melodic songs that contained a spirit of cool and punk rock authority that separated Hanoi from the pack. With frontman Michael Monroe's cover-girl good looks and undeniable charisma, Andy McCoy's effort-less virtuosity and gypsy jazz–inspired melodic guitar flair, and a group rounded out by picture perfect examples of pencil thin rock'n'roll chic, this was a band that was born to inspire — natural leaders, chemically fueled purveyors of true rock'n'roll danger . . . in other words, the real deal.

It was natural that Hanoi Rocks and Mötley Crüe would find each other as rock'n'roll comrades, young visionaries of music and fashion and chemical misadventure: Mötley, flush with the success of *Shout at the Devil*, and Hanoi, ready to embrace a similar success after so much well-deserved critical acclaim. But in one fatal moment, it all fell apart for Hanoi Rocks. On a trip to the liquor store to replenish supplies for a party attended by both bands, Vince Neil, under the influence of various substances, lost control of his Pantera and collided with an oncoming vehicle. Two young passengers in the other car were paralyzed, and Razzle died from injuries sustained in the crash. Hanoi Rocks would not be able to overcome the immense loss of their friend and drummer, and their seemingly imminent success was dashed.

While this put an end to Hanoi Rocks for many years, Monroe and McCoy did mount a comeback with a new Hanoi lineup in the early 2000s, and to my great thrill, my band Crash Kelly ended up becoming labelmates with them in the United States. My first exposure to Hanoi came in the late '80s, when Skid Row frontman Sebastian Bach was hosting a metal specialty show on MuchMusic (Canada's answer to MTV) called the *Power Hour*, and he played the video for "Don't You Ever Leave Me," an older Hanoi track that had been reworked by Bob Ezrin for 1984's *Two Steps from the Move*. In retrospect, watching that video was seeing the beautiful thing that '80s rock could have been . . . what it should have been. Glamorous and melodic, yet raw and heartfelt — a perfect balance of polish and swagger. Hanoi Rocks would go on to have an enormous influence on the later '80s Hollywood scene, their artistic promise ultimately being fulfilled by a young Guns N' Roses, who would right the wrongs of the production excess and formulaic imagery that had begun to plague '80s hard rock.

After a 30-day jail sentence, a stint in rehab, and a $2 million payout, a newly sober Vince Neil was back in the recording studio with his increasingly strung out Mötley bandmates, and *Theatre of Pain* was borne out of a sludge of substance abuse, cruel indifference toward Neil's emotional devastation, and Sixx's visionary need to "zig" as almost every other band in Hollywood tried to "zag" into Mötley's lane. *Theatre* has long been panned by critics as being somewhat of a letdown in terms of writing and performance, but I still hear this record with the fresh ears of an 11-year-old boy shivering in sweet anticipation. Mars, reintroducing the slide guitar he used to such crude effect on *Too Fast for Love*, employs a more traditional approach, his Duane Allman showing from underneath the alcoholic murkiness that one may attribute from some of the "sameness" inherent in his note choices. However, he more often than not delivers the goods, with particular highlights being his tremolo picked frenzy on "Use It or Lose It," his soulful slide display on "Save Our Souls," and his melodic restraint on the ubiquitous power ballad "Home Sweet Home." Slower piano-based songs were nothing new in 1985, in fact bands like REO Speedwagon were making complete albums full of the stuff, but it was odd to hear something so sweetly earnest and gentle from the self-described heathens of the Crüe.

Tommy Lee's delicate piano playing was so impressive, and his credits on the album were something I would marvel at with pride. All of a sudden, I'm hearing acoustic guitars, piano, and even my hero Nikki Sixx playing a *synthesizer!* It's strange to think how ill-regarded keyboards were amongst fans of hard rock and metal, while at the same time being ubiquitous on all these recordings . . . maybe it was an aversion to images of Duran Duran or Flock of Seagulls burned into our brains, looking all bored, foppy, and sneering like they were *better* than us lowly rock fans. (It didn't help that this was the messaging we were getting from the new wave–loving girls at school. The girls and boys who were into Mötley Crüe or Ratt tended to smell like an ashtray and look like they had been rolled around in the denim section of Thrifty's.)

I remember reading an interview in a long gone copy of *Faces* magazine where Tommy Lee excitedly described his drum sound on *Theatre of Pain* as being akin to cannons going off. And sure enough, through the use of the burgeoning sampling technology at the time (where the actual acoustic signal from the striking of the drums "triggers" a synthesized sound, often with massive amounts of reverb), the drum sounds on *Theatre* were positively massive. The funny thing with excessive amounts of echo or reverb is that, after the initial effect has been experienced, the resulting ambience can detract from the power of signal, and end up making the track sound smaller. This is a common criticism of much of the recorded hard rock output of the 1980s, and when bands like Nirvana and Soundgarden came out in the early '90s with more organic direct sounds, it was hard to argue against this point. However, in 1985, these sounds were fresh, vibrant, brand new, and exciting. It should also be noted that the digital harshness or brightness of these effects (and the other new digital outboard recording gear that was starting to be used at the time) was still being recorded to analog tape and mixed for analog media such as vinyl and cassettes (although by 1985, CDs had entered the marketplace and were well on their way to becoming the preferred format). Point being here that any digital harshness was often tempered by the natural low-end warmth and compression that arises from recording onto tape. CDs even came with warnings that the high resolution inherent in the format could "reveal limitations of the source recording," and this was often the case. Early CDs were not "remastered" to compensate for this higher resolution, but later versions did try to enhance the quality of representation. All this is to say that, in my humble opinion, *Theatre of Pain* sounds pretty bitching on vinyl or cassette but less bitching on a CD.

But that could just be the memories talking, the emotional clouding of judgment that convinced me that *Theatre of Pain* was far superior to *Too Fast for Love* or *Shout at the Devil*. I mean, it had to be, right? Every interview I read by any band always said that their new recordings were *way* better than what had come before.

God, I miss the days of believing rock stars.

So yeah, if Vince Neil is going to wear pink lingerie, and Tommy Lee is going to wear a sequined mohair suit, I'm in. Mick Mars in a purple sash? Fuck yeah, he looks amazing. Nikki Sixx in a polka-dot onesie and ballet slippers? Yes please. And if Nikki Sixx loves Italian theater, I guess 11-year-old Sean Kelly does too. Comedy and tragedy, entertainment or death . . . for a few months in 1985, *Theatre of Pain* was, in my mind, the greatest album of all time. Why? Because Mötley Crüe were my favorite band, and I simply believed that they would always get better with every album. Forever.

I still love *Theatre*, but I can certainly see the argument for it not being the shining star of their discography. Ratt and Dokken, on the other hand, came out in 1985 with albums that undeniably were stronger in every way from what had come before.

Invasion of Your Privacy takes the application of reverb and echo employed by Mötley on *Theatre of Pain* and expands on it in a more aggressive but pointed way. The album sounds like it was recorded in an empty hockey arena . . . and this is a very good thing. In this case, the ambience works with the more aggressive midrange and top end guitar sounds of DeMartini and Crosby (this would be Robbin's last album where he makes considerable lead guitar contributions, and he does so with great style and presence), and the articulate grooves and fills of drummer Bobby Blotzer. The precision of the riffs and the chord voicings in tracks like "Lay It Down," "You're in Love," and "Dangerous but Worth the Risk" work incredibly well with the cold (but never sterile) application of effects and ambience, the right blend of dirt and gloss. On this album, producer Beau Hill shines not only as a creator of high-energy sonics but as an expert arranger of the components of the songs, parts, and textures. Hill's production on *Invasion of Your Privacy* gives a high-tech, almost New Romantic sheen to Ratt's Aerosmith–Van Halen–Judas Priest jumbo, supporting the power chord crunch and rhythm section pound with surprisingly sophisticated (at times bordering on avant-garde) background vocals and cinematic synthesizers used not so much as parts as they are as blended colors on a palette. Beau Hill's sonic stamp is what often comes to mind when people think about the sound of the '80s, and you can hear his strong influence on *Midnite Dynamite*, the 1985 effort of hair metal outliers Kix (an excellent band from Baltimore, Maryland, that mixed AC/DC riffage with a Cheap Trick sense of power pop melody and esotericism), as well as his coproduction work alongside Michael Wagener on Alice Cooper's post-rehab comeback album *Constrictor*.

For such a commercially successful album, it's remarkable how unmelodic Pearcy's lead vocals are on *Invasion of Your Privacy*. Once again, this is by no means a slight. As we discussed, on *Out of the Cellar*, Pearcy's power lies in the rasp in his tone, the sneer in his delivery, and the attitude in his phrasing. These elements are what make him one of '80s rock's great vocalists, and each is maximized on *Invasion*. The melodic hooks come from bassist Juan Croucier and Hill himself, with added girth and punch coming from the "football" harmonies of the rest of the Ratt gang. *Invasion* is Ratt'n'Roll at its finest, pop song structure with a punch.

Dokken delivers on the songwriting promise of 1984's *Tooth and Nail* with their '85 opus *Under Lock and Key*, albeit at the expense of some of the metallic rage of the former. In what might be a bit of a nod to the formula utilized by Mutt Lange and Def Leppard, we often hear the angular, aggressive, and sophisticated guitar riffs in the verses, and instrumental breaks give way to pillowy background harmonies and boosted lead vocal levels in the chorus. You can almost hear the conflicts of ego in the mix levels, Don Dokken and George Lynch battling it out for some kind of musical supremacy throughout the album. It's a common criticism of many albums released during this time period, a smoothing of the edges that gives way to a new accessibility. I've read numerous suggestions over the years that Dokken songs were often just an excuse for brilliant George Lynch guitar solos and riffs, but on *Under Lock and Key* the songs are very strong, especially melodically. There is a really nice hybrid between Lynch's exploratory guitar figures and Don Dokken's Klaus Meine–inflected vocal phrasing and tone (so closely matched that Don was at one point brought into the studio to work on demos for the *Blackout* album as Klaus recovered from damage sustained to his vocal cords). The rhythm section of "Wild" Mick Brown and bassist Jeff Pilson bring an identity to the table that lifts Dokken above many of their contemporaries. There is an organic power and conviction in Brown's playing in particular that seem to put his spirit and soul on top of the sonic processing applied to drum tracks of the era — maybe it's that '70s thing. Pilson, like the man he replaced in Dokken, Ratt's Juan Croucier, was a strong enough vocalist that he could easily have fronted the band as well, and his vocal power, combined with that of Dokken's and Brown's, gave the band an identifiable background vocal sound that saves that harmony-drenched production from sounding like melted marshmallows.

Something about the European-tinged, melodic nature of Don's vocals and the sense of exploration inherent in Lynch's playing have helped tracks like "Unchain the Night" (warning . . . *never* do this, according to Don!), "The Hunter," "In My Dreams," and "It's Not Love" age better than other material from the era.

After the phenomenal success of Quiet Riot's *Metal Health*, it was understandable that producer Spencer Proffer would be a hot commodity, and a trio of albums that define a big part of the sound of 1985 would fall under his production helm.

Anticipation was running high and hot for Quiet Riot's *Condition Critical* when it was released in 1984. As I waited up late to catch a glimpse of the new video for the first single "Mama, We Are All Crazy Now" on *Friday Night Videos*, I was completely unaware that the song was, just like "Cum on Feel the Noize," a cover by U.K. glam rock pioneers Slade. But when it came on, I was thrilled to hear that familiar Quiet Riot sound and to see those omnipresent black-and-white stripes adorning Kevin DuBrow's mic stand and Frankie Banali's drum kit, the familiar logo splashed across each of the two massive bass drums that served as anchors. The iron mask from the *Metal Health* album was on full display, reminding us all just how much we loved *that* album, and man were we going to love *this* one too.

It sounded amazing, the video looked more expensive, and when I purchased *Condition Critical*, it had that very distinctive Quiet Riot sound, elements of which I would hear on the equally anticipated (to me anyway) W.A.S.P. album *The Last Command*, and on Canadian rockers Kick Axe's follow-up to their gold-selling debut *Vices*, *Welcome to the Club*. Spencer had basically created something that my good friend, and ultimate authority on heavy metal, Martin Popoff describes as the Pasha sound. It's a sound that is quite specific to that studio, a blend of clangy and metallic percussion that is rounded out with a very distinct reverb, satisfyingly chewy and gooey over-driven guitars, chorused and flanged clean arpeggiated guitars, judicious if generous use of synthesizer pads, and big gang vocal arrangements designed to encourage listener participation.

I believe *Condition Critical* is as good, and maybe even a better album than *Metal Health*. There are more songs that tap into Proffer's participatory rock theory, and those songs have brighter melodic moments that do a fine job of blending major key sunshine and the opportunity for shout-along moments. "Sign of the Times," "Mama, We Are All Crazy Now," "Party All Night," and "Stomp Your Hands, Clap Your Feet" give us four such stompers in a row, and in an era maligned for pushing out albums with one good song and nine pieces of filler, this is a pretty great ratio. This is followed by a fantastic power ballad in "Winners Take All," and a really interesting and dynamic metal workout with the title track, crunching harmonic riffage alternating with crystalline arpeggios in a menacingly slow prowl across Judas Priest terrain. Even filler like "Scream and Shout," "Red Alert," and "Bad Boy" are pretty strong.

And while the album would go on to sell three million records around the world, something about it didn't quite connect in the same way as its predecessor. I even remember my own feeling of muted excitement. I was thrilled to have it, and yet I wasn't hitting rewind as much. I wasn't co-opted into believing that this was a better record than its predecessor in the same way I had been with every successive Mötley Crüe album. Something had changed for me with this band . . . I didn't buy in as fully anymore to this new product, and I found myself going back to the three or four tracks on *Metal Health* that really moved me. Maybe it was the fact that Kevin DuBrow was trash-talking all the other bands I liked in every interview I ever read with him, or maybe it was the way he was moving onstage . . . he didn't look like Vince Neil or Stephen Pearcy; they felt and looked like something forward-thinking, something new. When I watch Kevin onstage now, with an understanding of artists that influenced him (Rod Stewart, Steve Marriott, Tina Turner), his gesticulations and stage mannerisms make perfect sense to me and seem very authentic and entertaining. But at the time, it just seemed a bit old-fashioned . . . especially when compared to the highly stylized stagecraft I was seeing from Ratt and Mötley Crüe. (I do have to say I always thought Rudy Sarzo looked amazing and played great . . . so much so that when I had the opportunity to work with him on my own Crash Kelly record, I asked him to show me one of his signature moves, where he pounds the upper horn of his bass guitar while holding a note with his left hand, the opening strings ringing in sympathy, creating a massive sound — one that I now know how to achieve myself, though it never sounds as cool as when Rudy did it for me.)

Crash Kelly opened a show for Quiet Riot years later in 2005 in a small bar (a former post office!) in Southern Ontario. The lineup at the time included DuBrow, Banali, and bassist Chuck Wright, who had played on a few cuts on *Metal Health* before leaving for pomp metal mongers Giuffria. A reconstituted lineup with so many original-ish members was a rare commodity all those years later, and I won't forget Kevin DuBrow's warmth and kindness as he generously shared stories of his time with Randy Rhoads with me after the show in the club's tiny upstairs change room. A few years later, as I walked down Santa Monica Boulevard in Los Angeles on a trip to promote Crash Kelly's second record, I would hear a shout of "Hey, Canada!" from across the street. It was DuBrow, accompanied by legendary bassist Glenn Hughes of Deep Purple. Kevin was once again warm and friendly, in proportionate measure to Hughes's disinterest. (And why would he be interested?) But Kevin still introduced us and made him shake my hand. In my brief experience with Kevin DuBrow, I met a man who through experience knew how precious and perilous the perception of the rock star could be, and was here trying to ensure that a fan had a good experience. I listen to those Quiet Riot records today with a renewed fondness, and I am grateful I had the chance to see that side of the man.

Tim Holmes goes on to offer a slightly back-handed compliment (a common theme in most critical reviews of '80s hard rock) when discussing the work of Twisted Sister:

> Twisted Sister, on the other claw, is plainly the clown heir apparent to the gaping vacancy left by Alice Cooper. Dee Snider and company fill it with all the banal good cheer and bad-boy rah-rah a kid could want. They tend to write songs that have a giddy, street-smart narrative approach and a gritty coherence that metal usually lacks. *Under the Blade* is not technically a new album but rather a remix for modern ears of an earlier LP. They've included, for all you Twisted hardcores, "I'll Never Grow Up, Now!" — the band's very first product, a single released on an independent label way back in 1979.

Twisted Sister came back on the scene with a reissue of their 1982 debut *Under the Blade*, remixed for an audience who had fallen in love with the more radio-friendly tones of *Stay Hungry*. I perceived the progression in sound and image between the two albums in the same way I had upon discovering *Too Fast for Love* after having been familiar with *Shout at the Devil*. In the case of Twisted Sister, the change seemed a bit less dramatic. The roots of what I had come to love about the band were there on *Under the Blade*, but the refinements in songwriting and production made *Stay Hungry* more palatable. Still, it was wonderful to have new Twisted Sister music, and it set up more of that sweet preteen anticipation for the release of brand new TS music later that year. In December of 1985, *Come Out and Play* was released in a deluxe vinyl package that featured a pop-out Dee Snider emerging from a manhole on the cover . . . the title and technicolor gang imagery of the album a nod to cult film *The Warriors*. *Come Out and Play* was an album conceived of and written entirely by Dee Snider, who had taken control of almost all aspects of the band's creative vision. Produced by Dieter Dierks, the album has a high-tech gloss that stands in stark contrast to their earlier albums. There is a sterile separation of the instruments on this recording, processed guitars and drums speak with clarity but seem to lack emotional connection to the overly ambient vocal production. While the overall songwriting efforts continue in the anthemic and melodic vein of *Stay Hungry*, they feel somehow more contrived and thought out. It didn't feel like Twisted Sister had stayed hungry, with tracks like "You Want What We Got" feeling more like an "I told you so" than a "fuck you." It all seemed to be coming from a different place than the one that brought us all together.

Singles like the band's cover of the 1965 Shangri-Las hit "Leader of the Pack" (a set list standard from their club days) and "Be Chrool to Your Scuel" (a duet with Alice Cooper that also featured Brian Setzer of Stray Cats on lead guitar, Billy Joel on piano, and Clarence Clemons of Bruce Springsteen's E Street Band on saxophone . . . just in case you didn't know that Twisted Sister had made it!) on paper seem like slam dunks for hits. But when stacked up against sonics coming from albums like *Invasion of Your Privacy*, *Under Lock and Key*, or the sleazy danger that was still inherent on *Theatre of Pain*, *Come Out and Play* just didn't sound or feel as rebellious.

The same can be said of the videos for said singles. Where the clips for "We're Not Gonna Take It" and "I Wanna Rock" were fresh, innovative, and hilarious takes on the cartoon violence of classic *Looney Tunes*, the video for "Leader of the Pack" just made the band seem kind goofy. And the zombie-splatter flick–meets–*Rock'n'Roll High School* concept of "Be Chrool" (complete with a super long intro scene sans music featuring the high-octane ramblings of then-hot comic commodity Bobcat Goldthwait) was simply too gross for MTV back in the day. I will say, it has actually aged quite well and, if anything, shows the magic of two of the best frontmen and performers in the world working off each other.

Come Out and Play was still a gold-selling disc in the U.S., with many strong songwriting moments. And I loved that pop-up album cover . . . still do. In retrospect, what I hear is a band that is trying too hard to show you that they'd made it. Understandable, considering the years of hard slog that Twisted Sister had put in. Just like with Quiet Riot, my love didn't die, it just kinda faded away for a while . . . shinier things had caught my ears and my eyes. I will say, though, having recently seen some footage from the epic yet ill-fated Come Out and Play Tour, that Dee's ultimate vision for the concept was never fully expressed to the public. On a stage that mimicked the violent New York City psycho-scape of the *Warriors* flick, all trash can, burned out buildings, and neon illuminated manholes, the fury of Twisted Sister live could have sold the concept and maybe even have seen the band rise to greater heights . . . if only we kids had known that such a spectacle existed. Due to a lack of ticket sales, the tour was ultimately scaled down and cut short . . . Twisted Sister had been the leader of the pack, but now they were gone.

This idea of artists with highly developed concepts of stage performance not quite fitting in with the current state of affairs is maybe most evident in the live performances of Kiss at the time. It must have been incredibly frustrating and confusing for the undisputed masters of hard rock showmanship and spectacle to find a way to simplify and restructure the look that had influenced the artists who were now their contemporaries, while at the same time trying to match a new type of flamboyance that was rooted in androgyny, glamor, and fashion as opposed to superhero fantasy or supernatural shock and awe. When Kiss lost the makeup (which, admittedly, by 1983 had become a shtick akin to Saturday morning cartoons), there was a paradigm shift in the band's fundamental roles. Of course, this also can be attributed to the fact that when original members Peter Criss and Ace Frehley left the band, the concept of four equally distinctive and powerful partners was obliterated, but it actually had more to do with the new realities of market demand.

Paul Stanley, with his powerful tenor voice, androgynous good looks, athletic and fleet-footed stage presence, and penchant for penning tunes that aligned with the more melodic side of rock'n'roll made him a natural candidate for the role of frontman. Gene Simmons's more imposing physical stature and head of wiry black hair provided challenges in terms of imaging, and his 1985 look often ended up resembling an episode of *Dynasty* gone horribly wrong . . . all shoulder pads and rouge abuse, Phyllis Diller as a linebacker . . . sequins on steroids. But to his great credit, Simmons provided a connection to Kiss's illustrious past by using his greatest natural asset, the longest tongue in rock'n'roll, as a reminder that Kiss had been around long before the current crop of rockers. In many ways, Gene may have been the one responsible for keeping diehard fans coming back and buying tickets to at least half fill the arenas that the band once filled with ease. While he may have seemed a bit lost in the sartorial sense in the mid-'80s, his lascivious flicking of that giant tongue at any given opportunity at concerts or promotional events was a defiant display of what Kiss once was, just as much as his cocksure, splayed-legged, chin-out posture was a symbol of a man who wasn't quite ready to give up his claim to being the ultimate iconic representation of the Kiss brand.

However, let's not forget, while Kiss may have been struggling, they had come back with the makeup off to deliver two platinum albums in 1983's *Lick It Up*, and 1984's *Animalize*. With Stanley taking more control of the production and direction, and the band having the wherewithal to find great writers to collaborate with, Kiss delivered strong songs in the mid-'80s that bear hallmarks of melodic and musical sophistication, even if lyrically they tend to navigate words mired in bawdy misogyny. "Lick It Up," "All Hell's Breakin' Loose," "Heaven's on Fire," and "Thrills in the Night" were genuine hits that all featured Stanley on lead vocals. The spontaneous wail that kicks off "Heaven's on Fire" is a perfect summation of how Stanley approached the '80s, singing higher and stronger than he ever had previously, the culmination of this approach being 1985's *Asylum* album. Drummer Eric Carr had already proven himself the perfect candidate for Kiss's approach to the '80s, a player with a flair for massive drum kits and overt gestures of technical proficiency, all the while playing appropriately for the song. And with Bruce Kulick on guitar, Kiss had a player who embodied the best traits of previous guitarists Ace Frehley, Vinnie Vincent, and Mark St. John. Kulick was a tasteful, melodically developed player rooted in the tradition of '60s British rock who had earned his sea legs as a touring guitarist for Meat Loaf during his massively successful Bat Out of Hell tour in the '70s. Kulick was able to harness the firepower that was expected of players in the '80s and executed by Vincent and St. John in their studio performances on *Lick It Up* and *Animalize* respectively, and blend it with Frehley's more traditional approach to craft exciting and powerful solos that were among the finest examples of a style of playing called "in and out in eight."

The best "in and out in eight" players take an allotted space of eight measures and are able to elevate a song by delivering solos that are melodic and memorable, while also providing the excitement that comes from demonstrations of technical mastery of their instrument. This can also be modified to "in and out in four" for slower tempos (for example, Steve Lukather of Toto's melodic master class on "Rosanna"), or "in and out and in sixteen" for bands that featured a particularly prodigious guitar hero (such as Steve Lynch's two-handed tapping clinic in Autograph's "Turn up the Radio," or Matthias Jabs's fleet-fingered fire in "Rock You Like a Hurricane" putting the "sing" in the "sting"). These players often didn't garner the big features in guitar magazines of the day, but they fulfilled a very important role nonetheless, and, in retrospect, their contributions to '80s guitar vocabulary were most memorable to the general music-loving population. Kulick's brilliant solos on the *Asylum* hits "Tears Are Falling," "Who Wants to Be Lonely," and "Uh! All Night" are textbook examples of the style, breaking up moments of flash and burn with soulful string bends and simpler patterns that repeat rhythmically, allowing the listener to anticipate and appreciate in a more meaningful way. Deeper *Asylum* cuts like "King of the Mountain" showed Kulick to be a master of post–Van Halen shred guitar as well, and also demonstrated his tonal consistency, conviction, and fluidity of phrasing.

The mid-'80s had quite a few masters of this approach. Matthias Jabs from Scorpions, with his solo breaks on tracks like "No One Like You" and "Rock You Like a Hurricane," is a prime hard rock example. Steve Lukather was doing it on a daily basis as a first-call L.A. studio musician on hits for Don Henley, the Tubes, Lionel Richie, and hundreds more, as well as with Toto. Keith Scott, backing Bryan Adams, was right there, too, with classic lead breaks in songs like "Somebody" (eight bars), "Heaven" (four bars), or "It's Only Love," where the playing is so melodically perfect that he's called on to work his magic in groups of four, eight, and twelve bars as he weaves in between the lusty and raspy vocal master class taking place between Adams and duet partner Tina Turner. Neil Giraldo was bringing it with Pat Benatar, Stuart Adamson was making it sound like bagpipes with Big Country, Englishman Andy Barnett was lighting up Canadian superstar Corey Hart's biggest hits with fiery leads that somehow managed to feel highly composed and yet completely off the cuff as well. One of my proudest professional moments came in 2017 when I had a chance to perform at Corey Hart's induction into Canada's Walk of Fame with Nelly Furtado. Nelly had crafted a very cool arrangement of "Sunglasses at Night," and I was thrilled when she wanted me to perform the iconic guitar parts, including Andy's jaw-dropping solo, verbatim, for her modernized take. A career highlight was getting to meet Corey, a man as humble and genuine as anyone you'd want to know. He told me that when I played the solo, it felt like he was back onstage in 1985. I couldn't have asked for a better compliment.

Okay, I know, this is supposed to be about hard rock . . . but to be fair, Barnett did end up going on to play with U.K. melodic hard rockers FM. And really, in the mid-'80s, mainstream pop rock and commercial hard rock were often not that disparate. Many hard rockers were taking their cues from the sounds those mainstream rockers were achieving on their recordings, and maybe they didn't see themselves as too far removed in the first place. Which is probably why a guy like session ace Tim Pierce could come into a session with a young up-and-comer like Jon Bon Jovi and lay down an iconic solo like the one he played on "Runaway." Pierce was already playing on albums by pop rockers Rick Springfield and John Waite, so it made sense that he would be a great fit to play on Bon Jovi's first big hit, a pop-inflected hard rocker that owed a debt to artists like Aldo Nova and Billy Squier, who had managed to crack the radio *and* MTV with catchy hard rock that was easy on the ears but still got the heart pumping. (It was only after "Runaway" started catching fire on regional radio that Jon found his ultimate six-string foil in Richie Sambora, himself a master of the "in and out in eight" formula.)

I recently watched a tutorial video on Pierce's YouTube channel where the incredibly successful session guitarist (he played with everyone from Michael Jackson to Madonna and Phil Collins) ruminates on what it would have been like if he had stayed with Bon Jovi. It speaks to serendipity on one hand, but also to the factors that ultimately separated the commercial hard rock bands from mainstream solo artists. I can't actually recall a solo male artist in the '80s who was marketed as hard rock or metal (Alice Cooper aside, and even he took his name from the band he was in!). Well, there was an AOR album from famed crooner Michael Bolton (1985's *Everybody's Crazy*) that came perilously close to hard rock thanks to the crunching guitars of Kiss's Bruce Kulick and fantastic production from Neil Kernon (the producer of wonderful-sounding albums by Dokken, Autograph, Queensrÿche, and many others). Michael wouldn't find the massive fame he would ultimately enjoy by hammering away in the rock quarry, ultimately making a case that male oriented hard rock only seemed to be accepted as a group commodity. And while Jon (Bongiovi by birth, Bon Jovi by marketing) could have very likely made his mark as a solo artist in the vein of Squier, Springfield, or Adams, it was clearly decided that a group approach (even if it was ultimately a benevolent dictatorship) was the best chance for success. Thus, we have Bon Jovi the *band* built around the man, coming together to finish their 1984 self-titled debut, a gold-selling album thanks to the crossover appeal of "Runaway." The fully solidified and road-tested lineup of Bon Jovi, Richie Sambora, Tico Torres (drums), Alec John Such (bass), and David Bryan (keyboard), shot for platinum success on 1985's *7800° Fahrenheit* with a fully American AOR sound that combined Def Leppard–esque pop metal ("In & Out of Love," "Tokyo Road") and mainstream rock balladry ("Silent Night," "Only Lonely") with a look and stage presence that bore a resemblance to the heavier rock acts like Scorpions and Ratt that they were supporting on tour. And while the album managed to match the sales of the debut, it wasn't the blockbuster success that had been expected of a band with this level of photogenic appeal, seasoned stagecraft, and songwriting and performance chops.

There would likely only be one more shot (to the heart) to match the corporate expectations that weighed heavy on the shoulders of New Jersey's second favorite son. And with 1986's *Slippery When Wet* breakthrough, Bon Jovi connected with his Jersey roots, and ultimately suburban youth everywhere, arguably in a more genuine way than Bruce ever had.

Bon Jovi is the true representation of Jersey's seaside suburban youth, speaking directly to kids who were more likely born to run to the shopping mall or into the arms of a solid union job than they were yearning to seek freedom beyond the confines of the New Jersey Turnpike. This time, Jon and his writing foil–consigliore Sambora worked with the assistance of master song doctor Desmond Child, the man who had helped Kiss navigate choppy '80s waters sans makeup and would go on to do the same with old-guard members like Aerosmith and Alice Cooper.

Songs like "Livin' on a Prayer" and "You Give Love a Bad Name" found the balance of hard rock and metal's guitars, drums, and visuals and mainstream pop's melodic vocals and keyboards that would come to be the standard bearer for hard rock's second-wave assault on the charts, a commercial reign that would extend even into the early part of the next decade. The whole album is a triumph of expert musicianship and impeccable songcraft coming together with a look and feel that was glitzy enough to separate the band from their audience for rock star effect, but denim and leather enough not to alienate them. This combination spoke to the hearts and wallets of the kids.

America, at least in the thoughts and emotions of many of its countrymen, was doing well and going strong, and this new pop metal confection coming out of Jersey was the soundtrack to an American dream that, even if it was not your reality, was worth fighting for. More importantly, the stories and characters in these songs gave relevance and voice to experiences that may have been less colorful and dramatic than a Springsteen epic but resonated in a more achievable and empowering way. Your struggle wasn't a tragedy . . . you live for the fight when it's all that you got, and losing your virginity in the back seat of a car could be a badge of honor.

Slippery When Wet feels so American in its sound, attitude, and lyrical content, yet it was created in and informed by the work that was coming out of a studio in a sleepy part of Vancouver, Canada.

Little Mountain Sound was to become a mecca for bands looking to make powerful artistic and commercial statements, largely because of talented producers and engineers like Bruce Fairbairn, Bob Rock, Mike Fraser, Roger Monk, Rob Porter, and Chris Taylor.

Fairbairn developed a unique approach by melding a horn player's sense of arrangement architecture with metal's crunching guitars and booming drums (often a result of pumping a signal of the drum tracks into a PA that was then placed in the studio's loading dock, the magical ambience captured by microphones and blended into the songs) with Canadian rock bands like Prism, Loverboy, and Honeymoon Suite, and forward-thinking, synth-heavy new wave artists like Strange Advance.

Bruce and his engineers went on to create influential records that put as much emphasis on melody and texture as they did on crunch and power.

The production values heard on albums by Switzerland's Krokus (*The Blitz* was a gold record in the U.S.) and Black 'n Blue may not have been massive commercial blockbusters, but they were indicative of the higher quality of product coming out of Little Mountain (as well as local studios like Mushroom and Ocean Way), and these shinier sonics caught the ears of Bon Jovi, a band already well aware of Fairbairn's ear for marrying hard rock energy with pop melodies and radio-friendly sonics due to his work with Loverboy.

There was magic happening in that city nestled in the mountains, and Bon Jovi had the perfect combination of songs and players to take full advantage of the skill sets and sounds there. I have a theory that *Slippery When Wet* is the perfect mix of two albums: Black 'n Blue's punchy and anthemic *Without Love* and Canadian band Honeymoon Suite's equally anthemic but more pop-tempered *The Big Prize*. After Loverboy's success, there was much experimentation to find the right balance between hard rock's metallic guitar tones and radio-friendly melodies, harmony, and keyboards. Bon Jovi almost hit it with *7800° Fahrenheit*, but with *Slippery* the balance was perfect, and as a result it would go on to sell 12 million copies in the U.S. alone, ultimately becoming a worldwide smash.

Mike Fraser: The common thread with all of that would be Bruce Fairbairn. And Bob Rock would have engineered all that, but Bruce is manning the helm . . . always a big song guy. He wanted the songs there, and if the songs weren't there, he'd send them off down to L.A. to write with Diane Warren and . . . [Jim] Vallance and [Bryan] Adams. He always made sure the songs were there, and he'd want it to rock, too, and then Bob wanted it to rock, and so they would make these pop songs rock.

I first heard *Slippery When Wet* in September of 1986, in the back sanctuary of the Pro-Cathedral of the Assumption Catholic church in North Bay. As I solemnly performed my duties as a senior altar server (most of my friends had long since bailed on the position) and prepared the water and the wine that would ultimately become the flesh and blood of Jesus Christ by way of the miracle of transubstantiation, I was about to experience my own transformation (the sanctity of which is debatable, but it felt like salvation to me). As I poured the wine and water into their delicate glass vessels, "You Give Love a Bad Name" came on over the crackling airwaves of AM 600 CFCH, North Bay's multipurpose radio station that served up news, sports, and a community-friendly blend of all things pop and classic rock. Shot through the heart is an apt way to describe how I felt when those a capella gang vocals announced their rousing chorus, like an excerpt from Handel's *Messiah* (if Handel had just come back from the Sunday afternoon "shower show" at a Vancouver strip club). "You Give Love a Bad Name" is a sequentially perfect slice of pop metal, each successive element better than the one before, elevating and priming your adrenal glands for the payoff of that glorious chorus. Thematic electric guitar lines doubled with an octave pedal take simple pentatonic riffs and turn them into siren calls . . . or whatever the macho New Jersey male version of that is. Tico Torres's deep, behind-the-beat drum grooves are solid and powerful, the deep crack of his snare driving the backbeat behind a unison guitar and bass riff that marches in lockstep to the Hitman's incessant groove. It's common knowledge now that bassist Hugh McDonald actually played on most of Bon Jovi's recordings, and ultimately became a member of the band after Alec John Such's departure in 1994. In my mind, it doesn't matter in the slightest. Alec is the one I see when I hear those lines; he handled the music with rock star aplomb and dynamite backing vocals. Not everyone is a studio ace.

Keyboards have long been a target of misguided vitriol for those crying "sell-out," but here they provide dark mood and a hint of menace, with long sustained notes floating airily and eerily over the top of the main riffage, and state-of-the-art (for '86) sound effects punctuating transitions to build energy. But David Bryan was not some mere sound effect slinger to be cast off in the shadows behind the curtains offstage. His raging, Jon Lord–inspired organ riffage actually kicks off the whole damn album. The intro to "Let It Rock" is all toccata and no fugue. As a faithful Catholic, I was no stranger to the power of a massive pipe organ, and to hear all of that majesty pumped through what sounded like a wall of Marshall guitar amps made listening to *Slippery When Wet* feel like a sacred event.

Slippery's greatest influence on me lies in the iconic guitar moments. Going back to the "in and out in eight" theory, Sambora's lead on "You Give Love a Bad Name" laid out for me an approach and techniques I could incorporate to fulfill the great change I was undertaking. I was going to move from music fan to musician, and in eight bars of tasteful tapping, wicked whammy, crisply picked pentatonic lines and unison string bends, I was shown the way. I didn't just need to listen to this music, I needed to *make* it. Something in Richie's approach made me feel that I could, the digestible musical bites of blues phrasing and flash were appetizing and easier to sink my teeth into than, say, an Yngwie Malmsteen solo. Bon Jovi was my hair metal Beatles, or Ramones, in that in them I saw a clear path forward. It involved lights and ramps, long hair and leather, denim and distortion. Sambora delivered this accessibility in every song, solos that were short, sweet (or nasty), and integral to the compositions. Not unlike the work of Elliot Easton from the Cars, they were mini compositions in their own right. Yes, in Richie, I saw a role I could fulfill in a rock'n'roll band, so I credit him for giving me the tools to serve as a foil to many amazing lead singers over the course of my career.

> **Scotti Hill:** Touring with Bon Jovi . . . Now, you're talking about some arena shows we did before Sebastian was even in the band. There was, I think, two of them? Maybe one or there was supposed to be two . . . Something happened, one of them was canceled or something. Anyway, we went out and did . . . a show on the Slippery When Wet Tour, it was Matt [Fallon] in the band. It was our first arena show, and you know, we were all working jobs, and then one night we go play this arena with Bon Jovi, and holy shit. Wow, man. And then back to work on Monday. . . .
>
> [Dave "the Snake" Sabo] grew up with Jon. They're still good friends, they speak almost every day. So we were kind of used to seeing Jon come around, and Richie would come around. Richie had Snake and I go over to the house one night for a guitar, sit-down jam, get fucked up, eat lobster, jam, you know? And it was pretty awesome, and that was the

night that I realized how great he is. I knew he was a great singer and I knew he was a good guitar player, but I didn't realize . . . He's in another league, man. And guys like Richie and Tico really cut their teeth for a long time in the clubs and went out, did it every night in cover bands or whatever.

So when we went on the New Jersey tour, opening act, that was nine months of education — back to school again. I can remember Richie saying, "See those kids out front? Don't play for them. Play for those kids in the back, upstairs. That way, your energy will fill the room." Like, wow, this is valuable information.

Sambora was a key player in bringing forgotten guitar affectations and playing devices from the '70s into the mid-'80s in an updated way. A seasoned session man with roots in Page, Beck, Clapton, Peter Frampton, and Johnny Winter, Sambora took a dusty old device like the talk box (an effect that routes an electric guitar signal through the player's mouth via a tube, the vowel manipulations, reflection, and reverberation of which is then captured by a microphone and sent back to the soundboard) and turned it into an incredibly fresh new sound, focused and pulsing, its "woah woahs" echoing the same hopeful incantations of the chorus. Word to the wise regarding talk box use . . . make sure your dental work is solid. The first time I used one was in the studio with Gilby Clarke. I was not prepared for the power of all those rock'n'roll soundwaves rocketing into my oral cavity, and the first power chord I hit felt like someone kicking me *inside* my mouth! It's a testament to the skill of my childhood dentists that the fillings in my cavity-riddled gob (too much Fun Dip, SweeTarts, and Nerds, clearly) stayed intact!

Sambora should receive royalties for all the Ovation guitars he must have sold for them. His acoustic intro to "Wanted Dead or Alive," alternating in intervals of a sixth down the D-minor scale, created a must-learn, "Stairway to Heaven" moment for '80s guitar players. Sure, plastic roundback guitars may not make for the warmest acoustic guitar sound, but they do a great job of busting up potential feedback problems when playing delicate figures on massive arena stages. It worked for Nancy Wilson of Heart in the '70s, and if the video for "Wanted Dead or Alive" is any indication, it worked for Sambora in the '80s.

I needed to make these sounds. Up until that point, I had been enjoying my daydreams of rock stardom, satisfied to play the solo to "We're Not Gonna Take It" on one string with my beat-up $85 pawnshop guitar but never actually identifying as a musician per se. This new impetus to replicate Richie's licks felt much more realized, and it created within me a hunger that I was compelled to feed. I needed a guitar with a Floyd Rose tremolo, with string action low enough to apply the two-handed tapping techniques and fast scalar playing I was hearing on *Slippery* and the other albums coming out in its wake . . . one with screaming humbucking pickups, accompanied by an amplifier that was powerful enough to create the sustain and growl that I needed as much as food and water . . . in that transubstantial spiritual, musical way, of course.

Transformational stuff, for sure. And yet, I'd had an even greater musical epiphany just a few months earlier, in 1986. That would come courtesy of an unthinkable breakup . . . the parting of the ways between Van Halen and their lead singer David Lee Roth.

Yes, Van Halen were definitely on my radar in the mid-'80s . . . *1984* was everywhere, and like countless other budding rock fans I had a copy of the album on cassette and played it in rotation with my Mötley and Ratt. But unlike the lustful anticipation that fueled my acquisition of *Shout at the Devil* or *Out of the Cellar*, *1984* was picked up as more of an afterthought, a post-lunch purchase at the Orillia Mall during a pitstop en route to an altar server trip to Marineland in Niagara Falls. The Lord works in mysterious ways.

I loved the album, I loved the songs . . . even the quirky ones like "Top Jimmy" and "Drop Dead Legs." I'm not sure I bothered with side B very much once I'd gotten past "Hot for Teacher." Later in life I would obsess over every last detail of that album, but at that point it was more appealing to rewind side A (not all the way to the beginning, the ominous synth swells and bleeps and bloops of the instrumental title track kinda freaked me out) and listen to the hits. The people I saw wearing Van Halen shirts were often older than I was, and while the band was currently on top in the mid-'80s, there was something about them that seemed like they were from another generation. I needed something that was mine, all mine.

At some point in early spring of 1986, as my world was opening up to more freedoms (a new-to-me 50CC Honda dirt bike, a promise of a summer filled with access to my dad's Evinrude motor–powered Springbok aluminium boat, and unaccompanied adventures at midways and bonfires), I became aware that Dave was out of VH, and a new singer was onboard (the split had occurred sometime in 1985, marred in all the usual uncertainty that comes from band breakups). I was familiar with Sammy from his ubiquitous hit "I Can't Drive 55," and had borrowed the *VOA* album from a hockey teammate. It's a good record, but for the most part, I filed it under "meh."

But when "Why Can't This Be Love" hit the airwaves, I was floored. The sound of Sammy Hagar's voice against Eddie's pulsing, swirling musical concoction of a riff (was that a guitar? a keyboard? a helicopter at the beginning?) was magic. I was transfixed, even by the weird, loping, electronic drum sounds coming from Alex. And those glorious vocal harmonies, especially from Michael Anthony, sealed the deal. I kept my ears and eyes open to any mention on radio or the musical specialty channels on TV for a release date for the forthcoming *5150* opus from the "new" Van Halen. Finances being what they were, and my 13-year-old ass being impatient to own a piece of the music, I would usually test the waters through the purchase of a vinyl single. Repeated spins of "Why Can't This Be Love" convinced me I needed the full album.

After one pass through my cassette copy of *5150*, I had a new favorite band. And out of this new realization, came a very exciting opportunity. The split between Roth and Van Halen had been a contentious he said–they said affair, the Van Halen camp accusing Roth of abandoning the band to focus on a movie career, Roth claiming the band had reneged on an agreement to take a year off. Both camps had gone on the offense in the press, taking swipes at the other with each side promising to come out as the victors in a battle for supremacy. There had been no love lost in previous years between Hagar and Roth, despite the fact that at one point Hagar's band Montrose had been a big influence on Van Halen.

Van Halen drew first blood by being first to market with their new lineup, and this undoubtedly played a big part in my unwavering support of the band the press had now christened Van Hagar. If it came from the mouths of Sammy, Eddie, Alex, or Mike, it was gospel truth. I didn't need to hear about rock'n'roll from some *movie star*. This new Van Halen was all about the *music*, man, and I lapped it up. I also was fortified in my stance because with each thorough listen through the album, I was finding new musical evidence that backed up my belief that Eddie Van Halen was a genius. The thick and melodious strains of his keyboards on "Dreams" and "Love Walks In," his innovative experimentation with a newly developed whammy bar system on rockers like "Get Up" and "Summer Nights," and the Who–inspired wild abandon and slip-and-slide lead guitar licks and tricks of the title track brought me so much joy, a true elevation of the spirit and soul. This was the first time that music transcended my previous experience with hard rock as a soundtrack to rebellion, a way to belong in a peer group, or as forbidden visceral excitement stemming from sexually charged lyrics or the sheer blunt force trauma of loud guitars and drums.

5150 will always represent the freedom of listening without expectation. Where bands like Twisted Sister and Bon Jovi ultimately had more to do with me taking practical steps toward my ambitions to be a professional musician, I have never listened to Van Halen with an aspiration to *be* Van Halen. I never slavishly copied Eddie's playing, even though his influence is set deep in my bones. I rarely played Van Halen songs with the various cover bands I was in. Van Halen was and is a band that I place above and beyond all others, and Eddie Van Halen in particular is a player that is more spiritual sanctuary for me than someone I ever thought I could emulate. And that goes for Sammy, Alex, and Mike too. They may have been singing about things we'd all heard a million times before, hot summer nights, love walkin' in, the stuff that dreams are made of . . . but something about those people, the sound and playing on that album, and the time and place in my life where I discovered it all, that will always place *5150* on higher ground.

My faith and devotion were fully committed on August 18, 1986, at the Exhibition Stadium in Toronto, Ontario. My sister and brother-in-law lived in a suburb of Toronto, and would kindly take my younger sister and me to stay with them and experience the marvels and wonders of the big city. That summer, I was offered a choice between two amazing opportunities. A salmon-fishing tournament on Lake Ontario . . . or the Van Halen concert. It is no coincidence that the summer of '86 was probably the last time I dropped a fishing line in water.

It was a long season of the sweetest anticipation as I pored over issues of guitar magazines with hyped up reports of Van Halen's 5150 Tour . . . early glimpses of the massive steel stage and light riggings heightened my exhilaration, as did pictures of the band sporting the brightest of '80s colors: billowy pink pants, wild animal–print bandanas, neon yellow *Miami Vice*–approved jackets, Hagar's freshly bobbed mop of blond curls. Where other acts of the time looked like they were wearing costumes, Van Halen just looked like they were wearing *fun*, throwing on whatever happened to be thrown at them. Naturally, my sights were also fixed on the guitars. And not just Eddie's iconic striped Kramer "5150" guitars, or his new Steinberger headless axe, outfitted with the TransTrem vibrato bar system used on "Summer Nights" and "Get Up." There was Michael Anthony's Jack Daniel's bass, and Sammy's own "55"-stickered Kramer and Dean guitars, as well as his Jackson Randy Rhoads Flying V, all slathered with fire engine–red paint jobs befitting the "Red Rocker." It was the look and feel of that coming-of-age summer on Lake Temiskaming, free, fun, and endlessly optimistic.

From the very back of the massive stadium, I took in not only Van Halen, but opening acts Loverboy and Bachman–Turner Overdrive. (I still remember my brother-in-law's nods of recognition and approval as BTO delivered a solid set of classic hits that, at the time, were unrecognizable to me.) Loverboy served up an excellent hour of successive hits as the summer sun baked the audience (judging by the aroma of the smoke swirling around us, many were already pretty baked), empty Pizza Pizza boxes, frisbees and beach balls being tossed around in euphoric celebration. And yet, all I can remember wondering was "Where is Eddie? Is he in the crowd somewhere?"

Finally, as the sun began to set, a barrage of Eddie's trademark whammy bar–manipulated elephant sounds and finger-tapped guitar licks scooped and swooped around the pounding drum fills of his brother Alex, Michael Anthony's bass rumbling and tumbling as spotlights swirled around the darkened stage, centered by the newly designed Van Halen logo and flanked by two massive scrims featuring the *5150* album cover. With the massive lighting rig flashing on and off like a signal for the start of the Rapture, and a booming Sammy Hagar call of "Hello, *Toronto*!!" the game was afoot. To be honest, the first two songs were a completely unrecognizable blur

... I was not yet familiar with Van Halen's storied cover of the Kinks' "You Really Got Me," nor was I aware of Sammy Hagar's "There's Only One Way to Rock" ... but none of that mattered. In the cacophonous fray and spray of notes coming off the stage, and through the lens of my brother-in-law's binoculars, I was catching glimpses of familiarity, those faces and sounds that had been changing me elementally throughout a glorious summer of discovery. And when the band finally hit the first note of familiarity with the plucky intro to "Summer Nights," I achieved full spiritual elevation. This went far beyond musicianship, songcraft, or stage presence ... I was witnessing and experiencing emotional virtuosity. To see Eddie Van Halen performing his majestic unaccompanied guitar solo under that full moon in Toronto, hearing for the first time the fragments I would later come to know as "Eruption," "Cathedral," "Spanish Fly," and "Mean Street," was one of the greatest gifts my brother-in-law could have given to me. As Sammy climbed the massive rigging, defying death as he screamed through his headset microphone, I was sure at times it was me alone he was pointing at, inviting me to rock, *demanding* that I rock. We were together, me and Eddie, Alex, Mike and Sammy and Jim, sharing this incredible moment. Been there, done that, got the T-shirt and the tour programme. To my brother-in-law's eternal credit, we stayed until the very last power chord had subsided, the last bows were taken, even as it meant fighting a drunk and stoned crowd on the long GO train ride back to the suburbs. I owe you one, Jimmy Z.

The Van Halen split also gave us David Lee Roth's glorious *Eat 'Em and Smile* album. Dave came out ready to fight with a lineup that included not one, but *two* lords of the strings in former Zappa and Alcatrazz alum Steve Vai on guitar and bass monster Billy Sheehan of Talas. Along with drummer Gregg Bissonette, the new DLR band upped the ante on showmanship, virtuosity, and fun. Thanks to a "live off the floor" production treatment from longtime VH producer Ted Templeman, DLR managed to fill the void that Van Hagar had left when they went skipping hand in hand down more melodic, keyboard-based laneways. The videos got crazier, the pants got tighter, guitars and martial arts kicks were flying all over a stage packed with enough speakers and lights to deafen and blind those fans yearning for Van Halen's glory days. Tracks like "Yankee Rose," "Goin'

Crazy," and "Shyboy" were a far cry from the melodic sophistication of Van Halen's "Dreams" or "Love Walks In," and for Dave fans, that was just fine. As a budding guitar player, it was great fun to see the kind of virtuosity that Vai and Sheehan so brazenly flaunted in a commercial rock context.

Yet, while their fleet-fingered unison runs may have been miles beyond what Eddie was doing in the current VH incarnation, they just didn't capture my heart in the same way . . . as brilliant as it all was, the framework of the songs didn't bring me back for as many repeated listens. Still, the beauty of music is that not every band can scratch every itch, and there are times to this day when I just need to throw on *Eat 'Em and Smile* to hear the energy and vaudevillian lunacy that only Roth and that band could create in one short, sweet, exhausting listen. It's a reminder of how exciting throwing down the musical gauntlet can be, something that would be heard in later recordings by Aerosmith, Alice Cooper, Whitesnake, and Mötley Crüe in landmark "comeback" albums.

As I was experiencing these transformations of self and spirit in 1986, hard rock's popularity was growing all around me. New music from bands like Cinderella and Poison was catching fire, and these two bands certainly shared a sartorial connection based on the outlandish clothing and makeup that was plastered on their *Night Songs* and *Look What the Cat Dragged In* albums respectively. And while there were some similarities in look and marketing approach (both bands would go on to sell millions of records to largely the same fan base), the differences in their musical approaches would end up carving out two distinct paths that yet another wave of musicians could choose to follow as hard rock entered its golden years in the late '80s.

The success of these newer acts also seemed to hold sway of influence over established veterans like Iron Maiden and Judas Priest as guitar synthesizers, keyboards, and electronic percussion made their way onto albums that now were exploring truncated arrangements and songwriting approaches. Albums like *Somewhere in Time* and *Turbo* seemed to be taking aim at the youth market of America who were buying newer pop metal confections in droves, but there was also a backlash from diehards who saw these explorations as concessions . . . a selling out to corporate interests that betrayed the pure metal integrity upon which these acts had built their loyal fan base.

I have to get out of this chapter, but I'm not done with 1986. There has to be a setup for the ubiquitous glory days of hair metal that we will explore in the next chapter. That means a deeper look at debut albums from new bands like Poison, Cinderella, and Tesla who were looking back on hair metal's past influences, and new albums from established bands like Whitesnake and Def Leppard who were moving forward into a world of technological and sonic innovation.

And then, on to the last three years of the '80s . . . the view from the top of the rock'n'roll mountain.

CHAPTER 8
1987 TO 1988

LOOKING LIKE HOT CHICKS . . . SELLING LIKE HOT CAKES

T rying to include every band I love is like trying to fit all of the sand on a beach into a tiny pail. It feels like so much of it's sifting through my fingers as I watch the pail fill up. Every grain of sand plays a part in the makeup of the beach, and every piece of music I ever purchased is attached to some kind of memory and bears some influence. I guess if you're going to build a sandcastle, you inevitably leave a lot of sand behind. Mind you, I'm still going to try to build a sandcastle worthy of a Ronnie James Dio stage set.

With that metaphor exhausted, let's enter the golden age of popular metal, where the charts were veritably littered and glittered with hard rock bands of every ilk. From raw and sleazy to epic and polished, these years saw wonderful variations on the moves and grooves laid out in previous years by Leppard, Jovi, Crüe, the commercially fading but very important Quiet Riot, and the mighty Van Halen, who in 1988 continued on with their successful singer swap.

First, let's rewind the cassette back to '86 to look at three bands and debut albums that I feel really set the tone for much of what was to come to be loved and loathed about pop metal in this period.

Poison's *Look What the Cat Dragged In* is as authentic a rock'n'roll record as anything that has come before or after. Whether "authentic" means "great" is a matter of subjectivity, of course, but what we get on this shoe-string budget of a record is the sound of a hardworking band of musicians who transcend arguably modest technical abilities through hard work, spirit, desperation to succeed, and great songs.

Singer Bret Michaels, drummer Rikki Rockett, bassist Bobby Dall, and guitarist Matt Smith moved to Hollywood from small-town Mechanicsburg, Pennsylvania, to take advantage of the Sunset Strip scene that had been set aflame by Mötley Crüe, Ratt, Quiet Riot, and W.A.S.P., bringing with them dreams inspired by great '70s rock like Starz, Kiss, Cheap Trick, the New York Dolls, and a Southern rock–inflected vocal approach influenced by bands like Lynyrd Skynyrd and Molly Hatchet. Initially starting their Hollywood ride under the name Paris, the band quickly switched to Poison after discovering that former Fleetwood Mac axeman Bob Welch had a project under the same name. They began building a reputation as a dynamic live act, winning over audiences garnered through the hard graft of constant flyering and self-promotion in the clubs. Like Kiss and Mötley Crüe before them, Poison engaged eager fans (often smitten young women) as foot soldiers who would go out and spread the word and, at times, support them with meals, shelter, and clothing in exchange for attention of varying degrees. This type of interaction would become the stuff of legend and cliché, this tale of wannabe rock stars living off the kindness of girls desperate to be a part of "the scene." Whether this is a case of exploitation or mutually beneficial social transaction is debatable, but it clearly worked to keep a number of struggling musicians alive, pampered, and promoted in this decadently aspirational pursuit of success.

When guitarist Smith decided to make the mature choice of heading back home to Pennsylvania upon discovery that he was going to become a father, a number of players lined up to audition for the up-and-coming Poison, now packing the clubs with their "Kiss on a budget" party rock. One of these players was a young Saul Hudson, a.k.a. Slash, who would have secured the gig had it not been for the striking presence of a loud-mouthed New Yorker born Bruce Johannsen but soon to become better known as one C.C. DeVille.

For all of the slings and arrows that befall C.C.'s abilities as a player (aspersions cast range from comments about his tone to his intonation to his tendency to overplay), I have always rated him very highly. When C.C. joined, he brought a power pop expert's sense of songcraft to the band, a legitimate vibrant punk rock energy, and a post–Van Halen flair that may not have captured all of the dynamic touch and musicality of Edward, but most definitely conjured something so many other gifted technicians in the scene missed: a sense of fun and joy. You can hear it in his melodic, enthusiastic, and extremely well-crafted solos in "Cry Tough," "I Won't Forget You," and, most famously, "Talk Dirty to Me."

In "Talk Dirty to Me," "Johnny B. Goode"–inspired double stops and string bends are utilized in hooky, repetitive themes that incorporate just the right amount of open string pull-offs and flash, all ending on a major pentatonic string bend lick punctuated with a double picked major arpeggio that sounds like an inverted (perverted?) take on America's national anthem. "Talk Dirty to Me" may have been have borrowed its riff-ripoff charm from Cheap Trick's "She's Tight," but the naive simplicity of Rikki Rockett's '50s rock'n'roll–cum–'70s glam inspired drum beats and C.C.'s Sex Pistols–meets–Chuck Berry approach to the rollicking rhythm guitars painted the perfect Hollywood backdrop for Bret Michaels's sonnet to behind-the-bushes teenage groping. Michaels had an ability to take Jim Steinman's model of writing about teenage lust and somehow make it sound even more innocent, fun, and dumb. The other trick to the crossover appeal was that Poison was able to make all this overt sexuality and macho posturing seem nonthreatening through ragtag self-deprecation and concrete imagery of Americana. I mean, how much trouble can you get in at the drive-in in the old man's Ford? Yup, Bret and the boys wanted action, but there were no promises they were going to be any good at it.

This sense of playfulness extends to Poison's use of imagery as well. Where bands like W.A.S.P., Mötley Crüe, and Twisted Sister slathered on the makeup with more than a hint of menace, Poison were good-looking boys who weren't afraid to present as pretty as possible.

I will always stand up for this record and Poison's equally successful multiplatinum follow-up *Open Up and Say . . . Ahh!* First of all, a trademark of any great rock'n'roll band is that you can hear distinct personalities in the playing. And on both of these albums, I still hear the innocence of a band of average musicians playing at their very best. When bassist Bobby

Dall performs a rudimentary walking bass line, I don't feel a need to chastise a lack of innovation. I just hear a player playing a simple but effective line in the spirit of the music he was influenced by. I hear a band who has rehearsed for hours to transcend limitations to get their ideas down on tape. It feels real and authentic. I'll even go as far as to say it's not a huge departure from the efforts of bands like the New York Dolls and the Sex Pistols. If "Talk Dirty to Me" had been recorded by, say, the Dead Boys (perhaps with a slight lyrical tweak), it would be considered a punk rock classic. The songs on *Look What the Cat Dragged In* are played with personality and joy and presented in an image-conscious package that is contrived and calculated in all the right ways. Sure, on album number two producer Tom Werman may have slipped in the odd supporting synthesizer and well-arranged, studio-slick backing vocal action, but the ratty personality was still pretty well intact.

Cinderella, on the other hand, incorporated a coterie of pinks and purples in the scarf-and-makeup laden look that adorns the cover of their debut album *Night Songs* — strikingly at odds with the bluesy hard rock that defines the heart of the band, a heartbeat heard loudest in the disciplined virtuosity and deep musical knowledge of lead singer, songwriter, and guitarist Tom Keifer.

Blessed with lips like Jagger, a mouth like Tyler, and a throat that gives AC/DC's Brian Johnson a run for his money in the melodic screech department, Keifer's prodigious vocal traits are equalled by his abilities as a multi-instrumentalist — a master of many a stringed-thing, the piano, and the saxophone — and a fantastic songwriter and arranger who can access the best parts of AC/DC, Aerosmith, Led Zeppelin, and the Rolling Stones while still injecting just enough heavy metal fury to make *Night Songs* sound au courant and exciting in the 1986–87 season. Backed by a talented band that featured equally gifted axe man Jeff LaBar, bassist Eric Brittingham, and drummer Fred Coury (with "secret weapon" Rick Criniti along for the ride on Hammond B3, backing vocals, and even in the videos . . . why not just make the guy a member?), Cinderella's debut was recorded by fabled producer Andy Johns, famous for his work on *Led Zeppelin IV* and countless other English classic rock albums. It was actually Johns's work on a hard rock album by Stone Fury that caught

Keifer's ears. Stone Fury featured the vocals and songwriting talents of German musician Lenny Wolf, who would go on to find success with the much-loved (and -loathed) Kingdom Come, whose member Jody Cortez is credited on *Night Songs* for his drumming contributions. It's strange how an album like Stone Fury's, which is brimming with great songs and excellent production, can be lost in time for being ahead of its time, yet can find success in the influence it has on other acts . . . cold comfort to the creators, I'm sure, but fascinating nonetheless. I wonder how fascinating Big Star, Sparks, and Mudhoney find that.

Of all the bands that are cast aside or dismissed due to image, it's always been my feeling that Cinderella has suffered the greatest injustice. Okay, sure . . . the name didn't help. Songs like title track "Night Songs" and "Nobody's Fool" are examples of stereotype-busting musical epics, dark and melodic minor-key explorations that incorporate acoustic and electric textures and dynamics that rise, fall, and rise again in organic bursts of classic rock grandeur. The drum and guitar tones acquiesce to the reverb-enhanced largesse of the time, but they never lose their natural wooden power and resonance, the spirit of Bonham, Kramer, Page, and Perry never lost in the swathe of synthesized artificiality that would take down other bands just a few short years later. Cinderella could also keep the adrenaline pumping with four on the floor stompers like "Somebody Save Me," "Shake Me," and "Push Push," up-tempo rockers with just enough of a nod to the propulsive dual guitar riffing of Judas Priest and AC/DC to allow them to develop within the hard rock marketplace, while at the same time lacing their power chords with the sophisticated voicings of the Rolling Stones, Bad Company, Free, and any number of classic '70s acts who placed value on chord tones beyond the root and the fifth. In coguitarist Jeff LaBar, Keifer had a technically adept foil who could shred in the style of the day but do so in a way that still favored dynamics and tasteful phrasing over a full-blown wank.

Where there is sometimes a trend for bands to get heavier with each successive album as a way to establish growth and integrity, Cinderella would move in the opposite direction. 1988's *Long Cold Winter* followed up *Night Song's* success with an even rootsier response, bringing acoustic guitars to the forefront on singles like "The Last Mile" and "Coming Home," and cleaner and brighter Stratocaster and Telecaster tones that blended with thicker Les Paul sounds to create a modern classic rock concoction that still fit within the popular hard rock context of the era. Songs like "Gypsy Road" and "Fallin' Apart at the Seams" feel more like classic Aerosmith than even Aerosmith themselves did at the time. Cinderella even managed to imbue their obligatory power ballad "Don't Know What You Got (Till It's Gone)" with a class and musicality that elevated it above much of the schlockier examples of the form.

As overblown as Cinderella's image was on the cover of *Night Songs*, at the time I thought they looked amazing, and even better as they tempered their scarves and spandex look with long leather coats and a simpler color palate on 1988's *Long Cold Winter* album cycle, a bit of cowskin to offset the snakeskin. Really, the animal prints and spandex look was peaking in 1987–88, soon to be replaced by more streetwise apparel that could veer between Punk-y sleaze and Pirate-y flow, scarves moving from being wrapped around a spandex-clad leg to being wrapped around the still flowing locks of lion-maned musos (in some cases, perhaps hiding a frighteningly receding hairline or growing bald spot).

The third band that brought things much closer to the street (by which I mean the suburban street that I lived on!) visually while keeping the riffs amped-up and classic was Tesla. *Mechanical Resonance* takes the British hard rock guitar riffs of UFO and early Def Leppard and combines them with vocalist Jeff Keith's Southern twang and rasp. Frank Hannon and Tommy Skeoch employed contrasting styles to great effect, Hannon taking a more crafted and composed approach that worked well with Skeoch's more angular and off-the-cuff style. Songs like "Modern Day Cowboy" and "Cumin' Atcha Live" established Tesla in the hard rock market with plenty of guitar hero moments and arena-ready heavy metal energy. This was very cleverly balanced with rootsier numbers like "Little Suzi" and "Gettin' Better" that featured beautiful moments of clean electric and acoustic guitars reminiscent of the preludes one might hear on classic Led Zeppelin, Peter Frampton, or Aerosmith records. These numbers could turn on a dime and become accessible rockers, songs that made you want to hum along as you stomped. Drummer Troy Luccketta and bassist Brian Wheat contributed to a collective feel that sits more in the pocket, like a '70s rock record does. This was key in establishing Tesla's rootsier take on

Def Leppard's approach to dynamics and would prove to work well as the band refined these elements further on later albums.

I learned a great deal about the art of arranging from Tesla, largely because I could actually approximate the tones (or at least get close to them) with the simple tools I had at the time. The parts were beautiful and expertly played, challenging but not so difficult that they couldn't be replicated with a little elbow grease. I could hear a bit of the finger noise during the naked intros to "Gettin' Better" and "Little Suzi," and these moments of intimacy and imperfection would make me feel that the pursuit of learning this music was inclusive and achievable, much like the image of the band themselves. It was quite refreshing to see a band who, while still retaining the long hair of rock'n'rollers, looked more like their audience, in blue jeans and high tops. It was a symbol of relatability that thrash bands like Metallica, Megadeth, and Anthrax had already tapped into, and it worked well with Tesla's heartfelt, down-to-earth rock'n'roll sound. I still was enamored with the glitz, glamor, and pageantry of bands like Mötley Crüe and Ratt, but it was nice to see people making music I loved that looked like they shopped at the same mall I did.

To give credit where it's due, Mötley Crüe were continuing to rebel against the spawn of their own influence, spitting in the faces of the acts who had ripped off the highly colorful garb of their previous look. In 1987, *Theatre of Pain*'s pinks and purples were discarded for a handful of grease (well, still Aqua Net, actually) in their hair and leather motorcycle gear on their backs as the band dialed in a more streetwise, down-and-dirty rock'n'roll look and sound on the *Girls, Girls, Girls* album cycle. The album spawned genuine hard rock classics, from the T. Rex–ish groove of the title track to the greatest appropriation of the Lord's Prayer ever in the mechanically driving "Wildside." Yes, yet another Mötley Crüe song throwing me into a state of theological turmoil.

With *Girls, Girls, Girls*, Mötley had once again managed to establish a "new" look for hard rock . . . or perhaps, more cynically, had managed to stay on top of trends that were bubbling under in the scene with upstarts like Jetboy and Faster Pussycat. It was a look that would come to be appropriated and interpreted as a defining image of late '80s Hollywood. Black leather jackets and pants, pirate shirts and scarves, and hair not quite as gravity defying. A darker, bluesier sound would also accompany that change. Not that there wouldn't be proponents of more colorful looks and polished tones still peddling their wares successfully, but the seeds for a seismic shift were being planted.

1987 was big for me as a burgeoning musician. It was the year I gave my first public performance in a rock'n'roll band at my high school talent show. For all of my love and exuberance for all things shiny and virtuosic, my bandmates and I gravitated toward a set list we could actually pull off with our limited musical abilities, and a look that we could throw together with the means at our disposal (matching lumberjack coats, blue jeans, and Cougar winter boots . . . turns out we were "grunge" five years before those Seattle bands would come along and blow our world apart). The songs we chose were all three-chord wonders and, oddly, all cover versions of cover versions. We performed our take on Canadian punk legend D.O.A.'s cover of Bachman–Turner Overdrive's "Takin' Care of Business" (a bit of a nod to that revelatory show in '86 where BTO had supported Van Halen, in my mind) and a hyped up version of Jimi Hendrix's Live at the Monterey Pop Festival–interpretation of the Troggs' "Wild Thing." No guitars were lit on fire during our performance, but extended ham-fisted guitar solos with the two scales that I had memorized (in the one key I had learned them in) were inflicted in abundance upon the audience that evening. Our closing number was a fairly spot-on rendering of British goth rockers–turned–AC/DC revivalists the Cult's version of the Steppenwolf classic "Born to Be Wild." Still not aware of how to make my electric guitar cut through the din of my dynamically challenged bandmates, and fearing that the audience would miss the opportunity to bask in my "mastery" of Billy Duffy's strangled blues licks, I had a heart-to-heart with the sound technician that night to make sure he'd watch me very carefully for the visual cue — I would point violently to the sky as a signal to turn up the volume during my guitar solo.

The show itself was a blazing success . . . not so much musically, as a recently viewed warbly VHS recording of the performance has revealed, but certainly in terms of an elevation in social status for the least "cool" members of the band (I had been smart enough to load the deck with at least three popular dudes, whose resumes ranged from high school football star to local drug dealer). The rush of performing for a screaming crowd and the attentions and affections of girls I had once considered to be miles out of my league may not have been my initial motivation for becoming a musician, but it turned out to be a lovely side benefit.

It was clear to me that night that while other bands were tackling more difficult, technically challenging fare like Pink Floyd, Rush, and even the massive Whitesnake hits of that year, our simple, blues-based, three-chord songs had really made an impact. Chalk it up to ADHD, laziness, or the inability to comprehend and interpret the guitar tablature of the more challenging songs from the guitar magazines I was now buying on the regular, but I was really connecting with the raw viscera that came from simplicity, at least as a performer. I still loved listening to Metallica, Iron Maiden, Yngwie Malmsteen, and other forms of technical music, but I found myself (and still do, in most musical situations) wanting to feel the rush of a 3-minute-and-33-second burst of raw power chords and steel fisted pentatonic guitar licks in the classic rock mold.

That cover of "Born to Be Wild" came from the Cult's 1986 album *Electric*, a record chock-full of classic hard rock energy broken down into its most primitive state. Coming off the success of their 1985 *Love* album, with singer Ian Astbury's bellowing gothic invocation of Jim Morrison's vocal stylings and guitarist Billy Duffy's highly effected, jangling, and psychedelic guitar riffs and tones, all anchored by the steady, throbbing rhythm-section pulse of bassist Jamie Stewart and drummer Les Warner, you would think the band would be content to carry on with this formula of '60s psychedelia draped in gothic garb. Actually, they seemingly *were* content to do that on their first go at recording *Electric* (that first version would later surface as the *Peace* album). When that first attempt, produced by Steve Brown, who had also hemmed the board for *Love*, lacked the excitement that Duffy and Astbury were looking for, the band sought out a producer with a reputation for capturing the music of the streets . . . even if that music was hip-hop and those streets were to be found in New York City.

Producer Rick Rubin had been making his name with rappers like LL Cool J, Run DMC and the Beastie Boys, enamored with not only the rhythmic flow and intricate wordplay, but with the organic editing process that these artists employed in finding material to rap over. By building on the innovations of DJs like Kool Herc and Grandmaster Flash, hip-hop artists were finding the best sections of rock records and taking "break beats": instrumental sections of classic rock, funk, and R&B songs that could be looped repeatedly to create tracks over which to lay down their raps. In doing so, audiences were exposed to instrumental sections that emphasized big grooves and minimalist power chord structures . . . the energy of rock, with more space. Really, this was a formula that bands such as AC/DC and Aerosmith were already employing, and a big reason why a song like Aerosmith's "Walk This Way" made such an amazing foundation for a band like Run DMC. As a rap and rock fan and budding entrepreneur, Rubin saw the power in this, and his concept to bring Run DMC and Aerosmith together to record "Walk This Way" is one of the greatest mutually beneficial moves in music industry history. It helped Run DMC crack the mainstream barrier that was keeping them off MTV, and it also helped a drug-addled and commercially waning Aerosmith rediscover its street cred and kickstart an unparalleled career comeback that continues to this day.

And in that spirt of street cred, simplicity, space and power, *Electric*'s unaffected nod to the great classic rock of the '60s and '70s found its way to wax. Songs like "Lil' Devil," "Love Removal Machine," and "Wildflower" rip and roar like a kickstarted Harley, an effective combo of a fundamental guitar riff, simple yet classic blues-inflected guitar solos, pumping eighth-note bass and drum foundations, and Astbury's wolf-child howling. There are hints of the majestic riffs of Cream and Led Zeppelin, but without the exploration or virtuosity that those bands were known to employ. Whether this is a detraction or an improvement is a matter of subjectivity, but to this writer's adrenaline addicted mind, it was a definite plus.

Electric is psychedelia with direction. A hard rock effort trimmed of all of its fat, pure snarl and sinew, an all-protein guitar-and-drums feast with the odd tambourine serving as an amuse bouche. Rubin's direct approach to rock production would produce similar results with the debut of Misfits frontman Glenn Danzig's 1988 debut with his band Danzig. Utterly lacking in any unnecessary reverb or ambience, Danzig was pure, throaty '70s proto-metal tone, every nuance stark and clear. As he did with Slayer's thrash metal masterpiece *Reign in Blood* in 1986, Rubin removes any unnecessary sonic accoutrements that stand in the way of the greater artistic picture.

Elementally pure, his productions live and die by the merits and raw elements of the art.

The sound of the Cult's *Electric* would prepare rock fans of the era for more albums from like-minded minimalists and purists and eventually pave the way for one of rock'n'roll's great changing of the guards, the emergence of Guns N' Roses and their debut album *Appetite for Destruction*.

It's sometimes hard to fathom that *Appetite* came about as early as 1987. Its dominance as the most important rock'n'roll album of the '80s lasted for the rest of the decade, and the first year of the '90s as well. At one point, Axl Rose, Izzy Stradlin, Steven Adler, Duff McKagan, and Slash were individually and, ultimately, collectively just like any other street urchins living off the kindness and gullibility of strangers, sating the suffering and boredom of their impoverished existence through many different means, chemical, sexual, and violent. While the romance lies in attributing excessive behavior in rock'n'roll to some Blake-inspired journey for knowledge and truth through the decimation of societal boundaries, the fact is much of this behavior probably arose out of boredom. From what I have seen in my own journeys, excessive behavior is a way to offset wasted hours of mind-numbing mortality that occupy the space between real life and "the gig." Time not used in service of the gig is meant to be burned up until it is once again time to wield the hammer of the gods and rule the stage of some rat-infested Hollywood club for 90 minutes, where the artist is awash in the transcendent bliss of the music, forgetting domestic realities. Maybe a bottle of Night Train and a bump of blow stolen from a stripper's purse was just something to do until the next chance to lose oneself in the real palace of wisdom . . . the rock'n'roll concert stage.

Then again, Guns N' Roses weren't jocks from the Valley who thought it might be fun to slap on some makeup and grow out their manes to get in on the Sunset Strip party . . . three of them were legitimate transplants from different parts of the American tapestry. McKagan had come from Seattle, already a veteran of that city's punk rock scene and no stranger to underground living and the vices that could kill just as quickly as they could thrill. Stradlin and Rose had made the trek to Hollywood from Lafayette, Indiana, Stradlin first throwing a drum set in a Chevy Impala and setting up shop with various ragtag outfits, first as a drummer, then as a guitar player. What he lacked in technical skill as a player he more than made up for in swagger and songwriting sense, taking musical and sartorial cues from the Rolling Stones, Aerosmith, Hanoi Rocks, and underground bands like the U.K.'s Girl. Axl, a friend of Izzy's in Lafayette, saw his friend's exodus to Hollywood as a chance to plague the demons of his own upbringing, and the wrath and consultation of the authority figures upon whose radar he loomed large. Armed with a combination of influences that included Elton John, Nazareth, Grand Funk Railroad, and Motörhead, Rose's deceptively pedestrian Midwestern rock tastes mixed potently with Izzy's simple swagger as they churned their way in and out of various bands and incarnations. (The Guns in Guns N' Roses is actually guitarist Tracii Guns, a schoolmate of Slash, and an important artistic figure in '80s rock through his work with the great L.A. Guns.) With U.K. born–LA raised guitarist Slash's mix of punk rock attitude, heavy metal–informed articulation and attack, and mastery of the lexicon of authentic '70s hard rock guitar licks bouncing off McKagan's highly developed street-wise bass lines and born-and-bred California surfer dude Steven Adler's arena-rock-meets-junkie-disco approach to drumming, the results were combustible. Slash was the child of an album art designing father and a mother who was a stylist who worked with many big artists in the '70s, instilling in the young guitarist (née Saul Hudson) a genuine bohemian flare and meter for the bullshit that permeates much of the music business.

In much the same way that the Cult's *Electric* album did, GNR's *Appetite for Destruction* debut stripped away a lot of the sonic polish and perfection that had begun to plague albums of the mid-'80s. Classic rock staples like "Welcome to the Jungle" and "Sweet Child O' Mine" are so ubiquitous now, it's easy to forget how bizarre and challenging the structures were. The dark rise and fall in dynamics, the Les Paul–driven guitar tones and '70s inspired musical figures, and Axl Rose's vaudevillian growl-to-histrionic-screech vocal range sounded so fresh and compelling against numerous riffs and grooves. There was no apparent formula at work on cuts like "It's So Easy," "Mr. Brownstone," "Nightrain," or any other piece on the record . . . it was riff after glorious riff, performed on the very edge of the considerable abilities and vision of the musicians. *Appetite* is a place where the collective influences have carved out such a unique place within the compositions, they actually transcend their origins to become something new. Sure, you might be able to spot an Aerosmith or a Nazareth reference easily enough, maybe a Michael Schenker or Joe Perry riff here and there, but in the context of the intention of the players to disregard anything other than creating, something altogether new was born. From the first time I heard *Appetite for Destruction* in my 10th grade religion class (yup, the Lord works in mysterious ways!) via a classmate's Walkman, I was transfixed by not only the intense rawness of the music, but in the range of emotion and timbre in the singing. Zero to sixty in the blink of an eye, eye, eye, eye . . . where do we go *now*?

Axl Rose said "fuck" in a much different way than I said "fuck." It instilled a danger into the music that was not the same as the danger I had experienced when listening to Mötley Crüe. I wasn't worried about my mortal soul when I listened to GNR, I was worried about ever running into these maniacs! It all felt completely thrilling and unhinged, and yet this manic display was bathed in some of the most glorious and inspired music I had yet to experience as a young rock'n'roller. Mike Clink's production perfectly captured this band on the edge. The stereo imaging of this record courtesy of Steve Thompson and Michael Barbiero's mix still stands as my ideal sonic picture. Izzy on the left speaker, spinning and churning his Neil Young and Keef inspired rhythms, thin and wiry, barely making the chord changes in some cases, but with the undeniable swing of a guitarist born to make this sound. Recorded in stereo, with a stronger presence in the right speaker was Slash, the vodka-and-orange-juice-laced virtuoso, spinning iron-fisted classic rock guitar licks that danced along the edge of his technique, at times spiky and gnarled, at other times fast, smooth, and graceful . . . and always melodic. His lines implied a sophistication and understanding of the best traits of the electric guitar solo, flurries of smeared speed licks blending with mournful string bends, throaty wah-wah pedal punctuations enhanced by singing vibrato, and the ability to land on the right chord tones at just the right moments. His pseudo-flamenco informed solo in "Sweet Child O' Mine" is a master class in this approach, and he soars like Paco de Lucía on opiates. His runs on rave-ups like "Paradise City" and "Nightrain" are impossibly exciting flights of guitar fancy, blistering fast guitar sequences that impress not because of their precision, but because we are never really sure if Slash is going to make it to the end. And yet he does, enticing and beguiling us along the way with the integrity, power, and conviction of his performance. You can't learn these traits at the Guitar Institute of Technology, they only come from lifting and dropping a needle over and over again on the selected grooves of the albums that move your soul.

If the acoustic playing that graces the second side of 1988's *G N' R Lies* album (a record pushed out to retail to capitalize on *Appetite*'s runaway success) is any indication, the band's combined record collection most definitely included copies of the Rolling Stones' *Sticky Fingers*, *Exile on Main St.*, and *Beggars Banquet*. Slash and Izzy (and Duff, who adds beautiful double-stop guitar lines on the album's monster hit "Patience"), weave in and out of each other's playing like the glory days of Keith Richards and Mick Taylor, creating a depth of expression that emotionally dwarfed much of the party rock of their contemporaries. The first side of the album is a reissued version of the *Live?!*★*@ Like a Suicide* album, a "live" recording of the band bashing out early songs like "Reckless Life" and "Move to the City," and a well-curated selection of covers from Rose Tattoo and Aerosmith. *Live?!*★*@ Like a Suicide* was initially released by the band's label Geffen Records as a limited run in 1986, intended to prime the pumps and establish street credibility for the band. Geffen even went so far as to hide their own major label affiliation with the band, issuing the album under a pseudo indie imprint, Uzi Suicide. Guns N' Roses would later repay an inspirational debt to Hanoi Rocks by reissuing selected titles from the Finnish band's back catalog on the imprint. These reissues were crucially important for me, as in Hanoi Rocks I could hear even more of the personality, rawness, and swagger that made me react on an *emotionally* visceral level. When I played Hanoi Rocks and Guns N' Roses songs on my guitar, my body reverberated in a different way . . . the licks and riffs fell under my hands far more naturally than they did with an Yngwie or an Eddie Van Halen riff. The great gift from Guns, the Cult, and Hanoi was the realization of the type of guitar player I was going to be.

The *G N' R Lies* album is marred by deeply unfortunate lyrical content. "One in a Million" is Axl Rose's racist and homophobic autobiographical rant on the trials and tribulations of a poor white boy from Indiana making his way in big, bad L.A. The thinly veiled misogyny of "Used to Love Her," apparently written about his dog, feels like a threat disguised as a joke.

When measured against the sweetness and vulnerability of "Patience" and "Sweet Child O' Mine," these songs certainly helped perpetuate the myth of Axl Rose's mentally dichotomous state, or as the marketing narrative would push, his dedication to artistic honesty and integrity. But even in the context of my mostly white, small city Ontario surroundings, this narrative felt hurtful, cruel, and abhorrent. I can't imagine how this complicated relationships within the band, especially considering Slash himself was of mixed race. How painful and conflicting it must have been to be experiencing such massive success while your bandmate uses such demeaning language against people with your background on your own record? I felt for Slash as he would squirm to answer interview questions about this inner conflict. I felt his frustration, disappointment, and hurt, the struggle between wanting to do the right thing, while also trying to control this creative monster of his own expression.

That's not to say I wouldn't jump off my ethical high horse to listen to the album. I continued to devour *Lies*, and I loved "One in a Million," even though I knew his perspective was wrong. I knew it would hurt people of color and LGBTQ people if they heard it (despite my strict Catholic upbringing, slurs of any kind directed toward other cultures or the gay community were not tolerated in our household). The truth is, the music was too thrilling to resist, and likely so, too, was the taboo nature of Axl's seemingly fearless expression of this hate-filled narrative. It fills me with shame to think of it now, and I find it increasingly difficult to reconcile as an adult.

Perhaps herein lies the real danger of Guns N' Roses . . . not the good danger of the playing, not the exciting danger of living life in the fast lane, this was the danger of making enemies of people who don't look like you or live differently than you do. I wrote of the potential hurt it caused in the name of art, in the name of "free expression." But how "free" is one's expression if it is hurting and demeaning others? I believe Axl Rose felt that rage and fear, a confusion stemming from ignorance and his own child experiences with abuse, rejection, and mental illness. But he was wrong. And his early views on women, race, and homosexuality will forever stain his reputation as an artist, even as he espoused radically different views in later years. As ashamed as I am to admit it, Guns N' Roses probably hurt my development as a person on certain levels too.

It's so strange how my mind has reconfigured the timeline of this era. GNR's all-encompassing domination can make it seem like they were first to market with this Hanoi-Aerosmith-Stones-Motörhead streetwise rock'n'roll thing. In truth, they were products of a scene that was producing many bands with a shared taste of the darker side of rock'n'roll. Bands like Jetboy, Faster Pussycat, and L.A. Guns were all contemporaries of GNR.

Faster Pussycat actually struck first with their self-titled major label debut, released two weeks prior to *Appetite for Destruction*. It's a wonderfully loose and trashy rock'n'roll affair, the twin guitars of Brent Muscat and Greg Steele working that old Aerosmith magic, making the most of tried-and-true guitar moves that stick to the brain like a flyer on a Sunset Strip telephone pole. The rhythm section of bassist Eric Stacy and drummer Mark Michals barely keep it together, but in the best possible way . . . and Taime Downe's saucy, pouting vocal performance has just enough melody to make the sleazy attitude memorable. Closer in spirit to the New York Dolls than almost any '80s hard rock band, Faster Pussycat were savvy enough to add a little B-movie kitsch to their pirate strut, thanks to some tastefully tasteless videos inspired by Russ Meyer flicks (the band is named after the Meyer's film *Faster Pussycat! Kill! Kill!*). They may have been serving up sex on a platter, but this was no jock rock, baby. Sure, the Tura Satana–esque beauties in their skin-tight, cleavage- and curve-accentuating catsuits were on full display, but these videos featured powerhouse women who could snap your neck if you approached them the wrong way . . . sex and violence by way of *Looney Tunes* or the Marx Brothers. This wasn't about the domination or subjugation of women, this was the theater of the stars of the Strip, an equal-opportunity sleaze-fest that felt like the fun side of rock'n'roll's dark underbelly.

Ultimately, Faster Pussycat worked because of the tunes, with tracks like "Don't Change That Song," "Bathroom Wall," and "Babylon," bump'n'grind shout-alongs without the hang-ups of misogyny. In 1988, they would go on to make an even better album with *Wake Me When It's Over*. A massive step up in quality of performance and production value, *Wake Me* is likely the best '80s rock iteration of the '70s Aerosmith era. Songs like "Poison Ivy," "Where's There's a Whip There's a Way," "Tattoo," and "Slip of the Tongue" roll and tumble with intertwining guitar riffs that suggest a band weaned on *Toys in the Attic* and *Exile on Main St.* flexing their musical muscles with newly developed arena rock chops. Producer John Jansen's production resists the urges of his sample-happy contemporaries, and the result is an album that sounds powerful and organic to this day.

The story of L.A. Guns and Guns N' Roses is exhaustive — a story of the type of personnel swapping that is very common amongst members of any musical scene. Shared visions can be short-lived and collective loyalties fleeting when any manner of distraction, be it aspirational, chemical, or sexual, gets in the way.

Tracii Guns formed L.A. Guns in 1983 with drummer Rob Gardner. They merged with members of another band called Hollywood Rose (which featured Axl Rose and Izzy Stradlin) in 1985. Guns and Gardner left that band shortly thereafter, making room for Slash and Steven Adler to come together in the classic GNR incarnation. Guns re-formed L.A. Guns with singer Paul Black, bassist Mick Cripps, guitarist Robert Stoddard, and drummer Nickey Alexander. When singer Black's excesses proved to be a roadblock to the band getting signed, L.A. Guns manager Alan Jones connected Tracii with U.K. vocalist Phil Lewis, whose band Girl factored as an influence amongst the hipper bands of the Hollywood rock set. Lewis may not have been in possession of a technically great vocal instrument, but the sound he made and the attitude in his approach convinced Tracii he was the man for the job upon a simple "check, one, two" test of his microphone at his audition. This instant acknowledgment of the power of taste and chemistry trumping formulaic copycat syndrome is one of the reasons that L.A. Guns' self-titled debut stands as a shining musical example of the late '80s Hollywood rock scene. Like Pearcy and DeMartini, Mars and Neil, Eddie and Dave . . . the combination of Guns's guitar and Lewis's nasally, bratty British vocals made a sound that captured the trashy triumph of the songs they were writing. If you're going to write a song called "No Mercy," letting up on the intensity is not an option, and the track pummels from start to finish. There is a 99% chance that a song with the title "Sex Action" is going to suck, but with Guns's dark, chugging riffs and Lewis's shouting and pouting, they become the one-percenters who make it work.

Key to the whole album is the ensemble performance of the recording lineup. The driving performance of bassist Kelly Nickels (who missed his first big break with his former band Faster Pussycat due to being sidelined by a motorcycle accident) and drummer Nickey "Beat" Alexander had a straight-forward punk rock menace but with enough spit and polish to shine in 1988's recorded music landscape. The grooves feel a bit like a Motörhead 45 RPM single played at 33 RPM, metal with a swing, punk with a swagger. And like the best of these bands, the virtuosic Guns had a songwriting and rhythm guitar foil to bounce off, the dark and mysterious Mick Cripps. In the mold of the great rhythm guitar players of the past, Cripps's mere presence seemed to add credibility and cool to the L.A. Guns . . . the churn to Tracii's chug.

But ultimately, L.A Guns was and is built around Tracii and his breathtaking playing. Tracii Guns is one of my favorite guitarists of the era for his embodiment of the best of '60s and '70s classic rock ideals à la Jimmy Page and Keith Richards, his musical interpretation of the attitude of punk rock pioneers like Johnny Thunders and Steve Jones, and the technical command and sonic largesse of players like Eddie Van Halen, Randy Rhoads, Mick Mars, and Chris Holmes. In the riffs and leads of the debut and great albums like *Cocked & Loaded*, *Hollywood Vampires*, and *Vicious Circle* that would follow, Guns combines all the aforementioned colors on his palette, and he paints with a freedom that feels connected to the roots of rock'n'roll, but with the vibrancy and technical flare of the early '80s guitar pioneers. He may not have been pushing the vocabulary of the electric guitar in the way that players like Lynch, DeMartini, Lee, Yngwie or Paul Gilbert were, but Guns forged his own path by staying true to the authenticity of the blues-based architects of the past, while remaining technically exciting to young players like me. And let's face it, he was and is a guitar *hero*. Decked out in black leather and pointy black boots, feet planted in a power stance, his two-tone hair matching his black Les Paul Standard with the white pickguard, he looked cool as fuck. And as with his look, in his playing I heard something solid and timeless . . . and perhaps this is why I keep going back to these albums. When Tracii Guns plays guitar, I believe he is the authentic product of a deep love of the classic players who came before him, and I believe in his authentic expression of these influences.

San Francisco transplants Jetboy were another band that were leaders of the scene that Guns N' Roses would ultimately claim dominance over. Their following was so substantial in the Bay Area that bands like GNR and Poison would support them when they came to San Francisco. Conversely, Jetboy would begin to build a sizeable Los Angeles audience when the favor was returned, ultimately becoming a club-packing headliner. Signing with Elektra Records in 1986, Jetboy's success was marred by lengthy delays and the eventual shelving of their excellent debut album *Feel the Shake*. Fortunately, they were picked up by MCA Records, but by the time of *Feel the Shake's* 1988 release, momentum was lost, and the bands that had once supported Jetboy were now miles ahead in terms of exposure and success. A shame, as Jetboy were a band that could have turned the hair metal stereotype on its head. They had a legit underground musical icon in their ranks (Hanoi Rocks' Sammi Yaffa), and founding guitarists Billy Rowe and Fernie Rod were a sympatico guitar duo weaned on classic '70s American rock'n'roll like Aerosmith and Cheap Trick, and a healthy helping of AC/DC. It was actually a chance occurrence involving a Jetboy guitar case and a guitar belonging to Malcolm Young that helped me reconnect with Billy Rowe. I had known Billy from our days being signed to Los Angeles–based Liquor and Poker Music, the rock'n'roll arm of heavy metal industry giant Century Media. Billy's band American Heartbreak and my band Crash Kelly had shared some bills together and were the more "power pop" influenced bands on a roster that included the Hellacopters, Backyard Babies, Hanoi Rocks, the Black Halos, and others. Both Crash Kelly and American Heartbreak wore these "power pop" influences on our sleeves, a fact that I think offended the "cooler than thou" sensibilities of some of our labelmates. At any rate, Billy and I bonded.

I was recently recording with Lee Aaron at Armoury Studios in Vancouver, a high-end facility that was once owned by songwriter Jim Vallance and ultimately transferred over to super producer Bruce Fairbairn. The walls of the studio are still adorned with the multiple gold and platinum records Fairbairn was awarded for his work with bands like Bon Jovi, Aerosmith, and AC/DC, to name just a few. After the completion of the

AC/DC album *The Razors Edge*, Angus and Malcolm Young had gifted Fairbairn with guitars used in the recording of the album. When these guitars were shown to me at the Lee Aaron session, I noticed that one of the cases holding Malcolm's guitar was emblazoned with the Jetboy logo. Sure enough, after tracking down Billy (who is now on the road as a member of Buckcherry), it turned out that the case did indeed belong to him at one point. His mind suitably blown, I figured it was a good time to hit him up to discuss Jetboy's role and place in the heart of the '80s Hollywood hard rock scene.

Billy Rowe: We discovered Hanoi Rocks and we were very into Lords of the New Church and early Kix, and at the end of it, bands like Japan. We basically were into bands that were really unsung heroes. Some were still trying to break the doors down, like Hanoi Rocks and Lords of the New Church. In San Francisco there was a small scene that was into that stuff, but you'd go to L.A. and it was just always another level up, you know, the next notch. So we used to go down there looking for a singer. We built relationships with friends who we met out in front of the Troubadour and the Roxy and the Whisky and the whole underground scene at the time. And so when Jetboy started playing in '84, within a year we were trucking it down to L.A. and doing gigs. And we were just one of those bands out of our genre in San Francisco that went down there first and actually built up a pretty strong following. By the time we were going down there, the scene was big . . . we all had record deals by '86, '87. The clubs were just busting at the seams with the amount of people who were going out. It probably was how it was like maybe at CBGB and Max's Kansas City in New York in the '70s with the punk rock stuff.

We were on bills with Jane's Addiction, not the Chili Peppers, but Jane's Addiction, for sure. And we would go see these bands when clubs like Club Scream came along. I mean, you could have Guns N' Roses and Jetboy there for two weekends, and then you could have the Red Hot Chili Peppers one weekend as the headliner or whatever. And then you would have the Cult or some goth band. Goth was also very intertwined with that whole rock'n'roll scene at the same time. When you'd go to Club Scream and you could hear Bauhaus, but then the Cult, and then Guns N' Roses and Gene Loves Jezebel.

Jetboy possessed that most coveted of commodities in the '80s hard rock scene: a unique lead singer. With his mile-high mohawk and punk rock look, singer Mickey Finn cut a much different visual than the preening pretty boys promenading up and down the Strip. He had a vocal style that was similar to L.A. Guns' Phil Lewis with a bit more control, and a Bon Scott attitude that worked well with the hooky and efficient AC/DC–meets–the Alarm songwriting and bare bones production. In retrospect, the production on *Feel the Shake* splits the difference between the over-the-top high-tech excess of bands like Whitesnake and Def Leppard and the rawer aesthetic of GNR and Faster Pussycat perhaps a little too well ... a bit too polished for fans of stripped back rock, while also lacking in the excessive punch and gloss of more over-the-top productions. Still, in 2022, Jetboy's songs stand the test of time.

There was a real smorgasbord of hard rock delicacies on offer during this fruitful period of hard rock. For every sleazy, bandana-sporting, gypsy rock'n'roll band, there were still bands trying to push the envelope of rock in an upscale, high-tech, multilayered way. When *Appetite for Destruction* was released in 1987, it was not an out-of-the-gate smash. It took a full year of pushing from Geffen to finally break the band on MTV, and as much as it would ultimately set the tone for a return to rock'n'roll's roots, two monster albums by Def Leppard and Whitesnake were shining multiplatinum examples of a super saturation of the pop metal sound of the early '80s.

Def Leppard's *Hysteria* and Whitesnake's self-titled 1987 albums represent the most loved and the most hated production qualities of '80s hard rock, depending on who you talk to. From my teenage vantage point, these were albums that inspired on many fronts.

The struggles to record *Hysteria* have been well documented. The pressures of following up the enormously successful *Pyromania* without producer Mutt Lange (initially) forced the band to look elsewhere and resulted in an aborted effort to work with Jim Steinman, a costly misstep in terms of both time and money. Mutt's return to the production chair renewed hope and momentum for the recording project, but that was soon marred by the New Year's Eve 1984 car accident that resulted in drummer Rick Allen losing his arm. As testament to Def Leppard's commitment and loyalty to one another as bandmates, a replacement for Allen was never considered. Through a combination of advancements in electronic drum technology (and Mutt being no stranger to the use of drum machines on rock records), as well as Allen's drive and resilience in relearning how to play drums on an adapted kit, the band carried on with the arduous recording under Lange's microscopically analyzing production eye. The result was an album that combined the ambitions of Queen, the orchestration innovations of Led Zeppelin, and the programming and sequencing techniques found on pop, hip-hop, and R&B albums. But most importantly, for all of its methodical overabundance and controlled layering of multiple elements, *Hysteria* worked because it still stayed true to Def Leppard's core elements as a band. Underneath the gloss and sheen are songs that come from the heart of '70s glam rock: Ziggy Stardust, David Essex, the Sweet, Slade, and Wings. There are also nods to the guitar tone innovations of Boston's Tom Scholz (whose direct recording invention the Rockman was used to capture the crystal-clear clean guitar tones that shimmer throughout *Hysteria*) and Eddie Van Halen, as well as the open and sophisticated chordal approach of the Police's Andy Summers. With the exception of Boston's debut, no album has ever blended distorted and clean guitar tones so successfully and seamlessly, a veritable guitar orchestra. As much as the warm, rich guitar tones of tube amplifiers are coveted amongst players, Def Leppard's use of direct digital recording processors helped create emotional warmth in the compositions. Beyond the equipment, the distinct yet complementary guitar styles emanating from the fingers, minds, and hearts of Steve Clark and Phil Collen interact in a way that brings to mind the magical interplay of John Lennon and George Harrison's chordal harmony approach. By layering different chords on top of each other, harmonies that would be beyond the reach of a single guitar player are employed synchronously to produce one big guitar part. With Clark's looser, low-slung guitar approach playing off of Collen's more technically agile style, *Hysteria* lays out a beautifully separated layer of very human guitar approaches, framed in high fidelity, upon which vocal melodies and multitracked backgrounds can be built.

As is the case with a band like 10cc, vocals are king on a Def Leppard album. For all the accusations of sterility and cold calculation that are hurled at this record by critics, *Hysteria*'s exploitation and multiplication of the organic warmth and emotional connectivity of the human voice is a primary factor in its mass popularity. It's also in the vocals that we find the rock'n'roll excitement and energy that other bands generate in more traditional ways. If you listen to the thick layer of vocals in songs like "Armageddon It," "Women," and "Pour Some Sugar on Me," you will hear that they are delivered with a snotty and snarling punk rock attitude . . . nothing soft in the delivery there. Sure, there is great emphasis and consideration given to vowel formation, articulation, and intonation, but the attitude is fully present, even when wrapped in a blanket of accessible sonics — the type that translate so well on radio and TV.

Attitude is what makes Joe Elliott one of rock'n'roll's truly great vocalists. Like Brian Johnson on *Back in Black* and *For Those About to Rock*, Elliott's willingness to allow Mutt Lange to push him to the very brink of his range and dynamic ability are what ultimately sold so many millions of copies of *Hysteria*. In Elliot, we don't hear the warbling vibrato of a metal singer or the silky smooth timbre associated with AOR giants like Boston. What we get is a singer with a great tone who can generate rasp and intimacy in equal measure. What I hear in his approach is years of listening obsessively to records and a subsequent appropriation of the emotional content found in singers like Paul McCartney, Brian Connolly of the Sweet, Marc Bolan of T. Rex, or Bon Scott. I believe that Joe willed and worked himself into becoming a great singer, rather than relying on prodigious natural gifts. He sounds like a man who would do anything to best serve the song he is singing, even if that means finding notes beyond his range. And like a true Yorkshireman, he isn't doing it for the glory or a pat on the back. He just needs to get the job done.

Going back to Spencer Proffer's theory of participatory rock, the rhythms created through Rick Allen's electric drum and Rick Savage's tightly locked bass lines are designed to connect with our innate rhythmic instincts. From the Burundi drum samples and glam rock stomp of "Rocket" to the slowed down and slightly syncopated take on Queen's "We Will Rock You" that makes up the heartbeat of "Pour Some Sugar on Me," *Hysteria* may not move in an organically human way (one that speeds up and slows down), but it does aid in the process of unifying the audience rhythmically. Like a social metronome, *Hysteria*'s adherence to strict time keeping may have been one of the factors that made it a worldwide smash.

Well, maybe that's a stretch . . . but let's face it, even the most rhythmically challenged of us can clap along with "Pour Some Sugar on Me."

There is no doubt that *Hysteria* was written and recorded out of an ambition to be the biggest band in the world. But not for one second do I believe that was for money or fame. I believe that Def Leppard's success was borne of a need to connect emotionally on the biggest scale possible in order to fulfill a sense of manifest rock'n'roll destiny. They had to be the band that people loved as much as the bands they loved.

I think scale and scope plays a huge part in the popularity of *Whitesnake 1987* as well. In this case, it was the vision of John Kalodner, the music industry mogul hand-picked by David Geffen who would become synonymous with connecting '80s hard rockers with the wants and needs of American hard rock audience of the late '70s and '80s.

Kalodner's strength came with his belief in star power, and his recognition of those who possessed it. He saw that power in David Coverdale, another Yorkshireman who had found fame when he landed the lead vocal slot in Deep Purple in 1974. After his successful run of albums with Purple, Coverdale would form Whitesnake, initially as a solo outfit, and would go on to incorporate some of England's finest blues-based hard rock players, including Jon Lord and Ian Paice of Deep Purple, Cozy Powell of Rainbow, and guitarists and bassists of considerable British rock pedigree like Bernie Marsden, Micky Moody, Mel Galley, Neil Murray, and Colin Hodgkinson. Whitesnake would build a dedicated fan base throughout the U.K. and Europe and ascend to headlining status in larger theaters and concert halls. However, it was the intervention of Kalodner and the injection of firebrand guitarist John Sykes that would see Whitesnake make the transition from classic rockers in the '70s hard-rockin' blues mold to the full-blown FM radio, U.S.-stadium-ready, and MTV-omnipresent superstars they would become. The first step in the process was the remixing of 1984's *Slide It In* album for the U.S. market. Where producer Martin Birch's warm, round, and fat production resonated with the organic girth of the best of '70s British hard rock tones, it was Keith Olsen's sonic facelift for the U.S. market that helped *Slide It In* cross over to gold record status. Sykes's photogenic good looks and fiery modern rock guitar sound (heard to stunning effect on Thin Lizzy's 1983 heavy metal–laced swan song *Thunder and Lightning*) had an assertive and aggressive quality that matched the power of Coverdale's vocals. It would turn out that Sykes could also compose and create riffs of a very high caliber, the massive guitar tones and vibrant performances he laid down on the 1987 album setting the standard that would be aped but almost never duplicated.

Built upon the bluesy hard rock riff framework laid out by Jimmy Page; the passion, largesse, and virtuosity of Deep Purple and Rainbow; and the authentic blues and soul vocabulary that lie at the heart of Coverdale's personal taste, *Whitesnake* felt like an album bursting at the seams with intensity. The performances of bassist Neil Murray and drummer Aynsley Dunbar are sophisticated yet powerfully restrained, and imbue the album with a timelessness that may have been overlooked with a lesser rhythm section. Sykes's tones are so powerful, new, and tied to the era (as the best example of tone, in my estimation), they could have overshadowed Coverdale's intentions to create soul-inflected, turbo-charged electric blues. Metal was the chosen delivery system for these riffs, but Murray and Dunbar keep it connected to the original intention.

The album's centerpiece is the epic "Still of the Night," liberally borrowing from the rise-and-fall dynamics of Zeppelin's "Whole Lotta Love," but supercharged by Sykes's aggressive, vibrato-laced power chords and blistering speed licks. John Sykes, along with a handful of players like Yngwie Malmsteen, TNT's Ronni Le Tekrø, Loudness's Akira Takasaki, and Dokken's George Lynch, was able to deliver flash and authentic fury in equal measures. His right-hand picking and left-hand legato techniques are master classes in intensity. Where other players might be able to pull off fast runs with the help of ultra-compressed high gain tones, you can hear that Sykes's sound is a result of the physical attack of his hands . . . a phenomenon referred to in the guitar community as "bone tone." You can hear this in his rhythm guitar playing, akin to that of Jake E. Lee in its ripping 16th-note staccato intensity and exemplified in songs like "Children of the Night" and "Bad Boys." Sykes could even make a power ballad like "Is This Love" burn white hot, while Coverdale employs the restraint learned from his vast knowledge of R&B artists like Bobby "Blue" Bland, letting the song simmer with his smoky baritone delivery, then builds the intensity before exploring the upper ranges of his instrument.

Of course, the story of Whitesnake's 1987 album's success is built upon one song in particular. "Here I Go Again" was a track that, along with the epic heavy metal bump'n'grind shuffle "Crying in the Rain," was originally released in 1982 on *Saints & Sinners*, but Kalodner saw an opportunity to resurrect it as a key maneuver in doing the same with Coverdale's fortunes in the U.S. market. "Here I Go Again" was actually given two facelifts, one that appears on the album proper, and one a rerecorded version that was released to radio. While three versions of the same song did offer a bit of confusion, it is the 1987 album version that would prove to be definitive. For the hundreds of guitar tracks (and thousands of notes) played by Sykes on the album, it was actually Dutch guitarist Adrian Vandenberg who would record the solo on this version, foreshadowing the formation of a new lineup that would ultimately take the place of the musicians who recorded *Whitesnake*. This lineup would not include Sykes, as a massive blow-up involving money, ego, and artistic conflict would see him leave the band in a fit of animosity.

The trilogy of Marty Callner (yeah, the Twisted Sister video guy) videos that featured Coverdale's soon to be wife, Tawny Kitaen, sprawled over cars, beds, and other inanimate objects would be largely responsible for the 10 million copies of *Whitesnake* sold in the U.S. alone. They also featured a lineup of the hottest rock musicians of the day, including Vanderberg, Dio's Vivian Campbell on coguitar, ex–Quiet Riot and Ozzy bassist Rudy Sarzo, and veteran drummer Tommy Aldridge.

Watching live footage of this lineup of Whitesnake, it is clear that each player is a masterful musician — the performances are big, bold, and exciting. And yet, such video footage never captures the same dimensions of the performances on the album. It feels like what it is . . . an outside interpretation of the recorded work. Of course, live performance is always going to be different than the controlled environment of the studio, but when you hear bands like Van Halen, Guns N' Roses, or any act that is performing live the music they themselves have recorded, you can feel their identities and ultimately make a connection to what they are saying.

This is no slight on the stellar Whitesnake lineup of '87, or those who were to follow. In fact, the look and performance acumen of those musicians were responsible for numerous formative concepts of great rock'n'roll stagecraft. And the work of each of these fine musicians in their other projects speaks volumes about their creative ability. But still, knowing what I know about the chemistry of music-making as a mature musician, I can't help but wonder what it would have been like to see and hear the original musicians of this landmark recording actually be the ones performing it live. Then again, with MTV, MuchMusic, and other media outlets at the time being what they were, many of us may never have heard this album had it not been for John Kalodner's marketing vision and intervention.

In fact, aside from that one turn by Vandenberg, what we saw on those videos did not feature any of the musicians we heard on the record.

In 1988, with Sammy Hagar now firmly entrenched, VH would release *OU812*, another multiplatinum number-one smash album, and headline their own festival style stadium tour, the Monsters of Rock. Taking their cue from a European festival of the same name, the tour would see Van Halen headlining over Scorpions, Dokken, Metallica, and Kingdom Come. Of all of these openers, my favorite back in the day was Kingdom Come, or as they would not so affectionately come to be known, Kingdom Clone. Their appropriation of the melodies, riffs, and affectations of Led Zeppelin were so brazen, they would make Greta Van Fleet blush, and the outrage factor was amplified when members of Kingdom Come took to outright denial in the press of Zeppelin's influence on their music. Lenny Wolf aped countless Robert Plant phrasing moves and melodic turns, James Kottak's drum fills and grooves impeccably mimicked the power of John Bonham, and Jimmy Page's iconic riffs were pillaged to extraordinary (and very pleasing) effect by guitarists Danny Stag and Rick Steier. Produced by Bob Rock, Kingdom Come's eponymous album was one that would inspire as much as it would offend, with Mötley Crüe and Metallica in particular taking note of the expansive and epic-sounding tones that Rock was achieving at Little Mountain Sound.

From a personal perspective, *Kingdom Come* was a perfect extension of what I loved about *Whitesnake*. The album took the heaviest, most obvious components of Led Zeppelin's sound and delivered them in a hard rock package that would whet the appetite of a teenage audience weaned on the sound of metal guitars. The playful whimsy of Zeppelin's light and shade may have been lost, but I was getting the adrenaline fix that I craved without having to sit through subtle sounds my 16-year-old brain wasn't quite ready to dig into. And I didn't have to listen to lyrics about Hobbits.

Kingdom Come was successful enough with their thievery that the album made gold status and earned them their slot on Van Halen's Monsters extravaganza. It's ballsy enough to have to deliver a two-hour headline set to 40,000 sun-baked fans who have already been subjected to six-odd hours of pounding drums, screaming vocals, and shredding guitar solos. But when one of those bands is a young and hungry Metallica (who would apparently dominate the merch booth in terms of T-shirt sales, foreshadowing a coming change), you would think a band of veteran rockers who were now embracing keyboards and pop song structures in a big way would be intimidated, at least slightly. Not Van Halen, though, who by this point were an untouchable institution, defying categorization and fearing no challenge coming from younger, louder, and faster upstarts. In 1988, Van Halen were still the sound of suburban American summer. Whether fronted by Sammy's sun-soaked bluster and surfer-dude vibes, or David Lee Roth's vaudevillian viking–abstract weirdness (waning slightly with the cold techno production values of his second solo album *Skyscraper*) Van Halen are quite simply in a class, or at the very least a space, of their own.

There was no shortage of inspiration for young guitar players in this period . . . the indie shredders of Mike Varney's Shrapnel Records were all over the pages of the major guitar rags, names like Tony MacAlpine, Vinnie Moore, Cacophony's Jason Becker and Marty Friedman, and Paul Gilbert and Bruce Bouillet of L.A.-based club band Racer X were all touted as torch bearers of the next wave of post–Van Halen players, this time adding their own twists on the technical innovations of Yngwie Malmsteen (who was now shooting for commercial heights with his *Odyssey* album, an AOR-laced collaboration with former Rainbow singer Joe Lynn Turner).

As much as I was finding that rawer, blues-inspired playing fell much more naturally under my fingers, I was still inspired to break out my metronome and practice furiously along with the metal mavens who were breaking all land speed records at the time. It didn't exactly move my soul to play this way, but there was great joy attached to the freedom that my newfound chops afforded me. It was just *fun* to move my fingers that fast, just as it was fun to hear these shredders continue to push the envelope. It made sense that all of these cats were appropriating the glam look of the day as well, pushing it further and further with bigger hair, more colorful clothes, and guitars with even crazier paint jobs and accoutrements (Michael Angelo's four neck guitar, anyone?).

Still, I was always more drawn to these more technical players when great songs were attached. Dokken's *Back for the Attack* was packed to the brim with the next evolution of George Lynch's playing and sound (no hiding behind processed bullshit here, Lynch's pure tube tone made his amps sound like they were on fire), but also featured some of the most inspired songs of the band's career, including the *Nightmare on Elm Street* theme "Dream Warriors," "Kiss of Death," and the obvious single choice, "Burning Like a Flame."

A player who I to this day reference when I have to construct a fiery, melodic solo with a splash of flash is the great Vito Bratta of White Lion. While Vito always wore his Van Halen influence proudly on his sleeve, he was one of the few guitarists of the era who consistently talked about songwriting influence and the importance of serving the song above all else. I was intrigued that Vito seemed to be just as passionate about Elton John as he was about EVH, and sure enough, the harmonic sophistication of Sir Elton is quite evident in many of the songs on White Lion's *Pride*, a two-million selling platter that incorporates plenty of ambience but also considerable space. Rather than beef up basic power chords with walls of overdubbed guitars, Vito could make one guitar part sound like an orchestra, and when he did add another layer, it was markedly different than the core part, a deviation to an acoustic guitar figure or a volume-swelled pad that took the song to a different place.

It's not easy to play the type of pianistic chord voicings that Vito incorporated on songs like "Wait" and "Tell Me" with a distorted electric guitar, but the effect is a magical one. *Pride* has the power of hard rock and the accessibility of classic pop. And while Danish lead singer Mike Tramp may have looked like a version of early '80s David Lee Roth with better cheekbones, he possessed a warm voice that made you believe that he felt a genuine connection to what he was singing. My memories of slow dancing to hit ballad "When the Children Cry" at a high school dance, the gymnasium walls slick with the humidity and hormones, are colored with my own inner conflict of making out to a song about the mess of a world we've left behind for the children of the future. As simplistic as those lyrics are, they stand above other power ballads by power of the intention of the content. It's a song with beautifully arranged classical guitar figures and a mournfully melodic electric guitar solo that doesn't waste a note.

Another band that stood out for me, largely for the guitar playing, was BulletBoys. Their 1988 Warner Brothers debut was produced by Ted Templeman, the man at the helm for the first six Van Halen albums. Coming 10 years after Van Halen's debut, it's hard not to look at *BulletBoys* as a case of history repeating. In 1988, Van Halen were fully ensconced in a more mature, keyboard-oriented, melodic pop songwriting vibe, and BulletBoys were seemingly set up to be a reimagination of the visceral excitement and rawness of Roth-era Van Halen. BulletBoys came complete with a blond-maned acrobatic frontman in Marq Torien, and a genuine guitar hero in Mick Sweda. Torien was also a gifted guitar player and no stranger to the Hollywood scene. He was an early candidate to replace Randy Rhoads as guitarist in Ozzy Osbourne's band in the early '80s. Sweda along with bassist Lonnie Vencent were members of veteran drummer Carmine Appice's decidedly unsuccessful glam metal experiment King Kobra. Drummer Jimmy D'Anda was a relative newcomer to the scene, but he played with the backbeat authority of someone much more seasoned.

Their debut may share a production and label history with the mighty VH, but aside from the odd Torien vocal affectation, BulletBoys were in possession of a sound of their own. Sweda's tone on the album is bone dry and warmly overdriven, a classic Marshall Plexi sound rich in harmonic content and clarity but in no way an easy beast to wrangle. To Sweda's credit, he makes it work, and the result is an exciting guitar performance that highlights an impeccable sense of phrasing, unique note choices informed by jazz and blues, and the excitement that can only come from a player who is pushing his technique to the limit. In an era where amplifiers and pedals with gobs of deficiency-disguising distortion, delays, and modulation effects were de rigueur, Sweda's solos and riffs in songs like "Smooth Up in Ya," "Hard as a Rock," and their cover of the O'Jays' classic "For the Love of Money" stand out in the mix, as do the deep groove and articulation in his playing. Where glam metal is often criticized for overproduction and studio sterility, BulletBoys sounded like four guys bashing it out in your living room, live and in your face, but still in full control of their playing. Perhaps this is a testament to Templeman's production aesthetic, a desire to stay out of the way of the foundational creation of the recording and add only what's needed after the fact. We heard it in his work with Montrose and Van Halen, and it is present in BulletBoys' debut as well.

Veterans and innovators of the hard rock scene were adapting and succeeding deep in the late '80s, finding new and contemporary ways to assert their relevance. While Judas Priest, Iron Maiden, and Scorpions may have lost some of their commercial footing, they were still moving a substantial number of albums and packing arenas the world over, thus retaining their stature as icons. Maiden's dalliances with keyboards and concept album fodder on *Seventh Son of a Seventh Son*, and Scorpions' heavily Def Leppard–influenced production work on *Savage Amusement* were valiant attempts at integrating modern technology into their classic sounds. Conversely, Priest tried to bring back the heavy on *Ram It Down* after the mixed reviews of *Turbo*, their synth-guitar-laden attempt to cash in on American commercial tastes. Bon Jovi continued their dominance of the suburban rock'n'roll market with *New Jersey*, an album full of songs that rival the quality of those found on *Slippery When Wet* and performances that positioned the band as mainstream crossover heirs to Springsteen's throne. Once again, Bruce Fairbairn, Bob Rock, and the team at Little Mountain Sound helped Bon Jovi create a record that separated them further from the heavy metal pack while still tapping into hard rock's ever growing commerciality. Kiss found themselves deep in the glam metal game, still hitting the platinum mark with the überslick and infectious *Crazy Nights*. With the *Lita* album, Runaways guitar slinger Lita Ford finally found the magic combination of songs and image that could showcase her as an accessible star without downplaying her considerable talents. *Lita* highlights Ford as a musical force to be reckoned with, and a platinum selling one at that, courtesy of hits "Kiss Me Deadly" and the stunning "Close My Eyes Forever," a duet with Ozzy Osbourne.

Speak of the devil, Ozzy also came roaring back in '88 with his latest guitar hero find, a young New Jersey hotshot by the name of Jeffrey Wielandt, soon to change his name to Zakk Wylde at the starmaking behest of Ozzy's manager and wife, Sharon Osbourne. *No Rest for the Wicked* is an album that saw Osbourne reach back into his Black Sabbath heritage to pull out a slew of dark heavy metal riffs, polished up to a pop metal sheen. At the time, Wylde's heavily '70s influenced guitar lines, pinging "pinch" harmonics, and incorporation of a plucky country influenced style of playing known as "chicken picking" were criticized in some circles as being a bit underwhelming, considering the gothic and dramatic flair of predecessors Randy Rhoads and Jake E. Lee. However, time has been kind to these recorded performances and has revealed the 19-year-old Wylde to be advanced beyond his years in terms of maturity and vision. His integrity, sticking to his guns and developing a personal style close to his own heart and influences, would ultimately serve him well. His playing on "Miracle Man," "Devil's Daughter," and "Fire in the Sky" reveal a guitarist with deep admiration for the obvious influences (his reverence for Iommi, Rhoads, and Lee are well documented) that color his playing, and the courage to incorporate less obvious choices into a hard rock idiom (you can hear the intense alternate picking and complex linear phrasing of fusion stars Al Di Meola and John McLaughlin in Wylde's highly developed right-hand articulation).

It was a wonderful second-stage coming-of-age situation for a guitar-obsessed teenager. To my ears (if not necessarily my eyes, what with every act starting to look very similar), there was a wealth of musical diversity inherent in this rock'n'roll "pop metal" subgenre. But time to move on — there are still heights to be hit, so on with the show . . . the last push of hair metal's dominance in the music industry is a big one . . .

CHAPTER 9
1989 TO 1990

My sister Pam is 13 years my senior, and by 1989 her collection of 45s and vinyl albums from the '70s were sneaking their way into my listening. I was starting to make connections between the glam rock, power pop, and pure rock'n'roll of bands like the Rolling Stones, T. Rex, Bowie, Brownsville Station, and Grand Funk Railroad in the contemporary hard rock I was listening to, and I was drawn to the sounds of these recordings. To me, they were the aural equivalent to the faux wood panelling and shag carpet in my parent's basement: warm, woody, and woolly. The guitars had less distortion, and the drums were drier and more present in the mix, which made the vocals easier to understand. Reading about the influences of my favorite guitarists of the '80s while I listened connected me to their teenage experience, thus deepening my appreciation.

Creem, Deep Purple, Led Zeppelin, and Jimi Hendrix were consistently being cited as influences on '80s rockers, so it made sense to dig in and find the roots of what I loved. I liked what I was hearing, but my ears were still not developed enough to fully appreciate the production qualities of those records. Also much like my parents' basement, it all felt and sounded somehow antiquated, rough around the edges, and prototypical. My ears had become attuned to the heavily saturated guitars, ambience-soaked drums, and multilayered vocals of '80s hard rock production, and something in my brain did not allow me to fully realize the sonic beauty and warmth of those '70s recordings.

As over the top as '80s rock music was becoming, there was still room to push the envelope, and a slew of recordings from 1989 and '90 would come to represent hair metal's defining moment in time, both commercially and sonically. With major label hard rock platters routinely selling double-platinum, record companies latched on to visual and sonic formulas that would emulate previous successes. Artists would end up sharing the same clothing designers, producers, session musicians, and supplementary songwriters to augment recordings and looks, creating a brand consistency in the genre. For every album a power ballad, to every band a lion-maned frontman and shredding guitar hero. And I bought it all, or at least what I could afford. In retrospect, it was the beginning of a sameness and interchangeability that would take root in '80s rock, making it hard for listeners outside of any given act's devoted fan base to differentiate between bands.

Fortunately, I was actually making pretty good money in high school playing in Northern Ontario bars on the weekends, supplementing that with the cash made playing guitar at masses, weddings, and even funerals, at the Pro-Cathedral of the Assumption parish. The summer of 1989 was particularly financially rewarding, as I was able to parlay my connection as a church musician into a gig working at the Catholic cemetery as a caretaker. I had read that Ozzy Osbourne had worked as an undertaker, so I felt that this would be a valuable talking point for any future interviews I would end up doing with *Circus* or *Hit Parader*.

I would sometimes play guitar at a funeral, change into my work clothes in the church basement, and then drive up to the cemetery to help with the interment . . . it was a real "soup to nuts" sendoff. Plus, I could offset any of the Catholic guilt brought about by the weekend's rock'n'roll indiscretions (I wasn't that bad, Mom, honest) by putting my developing musical skills to work in service of a higher ambition.

Martin Popoff said it best in his all-encompassing genre compendium *The Big Book of Hair Metal*: 1989 was the year that, in the wake of the massive success of Guns N' Roses, hair metal both reconnected with its '70s hard rock roots, in particular the streetwise sleaze and swagger of

Rocks-era Aerosmith, while also "trying harder" in terms of songwriting, production, and overall marketing and visual presentation. Sure, there were plenty of bands still chipping and dipping into the pools of rock'n'roll excess, but these tendencies were tempered with an adherence to a healthier lifestyle and look.

While many bands were hitting the gyms and tanning salons before they hit the clubs, they were also recognizing the opportunities that presented themselves on commercial radio stations and music video channels. These outlets were more than open to the latest offerings from hair metal bands willing to smooth the edges, or to pop stars willing to make their edges more jagged. Belinda Carlisle knew what that was worth when she incorporated an almost verbatim take on Bon Jovi's bass line pump and power chord strut in her hit "Heaven Is a Place on Earth."

Bands were often trying to give the impression of edginess while still adhering to principles of stylized refinement as they vied for the affections of the rock hungry youth gone wild. In many cases the musical results were thrilling and vibrant. Unfortunately, for every band that imbued their recordings, music videos, and live performances with genuine rock'n'roll energy and improved songcraft, there were a number of bands who fell prey to formulaic copycat syndrome, trading musical inspiration for corporate imitation.

Skid Row deftly navigated the waters of contemporary sonics and genuine rock'n'roll abandon. Their Michael Wagener–produced, self-titled debut album was the shot in the arm that propelled the final dominant charge to the top of the music industry hill for '80s hard rock. The video for their debut single, the anthemic "Youth Gone Wild," highlighted the light and darkness that was inherent in the band's sound and look, shifting back and forth between color shots of the band in high-energy performance, and black-and-white images of empowered youth rebellion. While Skid Row, genetically blessed with incredible hair and good looks across the board (especially in Canadian frontman Sebastian Bach), had clearly worked on their stagecraft and imaging, there was an element of street credibility that transcended formula. There was an authenticity in the way that Bach moved, the way the guitars hung off the shoulders of guitarists Dave "the Snake" Sabo and Scotti Hill and bassist Rachel Bolan, and how Rob Affuso attacked his drums that made it clear that *Skid Row* was born out of the band's own deep desire to create rock'n'roll, not from some record company playbook. Yes, the band had the benefit of Snake Sabo's childhood New Jersey connection to one Jon Bon Jovi, who had promised his former bandmate a hand up in the biz once he was ready. But the truth is, no one could have stopped Skid Row from making an impact once Sabo, Hill, Bolan, and Affuso hooked up the final piece of their puzzle in Bach. Image aside, Bach was in possession of one of the greatest voices to ever grace a rock'n'roll album and was blessed (or cursed) with the energy and passion of 10 men. The melodic viscera, tone, and range in Bach's vocal performances elevated a songwriting acumen largely forged by the partnership of Sabo and Bolan. In combination with the individual musicianship and obvious chemistry of the band's ensemble performance, the musical results were combustible and undeniable. The riffs, dynamics, and vocal performance on "Youth Gone Wild" mark it as the perfect choice for market introduction of Skid Row, as the individual traits of each band member stand out but never take away from the impact of the whole . . . you could feel each finger of the fist that was punching you in the face. The recording highlights the separation and stylistic distinction between the two guitar players. The parts and solos on songs like "Here I Am" and "Rattlesnake Shake" bring to mind the classic guitar duo moments found in bands like Aerosmith, Scorpions, and Judas Priest, where the individual identities complement each other for the greater good of the performance. A perfectly-tight-yet-loose feel is achieved, the guitar parts well-considered and -crafted but captured on record while the ideas were still fresh and exciting to the players. Further, "Here I Am" and "Rattlesnake Shake" have moments that feel like it could all fall apart, only to be saved by a perfectly executed pick slide or pinched harmonic yanking the guitars back into the groove of the song.

Sabo and Hill's complementary skill sets as players reveal themselves in the way that Snake's Van Halen and Michael Schenker–influenced technical abilities offset Hill's soulful, fluid and melodic playing. The trade-off guitar solo in "Youth Gone Wild" is so exciting, I couldn't decide which player I wanted to be more.

Scotti Hill: Actually, over the years, we've started to sound like each other, which is kind of interesting. But in the beginning, like especially on that first record, you can definitely hear our individual styles. Snake's influences are very metal, and the most metal my influences would go would probably be like AC/DC or Van Halen. His go much deeper . . . Metallica and stuff like that. I guess I come from a more melodic style. I grew up listening to the Beatles, and then I discovered some fusion and I became a Jeff Beck disciple. I loved guys like Steve Lukather and Neal Schon. I always wanted to play solos you could whistle. If I went in to do a ballad, I've got to play something you can whistle and maybe make a song within a song. The theory didn't always work, but that's the idea. And then Snake's more "charge into it" and aggressive. It really works well together. We would take a part in a song and say, "Okay, now we've been playing the same thing in part A; now we're coming to part B, so let's split off and do different things."

In retrospect, I can see that I've strived to incorporate a bit of both personalities into my own playing. To this day, that "Youth Gone Wild" solo sets a standard for elevation and excitement that I aspire to achieve.

Ballads like "18 and Life" and "I Remember You" were both melodic and memorable enough to secure heavy radio and video airplay, while never feeling saccharine. If anything, the latter song was a revelation of the band's ability to offer genuine emotional respite from the pedal down metallic assault of songs like "Sweet Little Sister" (with its transcendent, off-the-cuff one-take solo from Sabo), "Makin' a Mess," and the bass riff–driven punk rock energy of "Piece of Me" (complete with "Wooly Bully," '50s-style drum backbeat).

I asked Scotti Hill what references from the past helped to create the architecture of Skid Row's sound.

Scotti Hill: Well, it would be definitely two very important ingredients: there's Snake's heavy metal thing and then Rachel's punk influence, Ramones and Sex Pistols and all that. Not like deep underground punk, but it was underground in the '70s. Those two things are the two ingredients, and you've got these guys who are both really talented and you mix that up and you come up with these songs that they wrote. They wrote most of those songs, so that is a really, really key ingredient.

There are so many variables involved. You have a singer who's flamboyant and controversial and young and full of energy and excitement. Of course, you know with any band you have to deal with each other, you have to get past the alcohol and the drugs and the jealousies and the spats and the cliques and all the shit that nobody knows about. Being in a band is so hard, and you know this, but if anybody is listening, being in a band is just ridiculously hard. It's like being married to four people. I mean, being married to one person, hey, good luck . . . But being married to four? Holy shit. Really hard.

The song "18 and Life" was a bit of a cliché smasher in the hard rock world, a tragic story of gun violence that walked the line between ballad and arena rock, mirroring the emotional impact of a classic '70s Judas Priest or Scorpions epic. Its dark crystalline guitar arpeggios give way to cascading power chords, a soulful Scotti Hill guitar solo, and Bach's otherworldly vocal performance, a master class in whisper-to-scream dynamics and range.

It was hard not to be drawn in by the black-and-white album cover artwork, the band backlit against a brick wall, the tattered Skid Row logo splashed across the top in bright red. The back cover frames the band in a stylized take on the classic denim-and-leather look, but with striking differences that rang true and sympathetic with the music on the album. Bolan's nose-ring-to-earring chain, Snake's Joe Perry streaky blond highlights and Lords of the New Church shirt, Scotti's Ramones-inspired tight leather jacket — all worked in concert with their music in a way that felt comfortable, authentic, and effortless.

Scotti Hill: You look at that record and you see like a darkness . . . I mean, we called the band Skid Row and we thought it should look like skid row. We were doing so many photo shoots back when we first broke, that, after a while, we were telling the photographers, "No more brick walls, man. Please, no more alleys, no more brick walls, okay? Please." Everybody wanted to take a picture in front of a brick wall or in an alley or something like that. It's like, "Yeah, everybody's doing it." But the interesting thing is that for the debut album cover, Atlantic showed us a bunch of portfolios of photographers and they're like, "You've got to use this guy." [David Michael Kennedy] was from some town out in Arizona somewhere, he's like a cowboy dude. And they flew him to New York, and it's a big deal . . . he's got to have this and he's got to have that, and then we go down the alley and they're like, "Okay, back the car up, shine the headlights over here." And he goes *click*, and it's like, "You have it." "Really? That's it? All right. That was it." And look at the album cover. I mean, it's just us with the headlights . . . That logo was designed by Rob Affuso's ex-wife — she was a graphic artist — and before that, we had kind of a spray paint, really, really bad looking logo, and she redesigned that. She was paid for it, she was a pro. That was a cool logo, it stuck with us.

I wanted to *be* this, to *look* like this, and to *sound* like this. I believed Skid Row, and my faith in what I was hearing and what I was seeing was confirmed when I caught the band in concert in 1990, opening for Aerosmith on their Pump Tour. The thrill of Sebastian Bach's homecoming to Toronto's SkyDome was in the air that night, and the band attacked the stage with a punk rock freneticism I had never seen before. Tempos accelerated, guitars careening in and out of tune, and the towering Bach was a whirling dervish of hair, knees, and elbows. You could hardly call the performance slick and polished, but slick and polished never mattered less . . . Skid Row was transcendent that night. As Bach name-checked Toronto's streets (my current east-end hood even got a mention with the acknowledgment of "fucking Woodbine!") and tore through almost every track on their debut, I saw a more defined future for myself. Before my eyes was the physical manifestation of the perfect combination of ability and attitude, one that shaped my ideal of the perfect balance between musician and performer. For all of the groove, songcraft, and great musicianship that Aerosmith would display later in the evening, that night belonged to those punks from the gutters of New Jersey and the streets of Toronto.

> **Scotti Hill:** But you know, that's what we aim to do. We've always been a band that thrived as being the underdog and let's go beat up the headliner. Let's go make them work for their money tonight. And an interesting thing is when eventually we brought Pantera on tour, they were doing that to us. They put the fire under our ass. So that was really, that one, that was a good pair-up.

I purchased a VHS copy of the band's home video documentary, *Oh Say Can You Scream*. The video was a compilation of live performances and random footage of the band acting exactly how you'd expect young suburban punks experiencing rock stardom for the first time to act. Caught on tape is the infamous incident where Sebastian Bach, after being struck in the head with a bottle onstage in a concert in Springfield, Illinois, hurls the bottle back into the audience, and then follows up a threatening introduction to the song "Piece of Me" by jumping off the stage to take on his assailant. We are then treated to footage of the singer, sporting a bandage over the substantial head wound received from the bottle, in his tour bus as the police are waiting outside to apprehend him. What we don't see in the video is that when Bach threw the bottle back, he struck an innocent young girl in the face, fracturing her nose and skull, and then proceeded to kick another fan in the face when he jumped into the crowd, breaking his jaw. Bach was arrested, and eventually released on $10,000 bail.

For all the drama and rock star shenanigans and hijinks on the documentary, what I loved most about it was how raw and energetic the concert performances were. As I had witnessed at the SkyDome, a Skid Row concert was adrenaline on stun and meters in the red. Skid Row may have, at times, forsaken precision and tuning in the name of chasing the energy implicit in the songs, but they always managed to hit the musical marks needed to keep the train on the tracks. Of all the hard rock bands of that era, Skid Row prove themselves here to be masters of walking the line between the energy of early garage and punk rock with the power and precision of the best of early heavy metal. The best part is, it's all in the service of great songs. The band were close enough to me in age that I could see myself being a contemporary, and they would serve as an inspiration for me to find a way into a career in rock'n'roll, preferably in a city with streets that looked like the one on their album cover.

Waiting in hot anticipation for a new Mötley Crüe album was a sensation I was very familiar with at this point in my life, and 1989 was promising the best-sounding album yet from a now totally sober, lean and mean Mötley.

The Crüe had hunkered down at Little Mountain Sound in Vancouver, following the paths of both Bon Jovi and Aerosmith in seeking the biggest and best representation of their established sound. Working with Bob Rock, whose reputation was now firmly established as not only a first-class engineer but also a producer thanks to his work on Kingdom Come's successful debut, *Dr. Feelgood* tapped into a wide variety of classic rock resources, including Aerosmith, Mott the Hoople, and the Beatles, while still retaining the "gutters of Hollywood" swagger that endeared them to millions of loyal rock fans in the first place.

Bolstering their efforts were a team of accomplished Canadian session musicians and famous guest stars who helped to frame Mick Mars's inspired riffing and Vince Neil's strongest recorded vocal performance with brilliant background vocals, horn arrangements, and lush keyboards that were far more than window dressing.

Marc LaFrance: On that particular record, none of them were drinking, there were no drugs and alcohol, especially around the studio and stuff like that. When I was in the studio, which was mostly for background vocal parts, Nikki Sixx was there, and Tommy Lee and Mick Mars. A lot of times Vince might not be there, he'd do his vocals and he wouldn't be around as much, but those band members were there almost every day, and they were helping contribute. They had specific ideas of how they wanted to see things go. It was really quite an organic way that we worked, and working with

Bob Rock and them . . . I mean, if you came up with a part, they'd be open to it, so it was like a real collaborative thing. I remember it being a highly creative experience, for sure, with the Crüe guys. And it was the same with the Bon Jovi *Keep the Faith* album as well. Scorpions' *Face the Heat*, same thing, but that one was with Bruce Fairbairn. On a lot of these projects, the band members — especially the key band members — were always really involved. With the Mötley guys, Nikki Sixx knew what he wanted, but Bob Rock in a lot of those sessions was one of the key guys that I worked with. A lot of times it was just Bob and I in the studio by ourselves. If I was doing stuff around the lead vocals or whatever, I'm not there to steal the limelight from the singer, I'm there to support, so you have to be kind of a chameleon. Each voice, you have to sort of change your tone and try and sound like them. You're listening to their phrasing and stuff, so you're working around that. I mean, there was a few times where I would sing stuff and then he might copy me, but it was a lot of the times you're basically working around what's there.

John Webster: People say, "Oh, there's no keyboards on that record." I go, "Good. You didn't notice." [Laughter.] Take away keyboards on *Dr. Feelgood*, take off all the overhangs doubling up the heavy guitar riffs, and you'd know they weren't there. There was a lot of analog synth. We always added analog synth to guitars, and anything where there was a riff you could jump on. Mick Mars seemed really good. I just stuck my nose in the room ever so often, and every time I'd hear stuff, I'd go "wow." I have a feeling Bob brought a lot of that, because Bob really is the guy. He knows his shit, he knows guitars, he's got all the great instruments.

You can hear the intention of performance that Bob Rock demanded from not only the band but the ancillary musicians as well. Not a note is wasted, no part left to chance. Surely, the danger and looseness in the performances in early Mötley records offered a different kind of visceral thrill, but those albums were the works of a younger band with different ambitions and experiences. From the very first bars of the title track, the transition from rock stars to rock icons is apparent. With its relentlessly down-tuned guitar and bass chug courtesy of Mick Mars and Nikki Sixx, and Tommy Lee's sloshing hi-hat cymbal accents and massive sounding signature power grooves, the Crüe were out to make a legacy statement. Guns N' Roses may have had the more impacting album with *Appetite*, but Mötley had the more established history. With *Dr. Feelgood* the perception at the time was that they were still the kings of Hollywood, at least sonically.

The Mötley Crüe that was making *Dr. Feelgood* was an entirely different beast, one who had turned their hunger for the darker side of excessive behavior into an appetite for greater appreciation in the overarching history of rock'n'roll. Vince Neil's vocals had never sounded better or more melodically nuanced. The mixture and depth of guitar tones employed by Mick Mars blended a more organic '60s and '70s tonal approach with his signature metallic distortion to become something altogether more "classic." He also raised his game technically and brought a refinement and polish to the table that reflected his newfound sobriety. In the past, Mars has admitted to "playing through a fog," but on tracks like "Don't Go Away Mad," "Slice of Your Pie," "Without You," and "Rattlesnake Shake" (a popular title in 1989, apparently), the fog had lifted, and Mars's years of experience playing cover tunes in the '70s inform his strongest recorded performance up to that point.

You can hear the same intention and musical transformation in two of 1989's other massive, made in Vancouver rock efforts: Aerosmith's *Pump* and the Cult's *Sonic Temple*.

For Aerosmith, *Pump* was a crucial follow-up to 1987's *Permanent Vacation*, the album that actually signaled the proper comeback that was supposed to have taken place with 1985's rough and ready *Done With Mirrors*, a record that was high on vibe but ultimately low on songwriting that connected with radio. Wisely, *Pump* marries the darker side of Aerosmith's riff-rocking with the same attention to songwriting, arrangement, and collaboration that worked to such great effect on *Permanent Vacation*, and in doing so connects Aerosmith's artistically well-regarded past with their aspirations to connect with a mainstream audience.

> **John Webster:** Dude, listen to "Janie's Got a Gun." I think that was the first song I played on for those guys . . . I was working on *Feelgood*, both records were being made at the same time in the two rooms across from each other, and Steven [Tyler] came in . . . He was hanging out all the time doing background vocals [on *Dr. Feelgood*] 'cause he didn't have enough to do in his room. But he came over and said, "Can I borrow Webster?" 'Cause we'd met, but I was hoping to play on their record, I said, "Yeah, I'm done for the day." So the assistants dragged all my shit over to the other room. He's talking, he's saying, "I've got this song," and he said, "I can't get a vibe for it. I got to sing it. I got to get a vocal on this thing, [John] Kaldoner is coming up and blah blah blah blah blah." And then he plays me fucking "Janie's Got a Gun" without any keyboards on it, and I'm just sitting there going, holy fuck. I get to play on "day one" of the '90s! We just start down the road of adding [keyboards]. All that shit [happened in] just two hours. We finished it up, Steven came over and gave me a big hug and said, "Sit down, I'm gonna go sing it," and he sang it in one take, right there and then. I said, "Okay, we're not in Kansas anymore."

While the band once again worked with outside writers like Jim Vallance and Desmond Child, it was the core writing team of Steven Tyler and Joe Perry who brought the majority of the music to the table. While *Pump* continued the upward commercial trajectory for the band that had begun with *Permanent Vacation*, it more importantly showed that Aerosmith could still retain its core identity, even when enhanced by the production of Bruce Fairbairn and the usual cast of Vancouver session musicians. The interstitial instrumental compositions that lead into songs like "Janie's Got a Gun" and "The Other Side" played on sundry unique instruments from around the world, brought to the table by renowned composer and multi-instrumentalist Randy Raine-Reusch, gave *Pump* a unique and experimental Appalachian flavor. This suggested a connection to American music beyond the blues. Somehow, *Pump* established Aerosmith as both forward thinking and timelessly classic at the same time.

John Webster: You're always looking for that thing that is gonna make the record . . . Like putting an accordion on "What it Takes" . . . As I got more and more into working on [*Pump*], I realized these guys weren't scared of anything, so it just became more fun, I went well, let's pull out the goofy stuff because they're already using hurdy-gurdies and all kinds of other crap, so let's go there.

I was an Aerosmith fan before I walked in, but when I got to actually work on the records, and watch them work I just went, fuck, this is the real thing. Even with its weaknesses, and its internal politics. And they're fucking teenagers. And they still are, I have a feeling, knowing Steven. But I was never so impressed just watching and going, "Holy fuck, these guys are the real thing. Nobody's fixing this shit." . . . And yeah, Joey Kramer isn't the world's best drummer and drives Steven crazy. But when you put the world's best drummer on it, it doesn't sound like Aerosmith. It leaves all the room for the swing and the tambourines . . . Steven Tyler's an insane rhythm machine. He is just like, he picks anything up. He plays great keyboards, he's an incredible percussionist. He's got so much rhythm in what he sings that if you had, as they tried to have (initially), Steve Barone play drums on "Pink" [from 1997's *Nine Lives*], it doesn't sound very good. 'Cause there's too much swing coming from the drums. It doesn't leave any room for all the other stuff that those guys naturally put into their parts. They swing like motherfuckers. To me, that swing is the whole thing in music. It's really where the best rock music happens, it's not on a grid. And stuff moves around, and playing with feeling means very rarely would anybody quantize stuff, even when it was possible. So they still leave a lot of the feel in a lot of these parts, because that's what made it real. Sometimes I went, "You're gonna fix that, right?" And Fairbairn would look at me and go, "Fix what? You'll never hear that on the radio."

The Cult was another established band making their big stadium rock play in 1989 with *Sonic Temple*. Recorded at Little Mountain Sound with Bob Rock at the production helm, *Sonic Temple* was the Cult's attempt to connect the psychedelic melodic sensibilities of their early gothic days with the bone dry guitar crunch of 1987's *Electric*. The result was a success, with songs like "Firewoman," "Sweet Soul Sister," and "Edie (Ciao Baby)" ticking all the arena rock boxes while still retaining a credible sense of art-rock. Keyboardist John Webster and drummer Mickey Curry provide substantial support on *Sonic Temple*, making it another example of a band invoking their collective history while putting greater emphasis on sonics and anthemic songwriting. Guitarist Billy Duffy in particular really stretches his wings, upping his technical game to deliver his most polished guitar performance to date ... classic licks in the vein of Cream and AC/DC are delivered with a more fluid, saturated tone, his vibrato and note choice evoking a classicism that avoids the pyrotechnic displays of flash guitar that would come to haunt players in just a few years' time. Funny that both Mars and Duffy were considered technical "underdogs" in a sea of shred-ready guitar heroes, yet it's their recorded performances of the era that have withstood the ravages of time. All under the watch of the same producer at the same studio.

While one would be hard pressed to find a Bob Rock–produced album that didn't sound fantastic, not all of them rose to the levels of commercial success oft-associated with those hallowed halls at Little Mountain. The 1989 self-titled debut album from Blue Murder is one such example.

Blue Murder was formed around the songwriting and guitar-playing talents of former Whitesnake guitarist John Sykes, with a legendary rhythm section in former Vanilla Fudge–Rod Stewart–King Kobra–drummer Carmine Appice and Firm bassist Tony Franklin. While the band was initially slated to be a four-piece, with Black Sabbath castoff–future Badlands vocalist

Ray Gillen and numerous other hopefuls considered for lead vocals, the singing position ultimately went to Sykes himself, and the band was forged as a modern hair metal take on the classic power trio.

> **Marc LaFrance:** The *Blue Murder* record, that was one of the earlier ones that I did with Bob — and, of course, the Cult, *Sonic Temple* . . . I'm proud [of those]. When it's happening, you don't necessarily think it's that big of a deal, just because you're doing this every day. Now, I look back on a bunch of the work that I've done and . . . I feel mystified by how the hell I was able to be a part of all that stuff, but at the time, you didn't. You were working, you're sitting in the studio, waiting to do a jingle or something, and Bob Rock would walk into the studio and go, "Hey Marc, I'm doing an album next week, a band called the Cult. Can you come and do some background vocals?" I said, "Yeah, sure." And so that's kind of what it was happening there. And other days, you'd be working with Bob and you'd come and sit down and one of the guys from GGRP, "Hey Marc, we're doing a Chevy ad tomorrow, can you come and do that?" . . . they had a nice little kitchen in the back where you'd get sandwiches. So I'd sometimes just show up for a sandwich and coffee and get a gig.

Blue Murder is a thick slab of heavy riffs, epic keyboards evocative of *Physical Graffiti*–era Led Zeppelin (courtesy of Nik Green), the unique fretless bass stylings of Franklin, and the classic power drumming moves of Appice (an innovator of that sound and style). These elements are all brought to life in vivid technicolor thanks to Rock's production and Mike Fraser's panoramic mix. Heavier and bolder than both Whitesnake and Kingdom Come, and coming hot on the heels of the renewed Led Zeppelin hysteria that both of those bands helped create in the late '80s rock market, *Blue Murder* served up an intense interpolation of numerous Led Zeppelin–isms in a melodic hard rock context.

John Webster: Well, so first off, you have to know that Bob Rock is the biggest Led Zeppelin junkie you're ever gonna know. And I always start every keyboard instruction with, "What would John Paul Jones do?" So . . . yeah. From those two points of view, I'll guarantee you . . . there may have been a little bit of, "We're not gonna steer out of the skid." That [influence] was already there in their music, so why avoid it too much; let's just not directly rip-off "Kashmir." Bob and I are huge fans òf Zeppelin, so that's always where I go . . . Hammond [organs] and Mellotrons and Rhodes, and all the stuff that was on their records. People don't know there are keyboards on "Stairway to Heaven."

Blue Murder should have been a smash. And yet it wasn't. You could make a case for blaming it on the lyrics, dumber and more sex-addled than most at the time (and that's saying something). Or maybe it was the fact that audiences just weren't digging on a lead guitar–playing frontman. Yes, Cinderella's Tom Keifer fulfilled that role, but he had the virtuosic Jeff LaBar in the wings for those times he needed to pluck a delicate power ballad on the piano or grab hold of a scarf accessorized mic stand à la Steven Tyler for full frontman effect.

Closer to the truth is that Blue Murder, for all of their inherent musical talent, good looks, and production and record label resources, just did not put across the band chemistry that their more successful contemporaries at the time displayed. Did they make a special record? In retrospect, I believe they did. Listening back in 2020, the album sounds fresh and powerful, clearly evocative of the wet-and-wild sounds of the day, but delivered with fire and heavy punch. Still, there was always some burden associated with the band, the weight of a collective history that hampered any easy flow or chemistry. Perhaps the shadow of Whitesnake's self-titled 1987 record was too big for Sykes to get out from under. Or maybe the image of Appice cavorting in Rod Stewart's "Do Ya Think I'm Sexy" was still fresh in the minds of the disco despising heavy metal youth of the day. Or was it that Blue Murder did not have an obvious, knock-out radio single?

Sometimes shit just doesn't work out. It would take a few more years for Sykes to attempt a follow-up with a reconstituted lineup, but by 1994 the world (or most of it) wasn't exactly clamoring for a new Blue Murder record.

There were still plenty of bands working the more dramatic (if artistically simplified) side of Zeppelin's blend of heavy blues guitar riffs, hound dog howls, and melodramatic orchestral embellishment. John Bonham's son Jason got in on the action in a genetically authentic way with his band Bonham's Bob Ezrin–produced album *The Disregard of Timekeeping*. In the wake of the success of Kingdom Come's debut, bands like Great White, Badlands (Ozzy guitarist Jake E. Lee's excellent '70s-inspired supergroup), Tangiers, and House of Lords were making well-crafted albums, referencing elements of Zeppelin's influence that ranged from polished rootsy-ness to production-enhanced bombast. Kingdom Come themselves moved away from that sound on 1989's *In Your Face*, opting for a more direct hard rock–pop sound that highlighted the diversity of Lenny Wolf's songwriting. Unfortunately, whether intentional or not, the bad taste that was left in the mouths of press and fans alike from the band's occasional denial of Zeppelin's obvious influence on their songs and production would overshadow a very strong record. In a world where one had to wait weeks or months for information to disseminate via magazines or scheduled TV and radio interviews, a false perception could clearly linger and cause damage.

Alice Cooper was once again enjoying multiplatinum success with the *Trash* album, his take on the hair metal sounds he helped to create. Working with Desmond Child and a coterie of au courant guest stars like Slash, Joe Perry, Steven Tyler, Jon Bon Jovi, and Richie Sambora to name a few, the Coop unashamedly built upon his clean and sober late '80s reinvention by stacking the deck with big hair, big stars, and big choruses. Songs like "Poison," "House of Fire," and "Bed of Nails" sound very typical and formulaic on one hand, but they are steeped in high class musical architecture thanks to Child's careful song doctoring. More importantly, the whole album is imbued with Alice's confidence of character. You can't snow the snowman, and there is a feeling on *Trash* that Alice is completely aware that he's stealing back the clothes that were stolen from him and showing them off. Where Kiss were similarly successful on a musical front with 1989's *Hot in the Shade*, scoring a genuine pop hit with the Michael Bolton–co-penned ballad "Forever" and a video hit with "Hide Your Heart," they struggled with reclaiming their place in the hair metal jungle from a visual perspective; Alice seemed to walk right back in like he owned the place, while at the same time taking none of it too seriously. Tweaking his approach to blend in some sex with his dark theatrics, the Coop kept it fun and frothy, with custom-fitted black leather and a splash of color accompanying his trademark eyeliner.

As I was starting to set my sights on making music a career, I found myself increasingly drawn to the tunes that fell more naturally under my fingers. As much as I loved the incredible guitar playing I was hearing on White Lion's *Big Game* or Mr. Big's two-hand tapping take on classic '70s hard rock, I was really digging on the bands that, to my eyes and ears, represented a more "street" approach. In a post–Guns N' Roses world, I found myself less interested in wiggling a whammy bar or trying to impress with feats of speed and technical agility. I felt more and more connected to the nasty, raw, nitro blues–based early Aerosmith vibe that was gaining media attention thanks to the success of GNR. I still loved the flash of bands like Poison, but a leather jacket and some tight jeans seemed a bit more within my sartorial reach. More importantly, when I played along with a Guns N' Roses record, I felt like I was somehow connecting (as I did watching that Skid Row concert) to a tangible vision of my musical future. When I played a Slash lick, I could hear and feel how it connected me to a greater rock'n'roll roots foundation, something substantial that was built to last. In turn, it started to make other bands and music that I was listening to fall into a different category for me, music I loved as a listener, but did not aspire to re-create.

As much as I loved Winger and Warrant, these were not the bands whose songs I necessarily wanted to learn and play at the high school dance or the local bar. And truth be told, as a musician who has never been particularly technical-minded when it came to guitar gear and equipment, I couldn't really cop those types of sounds anyway. The same can be said for the playing. As much as both Winger and Warrant have been maligned (largely for being guilty of the crime of overexposure), their records are shining examples of high-tech hard rock production. In the case of Winger, a band comprised of legitimate virtuosi in vocalist-bassist Kip Winger (now a Grammy-nominated classical composer), Berklee College of Music–trained guitarist Reb Beach, veteran keyboardist-guitarist Paul Taylor, and fusion drummer Rod Morgenstein of the Dixie Dregs, both Winger's debut and their 1990 follow-up *In the Heart of the Young* were miles beyond what I could conceive of both technically and sonically as a player. I just had no idea how I could ever replicate the guitar, vocal, or drum sounds I was hearing in a live context.

Strangely enough, I relegated the music of Winger to music I would enjoy as a fan but wouldn't necessarily try to emulate in my own musical aspirations. When I listen back some 30 years later with more mature ears, I'm still blown away by the highly syncopated, note-dense riffs and lines, all punctuated by impeccable pop hooks. Perhaps it was just easier to write that stuff off as being "overproduced" or "too commercial," when in reality it was just too far beyond my scope as a player. Years later, I would finally be able to approximate some of those techniques and sounds with my band Trapper, a group I formed with my friend Emm Gryner, a well-respected Canadian artist and former member of David Bowie's band.

Warrant's debut was another Beau Hill–produced master class in glossy hooks and slick and polished delivery. To be fair, Warrant had a genuine ringer in session guitarist Mike Slamer to enhance the performances of guitarists Erik Turner and Joey Allen (both fine players who graciously accepted the help of a more seasoned studio musician, to their credit) and decorate songwriter Jani Lane's suburban pop metal confections. While the subject matter of Lane's lyrics is characteristic of what hair metal was offering on record in that they speak of love, lust, and the pursuit of the rock'n'roll dream, Lane manages to inject a level of vulnerability and suburban earnestness into songs like "Heaven," "Down Boys," and "32 Pennies" that aged better than the work of many of his contemporaries. I still don't know what a down boy is, but I know that Jani made me feel like I was one. Like Poison's Bret Michaels, Lane's gift as a writer was his ability to deliver garish lines that lit the fire of lust in a teenage hormonal heart while also honoring the innocence and the reality of your typical suburban teen's social standing.

Listening to Warrant felt like a celebration of the struggle between teenage desires and teenage reality. The highly choreographed stage moves in their videos and matching white leather outfits that were on offer in the videos for "Down Boys" and "Heaven," among others, were expressive and sartorial choices that helped Warrant stand out from the motorcycle jacket–wearing bad boys and the Day Glo spandex–adorned crew that were assaulting eyes (and arguably ears) at the time. It was great fun to watch Warrant strut in sync on big arena stage sets with blinding lighting productions. Cut together with images of the band dressed down and hanging casually with fans and friends alike, Warrant had a homegrown "aw shucks" vibe that offset some of the by now de rigueur cliché lyrical imagery inherent in their work . . . for every pair of street-lit silhouetted thighs, you also got a story about some dude scraping 32 pennies together in a Ragu jar to make ends meet.

Jani Lane's song made me feel that maybe there was a girl out there who might let me wrap my arms around her at night so I could feel her breathe. Beyond the well-crafted songs and polished recordings, was the aspirational feeling that I could somehow be "enough" by just being myself, a teenage suburban punk with dreams.

The infamous 1990 *Cherry Pie* is a record with an unheralded depth that has been buried by the perceived buffoonery of its title track. Lane apparently wrote "Cherry Pie" in a few hours after the powers that be at Columbia records pressured the band for a hit single. In many ways, the song represents the apex of pop metal, the moment where it reached its peak while simultaneously staring headlong into its eventual decline. "Cherry Pie" is an undeniably catchy sexist sing-along that demands frat-boy style participation. It has a wide open, stripper-approved drum groove, bone-simple guitar riffing, and a frenzied whammy bar guest solo by C.C. DeVille (apparently part of a bargaining chip in a deal that helped secure Warrant a support spot on a Poison tour).

The video for "Cherry Pie" is a super-saturated filmic feast for the eyes, hammering home the red-and-white color scheme of the album cover. It features hair metal–album cover model, video vixen, and author Bobbie Brown, Jani Lane's future and ex-wife, in various states of undress, being hosed down by the members of Warrant, who are dressed in glam rock firefighter regalia . . . I guess because she is so fucking hot. And while the song is undeniably fun despite (or more than likely because of) its insipid, juvenile sexuality, it actually takes away from the genuinely inspired songwriting on display in songs like "I Saw Red," a power ballad whose depiction of a betrayed male protagonist shows an uncharacteristic vulnerability that is mirrored in the song's musical dynamics. "Uncle Tom's Cabin" employs an abstract acoustic solo guitar intro, followed by Southern rock–inspired banjo picking that rolls into pounding heavy metal thunder for the verses, followed by an arena rock chorus that spells out a gothic tale of murder in a swamp, perhaps inspired by similar urban legends from Lane's home state of Florida. Sadly, as Jani Lane would go on to explain in a VH1 *Behind the Music* special, overzealous marketing of the album title and song would forever brand the talented songwriter as "The Cherry Pie guy." Lane tragically passed away on August 11, 2011, from complications arising from years of alcohol abuse.

I connected most strongly with particular elements of this period of hair metal, elements that informed my own desire to make rock'n'roll a career choice. These elements did not need to exist together in all of the acts I loved, but there had to be at least one present:

1. The fundamental idea of strong, pop songcraft (memorable songs).
2. The viscera of edgy, "street," Aerosmith-inspired performance and production.
3. A connection to my current reality and an aspirational suggestion that I could transcend that reality. A sense of relating to the small town–suburban teenage experience.
4. Strong instrumental chops that did not overtake the hooks or the songs.

Through Enuff Z'Nuff, a Chicago-based glam and power pop–inspired band, I was introduced to the world of power pop. On their 1989 self-titled debut, lead singer Donnie Vie, bassist Chip Z'Nuff, lead guitarist Derek Frigo, and drummer Vikki Foxx managed to pull together inspiration from the Beatles, Cheap Trick, Elvis Costello, and Big Star and supercharge it all with a Van Halen–esque virtuosity and energy that competed with the contemporary sounds of the day. Derek Frigo's note dense and fluid guitar lines may ultimately have served to attach songs like "New Thing," "She Wants More," and MTV hit "Fly High Michelle" to the hair metal era stylistically, but Enuff Z'Nuff's musical and vocal arrangements have more in common with bands like the Raspberries and Badfinger than those commonly found in the pop metal arena. Donnie and Chip's vocal blend was a wonderful marriage of raspy edge and melodic sweetness, tight and tuneful, emotionally connected in a way that evoked Lennon and McCartney or the Everly Brothers. The band adopted a pseudo-'60s look that capitalized on the twentieth anniversary of the Woodstock experience, and their use of neon colors, peace signs, and wild psychedelic effects brought a warmth and earnestness to hair metal's over-the-top exploitation of color. Chip Z'Nuff's bass lines, often performed on 8- and 12-string bass guitars, could take a deceptively simple three- or four-chord progression and refresh it with constant reinvention. Donnie Vie's rhythm guitar work was an evocative mix of Lennon and McCartney, finding sweet harmonic voicings that complemented Frigo's wildly ambitious playing. In 1989, this felt like an incredibly fresh and forward-thinking movement. The fact that it was not a multiplatinum smash was a mystery to me at the time. In retrospect, it may have been a case of a band employing too much musical content to be fully appreciated.

Chip Z'Nuff: The power pop influences that Enuff Z'Nuff carried were very diverse. A lot of our influences were from overseas, obviously the Beatles . . . you are what you eat, but we loved bands like Squeeze, we loved Led Zeppelin, they had a pop sensibility about them, very melodic band . . . loved Pink Floyd. Loved Split Enz, another great band.

So on our first record, we'd already recorded at the time about 250 songs, and then we signed our deal with Atco Records, we were discovered by Doc McGhee in Lake Geneva, Wisconsin, while Skid Row were doing their debut record, and we were were doing our first record. And [McGhee] was smart enough to know that perhaps

Derek Shulman, who used to be the singer of a band called Gentle Giant, would be interested in a pop rock band like Enuff Z'Nuff, and he sent our cassette tapes over to Derek Shulman who signed the band right away, which was incredible. Because we were, for years and years we were playing clubs in Chicago, opening for bands like Cheap Trick and BTO, Just trying to play . . . making no money whatsoever, just trying to get shows and reach an audience.

When we signed with Atco Records, our lives changed exponentially, in every single way; once we signed our deal, financially, we were good for the first time in our lives. Because we worked construction jobs, and now here we are, dressing up with our sisters' and mothers' outfits, scarves and T-shirts and bell-bottom pants. We were a colorful, very flamboyant band, and we just did that because we liked the look of it, no other reason . . . we didn't know anything about glam rock or glitter rock besides the bands we grew up listening to. Slade is another band I wanted to mention, and Sparks too. So it's just so many great bands over in the U.K. that tripped my trigger, and we loved the punk stuff . . . We love the Stranglers, we love Ultravox and the Sex Pistols. So there was a potpourri of music that we listened to at the time, but when we started making the records, we knew we had our own sound, once we went in the studio and started recording demos where I was playing drums and bass guitar and lead guitar and Donnie [Vie] was playing rhythm guitar and singing, and we had a four-track Fostex, we just recorded all the songs on that, bouncing all the tracks around, we didn't know what we were doing — we would try and navigate the best we could . . . we got lucky, we really did. We were a blessed band at the right place at the right time, and we had a different sound. In some ways it was good for us, in other ways, when I looked at the business how it is, we were a really difficult band to actually categorize because we were alternative before alternative.

A similar fate befell the mighty King's X, a band whose innovative use of drop-tuned guitars and dark yet melodic harmonic choices were a precursor to the grunge rock that would come out of Seattle at the end of the decade and the beginning of the '90s. A power trio consisting of guitarist Ty Tabor, bassist and lead singer Doug Pinnick, and drummer Jerry Gaskill, King's X came out of the Texas Christian music scene, although their lyrics delivered more subtle allusions to Christian ideals than the overt offerings of bands like Stryper. Like Enuff Z'Nuff, King's X also had a highly developed-harmony vocal approach, bolstered by Pinnick's soulful, church-inspired singing. Although only a trio, the King's X sound was thick and powerful, a combination of Tabor's unique guitar sound (the secrets of which he kept carefully guarded) and Pinnick's articulate and melodic bass lines. This was crunching hard rock, but always informed by a progressive and expansive approach that blended light and dark in a way evocative of the more progressive acts of the 1970s, while never actually sounding like them. Albums like 1988's *Out of the Silent Planet* and 1989's *Gretchen Goes to Nebraska* established a dedicated fan base and hinted at the prospect that 1990's *Faith Hope Love* would be the album that established King's X as the hard rock Beatles, the next massive band . . . and yet, it didn't happen on the scale it should have. The band had absolutely gorgeous ballads in such songs as "Summerland" and "I'll Never Get Tired of You," but I suspect they were simply too rich in musical information and lyrical depth to crack the mainstream code.

One band that did manage to crack that code was Extreme, the Boston-based hard rock band whom most know from their ubiquitous hit "More Than Words," a beautiful ballad built on a solitary acoustic guitar part and a magical two-part vocal harmony performance that, along with the band's other Top 10 Billboard hit, "Hole Hearted," is as responsible as any song for kickstarting the "unplugged" craze that would see heavy metal and hard rock bands introducing more acoustic elements into their sound.

"More Than Words" helped propel Extreme's second album, *Extreme II: Pornograffitti* to double-platinum sales in the U.S., with the song eventually topping the Billboard Hot 100 singles charts. However, ballad-driven success can be a double-edged sword, and while the acoustic elements of Extreme's sound were actually just flavors in a diverse stew of musical influences that deftly blended Queen, Aerosmith, and Van Halen with elements of funk, Sinatra-inspired crooning, and rap, "More Than Words" served to confuse many people who bought the album and were shocked at the heavy, swinging, funky rock riffs and grooves of songs like "Decadence Dance," "When I'm President," "Li'l Jack Horny," and "It('s a Monster)."

I became aware of Extreme through the proliferation of praise heaped upon the band's guitarist Nuno Bettencourt ever since the release of their 1989 self-titled debut album, a fine collection of pop-inflected metal produced by Reinhold Mack, the man who helmed Queen's funkier '80s oeuvre. Tracks like "Kid Ego," "Play With Me," "Little Girls," and "Mutha (Don't Want to Go to School Today)" showcased Extreme as a band who were not afraid to incorporate disparate influences and Bettencourt as a player with masterful command of his instrument. But for all the conviction and technical excellence on display on the debut, it was *Pornograffitti* that established Bettencourt as a dominant six-string force, one who would usher in the next decade of guitar playing in hard rock.

The pure, un-effected guitar tone and playing approach that Nuno employs on *Pornograffitti* is a marriage of the single coil–pickup clarity of early Yngwie Malmsteen and the Frankenstrat magic conjured up by Edward Van Halen on the early VH albums, all informed by the legitimate hard rock street funk of Joe Perry, the impeccable blues rock phrasing of Pat Travers (who makes a guest backing vocals appearance on turntable hit "Get the Funk Out"), and the right-hand, clean as a bell, funk wizardry of Prince. It is no exaggeration to suggest that Nuno is the most effective compartmentalizer of all of the best elements of the '70s and '80s rock guitarists that came before him. There is a deeply defined sense of swing and pocket in even his speediest of passages. From sweep picking to two-handed tapping, blazing fast alternate picking to perfectly articulated liquid left-hand legato flurries, Bettencourt somehow managed to offer it all up without wasting a single note to excess, every line serving to bolster and energize the lore of innocence lost and dystopian tales of misplaced sexual frustration that serve as the thematic fodder for a record that competes with Queensrÿche's *Operation: Mindcrime* for the title of hard rock's greatest concept album.

If Guns N' Roses' *Appetite for Destruction* served as a sonic palate cleanser from the pomp and polish of the overarching hair metal sounds that were au courant in 1987 through '88, two records served a similar function in 1990, bringing back for good the piano riddled swagger of the Faces and the strut and swagger of *Sticky Fingers* and *Exile on Main St.*–era Rolling Stones.

When the Black Crowes dropped *Shake Your Money Maker* in 1990, the first thing that caught my ears was a similarity to the sounds I loved from the 1986 debut by the Georgia Satellites . . . classic Fender and Gibson guitars pushing tube amps into overdrive, yet clear and ringing, untainted by digital effects or oversaturated distortion. The power was coming from the dynamics of the guitar players' hands, how they strummed, caressed, or dug into the strings. Formed around the songwriting talents of siblings Chris (vocals) and Rich (guitars) Robinson, the Black Crowes were a thoroughly modern take on a band out of time. Their look was a refreshing mix of the crushed velvet, tailor-cut suits, and flowing scarves of the '70s, eyeliner applied with just the right touch of junkie chic. The look and sound screamed classic rock'n'roll, even as the band were marketed alongside the glam metal of the day. But the music was something far removed. This was not a band that was trying to replicate massive arena sounds or a larger-than-life bombast, but rather an intimate, raw sound that brought the hips back to rock'n'roll. As a frontman, Chris Robinson was Steve Marriott, Rod Stewart, and Mick Jagger in a sea of David Lee Roth and Robert Plant imitators. There were elements of Plant in Robinson's vocal stylings as well, the conversational Plant who spoke of girls with flowers in their hair drinking all his wine, more so than the histrionic Plant who warned of Viking invasions or feigned orgasm in the middle of psychedelic instrumental freakouts. Robinson drew his power from soul singers like Otis Redding or Janice Joplin, his cool seemingly effortless. With his brother Rich providing the magical Keith Richards and Jimmy Page–inspired riffs and musical motifs in songs like "Jealous Again," "Twice as Hard," and "She Talks to Angels" and mixing them in with the punky rock'n'roll feel of a more musically sophisticated New York Dolls, the Black Crowes were able to not only thrive alongside the hard rock acts of the day, but also establish themselves as a musical force that would survive the inevitable changing of the guard that was to come. Classic and classy.

The Quireboys (or the London Quireboys as they were to be known in North America) were a band from England that had engaged a similar look and sound, a Dickensian take on classic U.K. pub rock. Fronted by whisky-throated belter and authentic British rock singer Jonathan "Spike" Gray, the Quireboys came close to topping the U.K. charts and made commercial inroads in North America with their debut album *A Bit of What You Fancy*. The liberally piano–laced swagger of songs like "7 O'Clock," "Hey You," and "There She Goes Again" was a refreshing lesson that simple elements played with style and soul trumped overly technical playing and glossily contrived production tricks. Another band that showed great promise, yet failed to make a commercial impact was the Dogs D'Amour, another English act. Sonically, the Dogs were even further removed from the metal and hard rock of the late '80s and early '90s than the Quireboys were, with an almost country and western aesthete applied to the strutting rock'n'roll of albums like *In the Dynamite Jet Saloon*, *Errol Flynn*, and *Straight??!!* Like his friend Spike, lead singer Tyla's vocals were drenched in raspy character, his tales of heartache and endearing alcohol-induced fuckups framed by the exquisite musical accompaniment of his bandmates, drummer Bam, guitarist Jo "Dog" Almeida, and bassist and multi-instrumentalist Steve James. Flipping through *Kerrang!* back in the day, I would read about the Dogs long before I heard them, but I immediately connected with the way Tyla could take an interview and make it read like a song . . . he made even the moderate success the band was achieving feel like some kind of romantic happenstance, a stroke of good luck that was predestined to fall apart at any moment. While the layers of eyeliner that the band wore were applied as liberally as any you might find on other bands on the Sunset Strip, the look was decidedly more pirate than pro wrestler. In the same way that the Quireboys conveyed a sense of timelessness, the Dogs seemed like a band who would somehow stick it out. And sure enough, both bands are around and playing to this day, and though the lineups may change, both are still fronted by Spike and Tyla, rock'n'roll street poets in the classic style. When my band Crash Kelly opened a U.K. tour for a freshly reformed Quireboys in 2003, I was struck by the authenticity of the band's approach to rock'n'roll as a lifestyle. It seemed like each day was lived as one graceful yet swaggering movement toward that night's concert — drinking, laughing, storytelling, but never forced.

It all seemed so natural, culminating in night after night of amazing rock'n'roll performances.

The music of the Black Crowes and the Quireboys was making its way into the set lists of the cover bands I was playing in at the time, sitting nicely in between our Rolling Stones and Poison covers. Poison was, at this point, also incorporating a slightly more organic approach with their *Flesh & Blood* album . . . even if certain stimulants seemed to be informing C.C. DeVille's lead guitar approach, which was becoming increasingly hampered by a tendency to play in a technical style that felt beyond his capabilities. Still, C.C. was delivering the riffs and memorable solos, as Bret Michaels's songwriting was maturing. For every "Unskinny Bop" and "Ride the Wind" that harkened back to glam metal glory days, there was a thoughtful ballad like "Something to Believe In" or "Life Goes On" that suggested something deeper. Poison were also adopting a scarves and bandanna look, but they still had a foot on the Sunset Strip, and their image still felt distinctly American.

Much is made of the homogenized nature of hard rock in the late '80s, but 1990 did see considerable diversity in the pool of record releases. Bands like Sea Hags, Salty Dog, Faster Pussycat, Jetboy, and Kill For Thrills were stripping the hair metal artifice off of their productions, introducing a sleazier, stylized biker element to their records and clothing, and in the process often sounding and looking more like old Aerosmith than the new Aerosmith did at that time. Ushered in on the tails of the Guns N' Roses revolution, these bands offered hard rock fans a street leaning alternative to the more accessible offerings of bands like Winger, Warrant, and Nelson. Unlike the line that would be drawn in just a few years' time with the grunge revolution, there didn't seem to be a need for audiences to choose between more commercially accessible hard rock and this dirtier, grittier throwback stuff . . . it all just kinda coexisted as a wonderful smorgasbord that fell under the protective glass barrier of "hard rock," the shared ideals being long hair, distorted guitars, and shared space in rock magazines and on MTV.

Gilby Clarke: I left Candy because I wanted to go more rock . . . it was just too pop, and it wasn't working at that point. So I started Kill For Thrills. When I started Kill For Thrills, I had no intention of singing, I was going to be the guitar player. We were a three-piece. It was a drummer and bass player from a different local band, and they were called Damn Yankees, and we were getting together, writing songs. Then we said, "What are we going to do about a singer?" And so the drummer goes, "Well, you know, why don't you just sing and let's get another guitar player?" So I said, "Okay, let's try that." And that's how that evolved. At that time bands like Warrant were coming up at the Country Club, and the Strip became "pay to play" — you'd have your headliner, then all the other bands would pay to play. The Strip and that metal scene really kind of got softened up, you know? Even Guns N' Roses and Faster Pussycat were making their marks, they were already national touring acts or just about to be, and so there was a different scene. Scream, Cathouse, English Acid, these were smaller clubs. Riki Rachtman had Cathouse, and Kill For Thrills was more that direction. Did we play the Country Club and Whisky? Yeah, we did, but it wasn't our scene. We were more of that underground scene that had Jane's Addiction. We played with Jane's Addiction at the Scream.

The Kill For Thrills thing was so fucked up. We got our major label record deal at our very first show we played. We opened for a band called Cathouse at the Whisky, and they were doing their industry showcase, they were playing for all the labels. They were popular, they were the headliner. We opened for them, and after we got off the stage — and by the way, we only had six songs — we had other labels in our dressing room. Seriously, I'm not exaggerating. "Oh, we need to talk. We need to talk. Who's your lawyer and blah, blah, blah." And literally got our major label record deal with six songs. I didn't even have 10 songs for the record yet.

Cinderella went further into their blues and classic rock roots with the excellent *Heartbreak Station*, an album that featured all manner of acoustic string instruments, Hammond organ, piano, horns . . . even a mouth harp on the hit single "Shelter Me." String arrangements throughout the album, most notably on the beautiful title track, were provided by Led Zeppelin bassist and multi-instrumentalist John Paul Jones, further connecting Cinderella to the '60s and '70s–era of classic rock. Really, the only thing that connected them to heavy metal or hard rock at this point were Tom Kiefer's AC/DC-inflected vocals. All manner of glam metal excess had long since been left in the past, and one would be hard pressed to find much (if any) finger tapping, sweep picking, or whammy bar dive-bombing at any point in their career. Tesla also continued their breakaway from the glam metal pack with *Five Man Acoustical Jam*, an album of live acoustic versions of lovingly curated classic rock covers and suitable songs from Tesla's own catalog. The album was recorded at the Trocadero Theatre in Philadelphia on a short run of shows that were booked to fill in off-dates on the band's support slot on Mötley Crüe's Dr. Feelgood tour. Even more literally than Cinderella, Tesla connected to '60s and '70s classic rock through faithful renditions of songs by the Beatles ("We Can Work It Out"), the Rolling Stones ("Mother's Little Helper"), and a cover of "Signs" by Canadian group Five Man Electrical Band that yielded a surprise Top 10 Billboard Hot 100 radio hit. The album also effectively showed the strength in Tesla's own songwriting, with the stripped-down versions of songs like "Love Song," "The Way It Is," "Gettin' Better," and "Paradise" taking on a new intimacy that connected with an audience that was getting used to all this pickin' and grinnin'.

Progressive-inclined hard rockers Queensrÿche had hit concept album paydirt with 1988's *Operation: Mindcrime*, but it was a delicately plucked acoustic guitar figure reminiscent of David Gilmour's work on Pink Floyd tracks like "Wish You Were Here" and "Goodbye Blue Sky" that drove the biggest hit on 1990's *Empire*. "Silent Lucidity" became a Top 10 Hot 100 single for the band and married elements of the glam metal power ballad to the more exploratory leanings found in Bob Ezrin's production work on *The Wall*. Queensrÿche had already demonstrated an ability to meld high caliber musicianship with concise songwriting, and *Empire* was a considerable evolution of the latter that did not come at the expense of a dumbing down of the former. Songs like the ominously plodding title track "Jet City Woman," "Another Rainy Night," and "Best I Can" all impacted at rock radio and music television, helping Queensrÿche achieve triple-platinum status for sales over three million copies in the U.S. alone. *Empire* was a record for audiences looking for progressive rock with a heart and melodic hard rock with a brain.

Other interesting fusions were happening in this two-year span as well . . . the Southern fried Texas boogie of Dangerous Toys brought together the machine gun tongue of former Watchtower vocalist Jason McMaster with a sound that could swing like a Texas playboy and rock harder than any of the GNR wannabes the Sunset Strip was producing. Yup, McMaster shared similarities to Axl Rose in terms of range, timbre, and phrasing. They even shared certain physical attributes: the long, wispy red hair; lithe build; and serpentine gesticulations.

But McMaster was no copycat, and Dangerous Toys' debut was informed by the legitimate blues of their Texas environment while still bringing a metallic classicism that evoked vintage Alice Cooper (topically, at least . . . the music has more in common with Jake E. Lee–era Ozzy) on "Scared," the homage to the man himself, and the accessible side of classic Judas Priest with "Queen of the Nile." The stop-and-go, turn-on-a-dime grind of first single "Teas'n Pleas'n" is perhaps the best example of guitarist Scott Dalhover's approach, his tone as dry as a rib bone with the meat and sauce sucked off it. Where the faint-of-heart guitarist might shy away from some of the burning licks and fast riffs that are all over this blinder of an album, Dalhover plays with the precision of a metal maven and the tonal authority of a Texas tonemeister. In short, he is a brave guitar player.

Jason McMaster: That's a huge compliment, and you know what? You're exactly right. It's something that I feel like I, as a member of, you know, standing right next to Scott all these years, that I take for granted — that he likes effects, but he's not overly using them. As a matter of fact, when he turns on a flange or Phase 90 or . . . something that's making it move around a little bit, it's usually on a clean tone. And you can hear that on the first record, the second record. When there's a clean tone, he's got some kind of help, you know, he's got waves going on, and I love that. Who doesn't?

The thing, to backpedal to what you were saying — yeah, it is brave guitar playing . . . Scott as a player constantly learning about the craft, constantly learning that less can be more. Constantly learning that really coming straight, maybe in the studio coming straight, as clear from the guitar to the amps as much as you can stand — because everybody likes toys, you know — is important. . . . If there's too much shit in between, you're not a brave guitar player at all.

Throughout the record we get authentically reverential nods to the first three Van Halen albums, early '80s Scorpions and Priest, and dollops of up-tempo Bon Scott–era AC/DC. Combined with great songs, a unique and almost quirky lyrical take, and meaty production courtesy of Max Norman, the *Dangerous Toys* debut is a must-have album from the era that has lost none of its edge over the years.

Jason McMaster: The first Toys album was recorded with Max Norman. There was a part in "Teas'n Pleas'n" on the demo that was just full [bonsai], and to recreate — it was a vocal part — to recreate that in the studio was a bit of a bear because we kept listening to it, going, "The demo's better. The demo's . . . We've got to beat the demo. We can't beat the demo. What are we going to do?" And I suggested to Max, I was going, "Let me cut this track . . . with an SM58, and let me hold it in my hand like I do live."

And he was like, "You're out of your mind. I'm not letting you do that." So we went around and around and around, maybe a couple of days, and he finally let me do it, and he had the tech, and he didn't tell me that the second engineer was going to come in with a roll of duct tape and tape the cable to my arm and my body because he was so worried about there being any kind of rattle or noise. And I'm like, "Fuck that! Rock and roll is rattle and noise." You know, in my head, I'm going, "Okay, whatever, you're the boss. You're going to make more money off this record than I ever will anyway, with all the points we're giving you." You know? And it was well worth it, of course. But the point is, is that song I cut with a 58 . . . He knew I was right that we weren't getting the magic, and we had to . . . try to recreate what the hell it is that I do, or I did. So I said, "Let me try this."

Even though when we got the demo, I didn't have a 58 in my hand. You know, it wasn't the same exact thing, but in order to do that, I was like, "Let me perfect it and do what I do live." And yeah, it's a mental thing. Let me throw shapes when I do this. Let me do my shuck and jive in order to get the track to be correct. And note it's the only track on the record that I recorded with a handheld microphone, but it's also the biggest song.

Charlotte, North Carolina's FireHouse issued a self-titled debut album in 1990 that could be the best example of sonic clarity, punch, and separation in the whole genre. When a FireHouse song would come on the radio, David Prater's production work made it feel like each instrument was laid out on a table, buffet style . . . separated delicacies that I could clearly hear and taste in their individual states.

"Don't Treat Me Bad" takes two or three Bachman–Turner Overdrive songs and applies a glossy glam metal treatment, made all the more enjoyable with those happily strummed acoustic guitars that were now ubiquitous on hard rock albums with commercial ambitions. Big rock anthems like "Rock on the Radio," "All She Wrote," and the now mandatory power ballad "Love of a Lifetime" would become everything that the music industry and, ultimately, audiences would rail against in just two short years (at least in North America . . . FireHouse would continue to find success in Japan, as would many other bands from the era). Polished-to-perfection songs about rocking out and bad boys and girls shaking and tumbling in the sheets may have been as cliché as they come, but the album stands apart thanks to the strength of the individual performances. Singer C.J. Snare was delivering vocals that had the rasp and attitudinal character of hard rock but still sat beautifully in tune upon the puffy clouds of expertly arranged vocal harmonies found throughout the album. In a world before Auto-Tune, his ability to maintain integrity of tone and intonation in the upper reaches of his vocal range ranks alongside Brad Delp's performances on the first Boston record as the high-water mark of what a human voice can do.

Guitarist Bill Leverty has all the tricks in the post–Van Halen guitar arsenal at his fingertips, and he employs them to great effect on *FireHouse*. The difference here is that Leverty has the taste and arrangement sense of a man raised on classic '70s rock, and any flash in his playing serves as an energy elevator that works in deference to the songs, rather than a showcase for noodling. Certainly, this album is built upon a foundation of Def Leppard and Bon Jovi, with a thick coat of production sheen, but in this case there is a pretty moist and delicious song cake under the icing.

If FireHouse represented the state-of-the-art example of everything that commercial hard rock had been up to that point, bands like Mother Love Bone, Electric Boys, Love/Hate, Pantera, Jane's Addiction, and Alice in Chains were bubbling under and suggesting a new direction, a way forward. Two of these bands would be swept away by the waves of the massive change that would befall rock'n'roll in the '90s, three would go on to become part of rock's next revolution, and in the case of Mother Love Bone, their dissolution would result in the formation of one of the most enduring and successful groups of all time.

You can hear the band that would ultimately become Pearl Jam in Mother Love Bone's 1989 EP *Shine*. Formed in Seattle out of the ashes of punk and proto grunge bands like Green River and Ten Minute Warning, Mother Love Bone was made up of future Pearl Jam members Jeff Ament and Stone Gossard on bass and guitar, respectively, along with guitarist Bruce Fairweather, drummer Greg Gilmore, and lead singer Andrew Wood. With a sound that harkened back to the riff rock of the 1970s, Mother Love Bone's connection to '80s hard rock lay mostly in the flamboyance of frontman Wood, a man who made no bones about his ambitions to be a "rock star." However, Wood's ambitions seemed to be tied to a different ideal of what constitutes a rock star, and his evocations of the spirit of Freddie Mercury, David Bowie, and Marc Bolan separated him from singers who modeled their presentation and performance on Vince Neil, David Coverdale, Bret Michaels, or some combination thereof. In songs like "This Is Shangrila," "Stardog Champion," and "Holy Roller," Wood's lyrics talk about sex, drugs, and fame in far more empathetic and spiritually aspirational tones than one finds on a Poison or Mötley Crüe album. It's not the all-conquering alpha male, more the messianic figure who transcends his human frailty, pain, and vulnerability through re-creation on the stage.

The guitar riffs and production on *Shine* and their 1990 full-length debut *Apple* had more in common with Kiss and Black Sabbath than they did with Van Halen, another marked difference. Sadly, Wood overdosed on heroin just days before *Apple* was slated for release, bringing an end to the band.

Gilby Clarke talks about the tour with Mother Love Bone that never was, and one can't help but wonder if an alternate course for guitar-based rock'n'roll in the '90s could have been charted had Wood and Mother Love Bone survived.

Gilby Clarke: That's how crazy it was. Now they probably saw us as, like you said, hair metal. That term wasn't used at that point but they were capturing that era, and it's like, "Here's a new, fresh band that nobody's ever heard about. They look good and all that . . ." But if you even look at pictures of Kill For Thrills, we didn't look like Poison and Warrant. We didn't — we had almost like a grungier kind of look. But we got a record deal. We made our record, and then we knew that our record wasn't coming out for a year, and we didn't know what to do during that time, but . . . *RIP Magazine* was huge at that time, and they had a tour booked that was Kill For Thrills, Circus of Power, and Mother Love Bone.

So what we used to do was . . . there were some really good bands coming out of New York. So when they came to L.A., they had no following, and vice versa. When we went to New York, we had no following, so with Circus of Power, they would open for Kill For Thrills in L.A., and then we would go to New York and would open for Circus of Power, and we had this little world together. When *RIP* did the thing, we were set. We had a major label record, we had a world tour presented by *RIP* and then the singer of Mother Love Bone died a week before the tour went out. And just killed it. Tried replacing the band, but the tour never ended up going, it just killed the momentum.

But the reason I'm bringing this up is this shows you what Kill For Thrills was. We weren't the band to play with all those, like you said, the Warrants and all those bands at that time. We were the band to play with Mother Love Bone, and basically what music was changing into. Like our drummer was very anti-glam, he hated that stuff. Honestly, I didn't really care. I liked Guns N' Roses, I liked Faster Pussycat, I liked L.A. Guns. I liked those bands, I didn't really like some of the other bands that came up at that time. But we were kind of anti-that a little bit, you know? We did wear cowboy boots, but we did it a little bit differently. We were already wearing [flannel]. Which became the grunge thing. Like I said, we were already doing that kind of stuff. But once again, we weren't trying to be grunge. I saw Alice in Chains . . . Kill For Thrills played [Cathouse] and the next week Alice in Chains played. And I saw them, and I never thought they were any different from what our scene was. Like I didn't think grunge or anything, I just thought they were a new rock band that just weren't wearing glam clothes, you know?

With a tribute album by the same name, Temple of the Dog supergroup featured members of Mother Love Bone, Ament and Gossard, along with Soundgarden's Chris Cornell and Matt Cameron, and Eddie Vedder and Mike McCready, who would soon join together with Ament and Gossard in Pearl Jam. Soundgarden had already been making waves and drawing major label attention as early as 1988, and 1989's *Louder Than Love* on A&M Records was an underground favorite. As much as people point to Nirvana's *Nevermind* as the album that killed off the '80s hair metal scene, the roots of a darker, "alternative" form of heavy guitar–based hard rock was already well on its way to mainstream acceptance. *Louder Than Love* and *Temple of the Dog* marked two albums of the genre that would become known as grunge's earliest commercial strikes. Major record labels were looking for the next sound and found it in the oft gloomy and rainy environs of Seattle, Washington, where bands like Soundgarden, Nirvana, and Mudhoney were impacting and coalescing on indie label Sub Pop.

Alice in Chains, taking their name from lead singer Layne Staley's former band Alice N' Chains, were born of glam but ultimately found their success as part of the newly anointed grunge movement. I clearly remember hearing 1990's *Facelift* album, and seeing videos for hits like "We Die Young" and "Man in the Box" and noticing the heavier, darker, down-tuned guitars and lower-range vocals. Still, Alice in Chains retained a connection to the slick sonics of glam metal production, and *Facelift* felt very much like a forward-thinking extension of what bands like Mötley Crüe and King's X were doing on their records, at least sonically. But as with Soundgarden, there was something more ominous in the lyrical content, something that wasn't necessarily sinister, but serious. But when I watched videos for songs like Soundgarden's "Hands All Over" and Alice in Chain's "We Die Young," I still saw long-haired dudes in some combination of the traditional lead singer with guitars and bass and drums format that I had been accustomed to. Alice in Chains probably had the biggest connection to hard rock bands from Hollywood, largely due to guitarist Jerry Cantrell's guitar playing. As opposed to Soundgarden's Kim Thayil, or Mother Love Bone's Gossard, Cantrell's tone was more saturated, his riffs more metallic in the '80s sense. His fingers and facility betrayed a more than cursory knowledge of the licks and riffs of Eddie Van Halen, Randy Rhoads, Warren DeMartini, and George Lynch. But he was also employing a restraint that suggested knowledge of '70s players like Tony Iommi, Jimmy Page, and Ace Frehley . . . shorter and more succinct lines that would come to serve him well in a few years' time, when highly technical guitar solos became less integral to hard rock productions.

Another band who fully embraced a glam metal look and traditional heavy metal sound in their early days, but ultimately transformed into something harder, was Arlington, Texas, groove metal combo Pantera. Consisting of brothers Dimebag (formerly "Diamond") Darrell and Vinnie Paul Abbot, bassist Rex Brown, and vocalist Phil Anselmo, Pantera's 1990 major label debut (the band had issued four independent albums from 1983 to 1988), was a massive evolutionary step for heavy metal music, and a case could be made for Pantera being the one band that managed to forge a completely new path for heavy guitar–based rock while remaining loyal to the ideas of the '80s rock that came before it, namely highly technical guitar solos and wildly excessive behavior. Producer Terry Date played a big part in Pantera's transformation, bringing the aesthetics of acts he had worked with before, namely Soundgarden (modern alternative metal), Metal Church (traditional melodic heavy metal), and Overkill (American power metal influenced by skate punk and thrash metal) to Pantera's inherent Texas power groove. Like Dangerous Toys, Pantera swing just as hard as they stomp. Phil Anselmo also brought a hardcore look and vocal approach to *Cowboys From Hell*, and that influence is seen and felt in the crowd-surfing and moshing that takes place in the video for the riff-heavy title track. All this aggro is offset by Dimebag Darrell's virtuosic playing, unashamedly revealing the influence of Van Halen, Rhoads, and all who came in their wake, but also informed by that very specific blues inflection that is unique to Texans. In a way, the actual sound is not that far removed technically from *FireHouse* . . . clean, heavily compressed, with tons of separation between the instruments. The difference comes in the violence and rhythmic complexity in the instrumental performances, the aggression of the lyrical content, and the guttural nature of Anselmo's vocal performance; the influence of Rob Halford and Bruce Dickinson, however, is also present in his more melodic moments, "Cemetery Gates" being one example — a song some might label a power ballad but would be more apt in calling it a power *metal* ballad.

Another glam metal–adjacent band was L.A.'s Jane's Addiction, a strange mash-up of Valley kid metalheads and gothic art-rock weirdos. Fronted by lead vocalist and future Lollapalooza festival main man Perry Farrell, Jane's managed to create a unique blend of alternative rock that smeared the psychedelic-cum-metallic guitars of Dave Navarro like paint all over the exploratory '70s rock canvas laid down by drummer Stephen Perkins and bassist Eric Avery.

Farrell's nasally strained major key vocal melodies and scattershot harmonies sat atop the band's dangerous concoction, and it sounded like what I imagined drugs felt like (later experimentation confirmed this to be fairly accurate). As with Soundgarden and Alice in Chains, the lyrics on 1988's *Nothing's Shocking*, the band's major label debut for Warner Brothers, and 1990's commercial breakthrough *Ritual de lo Habitual*, were as far removed from *Cherry Pie* as you could get . . . sex and drugs took on a darkly spiritual aspect, seemingly connected to real people with real feelings as opposed to disposable playthings, especially in the depictions of women. Where glam metal always seemed designed to be an escape from the pain and reality of modern existence, this new alternative form of guitar-based hard rock often dove headfirst into the struggle, and in doing so connected with the reality of what youth were feeling. Where Warrant and Winger offered aspiration and escape, this new school was bridging the gap between the lyrical weight and socially inclusive worldviews of bands like R.E.M., the Cure, and the Smiths and the highly developed, classic rock informed musical chops of glam metal (albeit with emphasis on the riffs and the rhythm section inter-action, and more judicious editing in the lead guitar playing).

It seems almost inconceivably naive to look back on this in light of the music these bands were making and how history would eventually come to see them, but at the time I didn't really see a huge gap between any of them. If anything, I only saw the connections . . . I was excited to see where bands like Skid Row and Guns N' Roses would go in light of the changes that were happening in music. As I prepared for my own journey to cast aside the Top 40 cover circuit and move to Toronto to throw my hat into the ring of the "original music" scene, I didn't foresee the massive changes that would shake my faith in the musical foundations on which I'd built my life. Now, the changing of the guard wasn't quite as cut-and-dried as history has made it out to be, and there was still plenty of vitality and creativity left in commercial hard rock . . . but like any good party, there comes a time where everyone gets kicked out and the cleanup begins.

CHAPTER 10
1991 TO ????

**"I'VE WORKED TOO HARD FOR MY ILLUSIONS
JUST TO THROW THEM ALL AWAY . . . "**

It really did feel wonderful: being a fan of hard rock and heavy metal in the early nineties. The style was ubiquitous, and you could hear the influence of crunching power chords and shredding solos on albums from a wide range of artists: Cher, Richard Marx, Belinda Carlisle, and Janet Jackson, to name a few. It felt like bands were seizing their moment at the top of the heap to create the best sounding albums of their careers. When I listen to these recordings, I feel . . . comfort. It's like a warm bath, bringing me back to a time where my world was a perfect combination of future opportunity, the imagined freedom of looming adulthood, familial support, and the security of thinking that I had this rock'n'roll thing figured out. In the grooves of those records I hear a similar comfort and confidence from the artists. It's the sound of musicians and producers who had found the key to delivering high-fidelity emotional content via a magical blend of melody, harmony, expansive instrumental technique . . . but still without much variation on the lyrical themes. The street-wise impact of Guns N' Roses and the surging mainstream popularity of bands like Metallica had toughened up the look and sonics a bit, but there was still plenty of long-haired, choreographed, formulated pop metal pouring out of the mainstream music business. There was a reassuring, personal expectation that I was going to like almost everything that was being released. Van Halen's *For Unlawful Carnal Knowledge*, Ozzy Osbourne's *No More Tears*, and Metallica's "Black album" saw these iconic artists retain their core identity while refining and delivering music that displayed many of the sonic traits of the hit "hair metal" that had come a few years earlier, with a focus on efficient and concise songwriting that maintained the integrity that made these artists great. Somehow, these recordings sounded almost as warm and powerful on a radio as they did blaring out of a CD player, a testament to the trial and error of talented engineers and producers who were fully embracing and marrying the technology of the past and present. Frank Gryner is my bandmate in the band Trapper. He is also a successful producer and engineer who has worked with Rob Zombie, A Perfect Circle, Tommy Lee, and many others. He suggests that the early '90s were also a time when the artists themselves were becoming more aware of studio techniques, and elaborated on how that environment could function as an extension of the art.

> **Frank Gryner:** I think a lot of the bands in the '80s were really oblivious to the recording process. They went to the studio, they knew about playing music, they knew about getting on the stage and doing their thing, [but in] the studio they had to trust all these technical people, producers and engineers especially, to get that kind of sound, and a lot of times they weren't really actively involved. The first few times they went into the studio with a big producer, they just did what they were told. Some of those guys really adapted well to that process and embraced it, and by the time the late '80s, early '90s came along, they were taking into account what could be done in the studio as part of the art form. You see this with guys like Nuno Bettencourt who really embraced the art of recording.

Some of my all-time favorite albums came out of the pool of early '90s releases. Melodic rock manifestos like Mr. Big's *Lean into It* and Enuff Z'Nuff's *Strength* are pristine examples of masterful power pop dressed up in hard rock regalia, all soaring and soulful vocals, guitars that ring and jangle as much as they shred, with more than their fair share of dynamics and balladry. Mr. Big found the top of the Billboard singles chart in 1992 with their ubiquitous acoustic ballad "To Be with You," and won over music video audiences with the dreamy clips that accompanied the swirling psychedelic pop of "Green Tinted Sixties Mind" and "Just Take My Heart." Enuff Z'Nuff artistically topped the pop metal mastery of their debut with 1991's *Strength*, an album that delivered even more of everything that had hooked me with the debut. Yet, where Mr. Big rose to platinum success, *Strength* failed to make a commercial impact. Perhaps there was just *too much* of a good thing to focus on. It is a record that overflows with highly developed melodic orchestral and production ideals, maybe to the point that with so much Beatles, Cheap Trick, Big Star, Van Halen, and Elvis Costello influence inherent in the compositions, audiences had a hard time finding enough *Enuff Z'Nuff* to latch on to.

But 1991 was a time of commercial hard rock for the masses, a safe space for housewives and leather-jacketed hoodlums alike. And for every iconic artist who had already established themselves, there were a slew of up-and-comers who were being afforded huge record company budgets to make their own lavish productions. For every Alice Cooper or David Lee Roth album that adopted the sonic tricks of the bands and producers they themselves had once influenced, there was a Kik Tracee, Bang Tango, Danger Danger, Tora Tora, or Tuff taking their well-earned shot and, for the most part, delivering really solid albums that ticked all the expected boxes. The influx and saturation in the marketplace was so strong it felt like long-term commercial dominance was guaranteed. But as history always has shown, change was inevitable.

It wasn't a change I particularly welcomed at the time, but I believe I get it now.

I've recently become enamored with the music of the Replacements. This is a band I have not given much thought to in my life, and they certainly wouldn't have been on my radar during their heyday. My ears, mind, heart, and ambitions just wouldn't have jibed with the rawness of what the Replacements had to offer. However, as I enter my 50s, I find myself craving the immediacy of live, imperfect performances. I haven't abandoned my love for a carefully thought out, perfectly executed recording or performance, but the feeling of a band playing beyond their technical abilities in the pursuit of some higher artistic ambition seems to fuel a different part of me, one that maybe I never felt I was allowed to love or acknowledge as a "trained" musician. Perhaps it's a club that I felt I wouldn't or couldn't have been accepted into as a card-carrying fan of commercial hard rock and heavy metal.

Anyway, on the very day I began writing this last chapter, I went to a record store and found a copy of the Replacements' 1984 album *Let It Be* (yeah, the one with the cover of Kiss's "Black Diamond" . . . sloppy and out of tune, but performed with a non-ironic reverence that transcends musical limitations).

On my way out of the shop, I stopped and picked up a slice of pizza, something I would do in my record store hunting days of yore. As I jumped in my car, I threw the steaming slice on the passenger seat and impatiently cued up *Let It Be* on Spotify, fearing that a full-blast review of the album on vinyl would be scuppered by various home life interruptions. As the music blared out of my Honda CR-V's speakers, I took one look at the pizza and tore into it, a mess of cheese and sauce and toppings spilling out onto the leather seats, greasy and way too hot. One hand on the slice, the other hand on the steering wheel, trying to avoid collision with Danforth Avenue's hipster cyclists and oncoming traffic. It was an impulsive, dangerous, and sloppy move, but the combination of that music and that pizza burning my mouth was magical.

The so-called hair metal of the '80s has brought immeasurable joy and growth to my life, but by 1991, maybe the pizza was starting to get a bit cold. It still tasted great, but in some cases, a formulaic sameness had set in . . . we were being force fed the fare of franchise chains when the world was ready for a slice from a kick-ass mom-and-pop shop in Little Italy. An overabundance of power ballads, tried-and-true visual pastiche, and reliance on songwriting and production clichés had oversaturated a market whose prime demographic was growing older and growing up. What had once seemed relatable and rebellious now had a whiff of corporate interference about it . . . a creepiness that comes with the realization that someone old enough to be your dad was trying to sell you on sex, drugs, and rock'n'roll.

John Webster: There was an era there, where it was Mickey Curry and Keith Scott, myself and Huey [McDonald] playing bass where we did a lot of sessions together. If it was a Desmond Child song, they would have charts or whatever, but we'd just say "Where is the modulation, before the solo or after the solo?" That was the only question, 'cause we knew exactly what was coming at us. Yeah, and there [were] usually some clever moves in it, but it just was I, vi, IV, and V [chord progression], pick your order.

A great song is still a great song, and with the passing of time, production indulgences and songwriting clichés are forgiven and even embraced as the cream rises to the top in our collective acceptance of the music of the past. But in that moment, so much of what was coming at us started to feel like a case of commerce over art. It all got a bit . . . professional.

The last recorded collection of consequence from a band weaned on the strippers and hairspray of the Sunset Strip were the twin Guns N' Roses LPs, *Use Your Illusion I* and *II*. Released as separate albums on September 17, 1991, both featured two new members, keyboardist Dizzy Reed and drummer Matt Sorum.

Sorum's pounding and powerful drumming signaled a distinct change in feel and attack, resulting in a far more "locked in" performance. It could be argued that the power inherent in Sorum's approach was perfect for a band trying to retain its relevance in a new era, especially after releasing one of the biggest selling debut albums of all time, with *Appetite for Destruction*. Still, for all of the technical prowess that Sorum brought to GNR, something had elementally changed in the band, a feeling of *swing*, and an alteration to the combustible chemistry that Steven Adler (who had been fired from the band for excessive drug use) had once brought.

Alan Niven: Steven's brilliance was he's not a good drummer. But my God, he had . . . *ebullience* is the word that I use with him. He loved what he was doing and who he was doing it with, and that came through in his feel, and he could swing. Every drummer since him has had hands of concrete. They just pound . . . Steven had enthusiasm.

The sprawling effort of the combined *Use Your Illusion* albums were a lot to take in, but as a member of the audience starving to hear anything new from this band, it was a welcome deluge of punk rock ranting, orchestral balladry overload, and Slash licks on stun. Izzy Stradlin and Duff McKagan took turns on vocals on a few cuts, and Axl Rose's unhinged ravings at everyone and anything he felt had wronged him during the band's tumultuous ascent in the late '80s felt like a raw and personal insight. When I finally did see the band live for the first time in 1991 at the CNE Stadium in Toronto, they came onstage very late, but ultimately stayed to deliver a marathon set of music that felt immediate and dangerous, despite the addition of ancillary backup singers, horns, and two keyboard players.

On that tour, the support act was Skid Row, whose new album *Slave to the Grind* had come out on June 11, 1991, and debuted at the number one spot on the Billboard charts. Having upgraded the nosebleed tickets I had via a scalper, I ended up with great seats just a few rows from the front. I noticed I was sitting beside a bearded gentleman with a laminated pass that said Bierk on it. The man was accompanied by a lovely elderly lady. Having clocked that Sebastian Bach was the stage name for lead vocalist Sebastian Bierk, I put two and two together to glean that this was in fact his father, famed artist David Bierk, the man who had painted the artwork used on Skid Row's new album. After I awkwardly introduced myself, the gracious Mr. Bierk introduced me to Sebastian's grandmother, and it felt very special to share in the obvious pride the two felt at watching their son and grandchild absolutely own his adopted hometown audience that afternoon.

Slave to the Grind was a spitting, scratching beast of a heavy metal record. With Michael Wagener once again at the production helm, the band opted to go in an even heavier and more aggressive direction, making a record that was more aligned with the viciousness of the live show I had witnessed a few years earlier and the lifestyle that was celebrated in the wake of their first years of touring, and risking alienating the mainstream fans who'd fallen in love with the softer side of songs like "I Remember You." When I spoke with guitarist Scotti Hill, I told him that even the ballads on

Slave to the Grind burned with a lyrical and musical intensity that far surpassed anything on the excellent debut.

> **Scotti Hill:** Well, you know, that means a lot because that's how I wanted it to be. I was playing for other guitar players. I wanted somebody to feel the way Neal Schon makes me feel, you know? When we left for that first tour after our first record, we were "this guy," and when we got home 16 months later, we were "these guys." We were different. Our tastes in music were different. We had experienced a lot of things. We had a little more pull and a little more power to do kind of what we wanted to do. And everybody's like going, "Oh, what are they going to do next? What are they going to do next? Sophomore jinx." You know what? . . . . Fuck how deep the water is; jump in. Let's just jump in. Let's make a record that sounds like the music we listened to on the bus all night long. We're fucking cranking it all night. Let's make that record.

And what was spinning on that Bach-analian bus that could have fueled such an intensely heavy album?

> **Scotti Hill:** It was everything. It was all that stuff. It was Priest. It was Motörhead. It was fucking Cro-Mags. It was fucking punk rock. It was Metallica, Slayer . . . we were listening to all that stuff, and we said, "Let's make a heavy record, let's make a record of *our* band." Well, [*Slave to the Grind*] is the record of our band in that point of time. We went to Fort Lauderdale and partied our asses off and just stayed out till six in the morning and go to the studio at eleven in the morning . . . It was excessive, but that's what we wanted. That's the record we wanted, and I don't even know what the label was thinking because at that point [after the success of the debut], we could kind of do what we wanted and we had their support and made the record we wanted to make.

And, you know, we're all proud of it. It was a cool record. It was a fun record to make, unlike *Subhuman Race*, which was not much fun at all. But *Slave to the Grind* was a lot of fun, and that was our vibe. If I had to put it one way, we were making the record of the band we were at that moment.

Interesting to note that in a year where so many hard rock artists were acquiescing to formula, Skid Row would hit number one on the Billboard album charts by making an album that uncomprisingly went against the sonic grain of what had made them successful in the first place. I asked my pal Mitch Lafon what he thought about artists bucking against formula and fan expectation . . . and why some bands become iconic, while others are not remembered in the same light.

Mitch Lafon: I'll tell you two things about that. First of all, you look at U2, you look at Madonna, you look at David Bowie, you look at Prince. They never really fit into a genre. They were genres unto themselves. There's no other Madonna . . . Madonna is not a dance artist, Madonna is not a pop artist, Madonna is Madonna. U2 is not just a rock band. You listen to the first Prince record, to the second Prince record, to the third Prince record, to the fourth . . . there is such a diversity. And same with Duran Duran, same with Metallica. And there's a lot of moving parts. U2 — they never did the same thing; fans expected them to change . . . I don't think a U2 fan wanted to hear *The Joshua Tree* eight times over, right? There was an expectation that they do something [different each time]. Madonna was culturally avant-garde and culturally significant, and fans wanted her to be cutting edge, they didn't want her to do "Holiday" [on] eight albums in a row; whereas Warrant fans and Poison fans, which I am one of, we kinda like to hear "Cherry Pie" probably done 18 times over just with different lyrics and just called something different — there was a safety to that, it was like a weighted blanket, if you want.

In retrospect, some of the best-sounding "hair metal" albums ever came from the period between 1991 and 1995, when many of the bands were supposed to have gone the way of the dinosaur. (Check out Warrant's *Dog Eat Dog*, Europe's *Prisoners in Paradise*, or the John Corabi–era self-titled Mötley Crüe album.) Some were successful, but most failed to reach the heights of efforts that came before. It must have all seemed a bit unfair to these artists . . . years of figuring out how to harness all of this new recording technology to create massive arena rock sounds that still retained clarity across the frequency spectrum, soon to be replaced by a return to the more organic production treatments of the '60s and '70s. A nose-to-the-grindstone adherence to the rules of hard rock success, perfecting the look, the songwriting, the attitude . . . all to be taken away by a handful of bands from a certain rainy Northwestern locale.

So much has been written about the demise of hair metal, an entire genre felled by the swing of Kurt Cobain's mighty axe. The four chords that kick off Nirvana's "Smells Like Teen Spirit" are not at all that dissimilar to those found in the chorus of Boston's "More than a Feeling," a song that kicked off the trend of high-production gloss that would inform so much of '80s rock's recorded output. But the menace and vitriol with which those four chords were performed by Nirvana, along with a distinct rejection of hair metal's image and perceived artifice, made all the difference to a new generation of kids who were looking at a future much different than the one celebrated in the abundant 1980s. The threat to hair metal had been bubbling under for years, lying in the weeds of college radio, various homespun alternative scenes, and even in the lower ranks of major label rosters. Sure, the music industry, like all industries really, is predicated on exploitation of previous success, but also on the acceptance of inevitable change . . . and the search for something new and fresh. Enuff Z'Nuff bassist Chip Z'Nuff recalls a record company incentive that ultimately foreshadowed a change in his own band's fortunes.

> **Chip Z'Nuff:** You mentioned Stone Temple Pilots . . . that's a band I discovered when I signed to Atco Records. The first thing the label said to me was, "Hey, if you find any bands and bring them to the label, we'll give you a point." And we said,

"Well, what's a point?" A point is a sales percentage point on the record, so if a record gets 10 points, I would get one point on the sales of that record if I found a band. And I always went out to look for new bands. I liked to produce bands that were just starting to try to get some action happening, even in the early days, so when we signed with Atco Records and they flew us to Los Angeles to meet with our constituents, the very first night I was out, I went to the place called Whisky a Go Go and there was a band there called Mighty Joe Young playing . . . and it was fucking Stone Temple Pilots! I didn't know it was the Pilots, I just saw a four-piece band kicking ass and heard all these pop rock songs, à la Enuff Z'Nuff, Cheap Trick. And I went back to the label the next day, spoke with Karen Dumont, our A&R representative over there, and I said, "I found a band already!" They're like, "Ahh come on, we just told you the story that you if you find bands, you get rewarded." And I said, "No, no, no, I'm not looking for that. I don't care if I get anything on it. These guys are great and they deserve a deal! They're called Mighty Joe Young, four-piece band, pop rock, straight ahead. No tapes, no sequencers, no guys [playing] backstage." It was just for cats plugging in and playing, and they were happening, and the label sat on their laurels and didn't move quick enough. Atco was a subsidiary of Atlantic Records, and Atlantic was smart enough to pick them up and sign that band . . . I'd be sitting right now in Burr Ridge [one of the wealthiest suburbs in Illinois] . . . If we would have done that deal, I would have made a Brinks truck full. I was one of the first guys to discover that band, bring it to my label, and unfortunately, that deal didn't happen but I still have the story to tell.

Just as a young and hungry Def Leppard had put Kix on high alert in the early '80s with their visionary *Pyromania* album, so, too, did Nirvana's *Nevermind* pose a similar, and even deadlier, threat to the Maryland band's fortunes and future.

Brian "Damage" Forsythe: Yes, in fact when I told you about the *Cool Kids* things with the *Pyromania* cassette, same thing happened with *Hot Wire*. I felt it was a better record than *Blow My Fuse*, and because of the success of *Blow My Fuse*, I figured it was going to be, "Okay, now we're gonna finally break through" . . . This was the one they bumped us over to East West Records, so we met with the CEO of East West and we're up in his office and he's talking to us about all these big plans for *Hot Wire* and then he goes, "Oh wait, I want to show you guys something." He opens his desk drawer, pulls out a CD — the Nirvana CD — and he holds that up and he goes, "This is gonna be huge." It was a flashback to the *Cool Kids* record, and we were like, "Uh-oh." Like we knew it, at that point.

And you know it was weird because when they did put us on East West, we thought we'd get more special attention, being on a smaller subsidiary of Atlantic. At first we did, and we were kind of like the big fish in the small pond kind of thing. They put a bunch of money in, they'd fly Steve and I out to the West Coast to do *Headbangers Ball* on MTV, and they gave us really good tour support right off the bat, but then really quickly it started to fade. We were right in the middle of filming a video for "Tear Down the Walls," which we figured was the follow-up to "Don't Close Your Eyes" [the breakthrough power ballad from *Blow My Fuse*], that this is going to be humongous. We were filming it at this college in Prosper, Maryland, and midway through somebody comes up and says, "Hey, so-and-so called from [the record company] — they said, 'Eh, that's it.' Shut it down, they're done. They're not going to put any more money into this." So we had to just scrap it and that was it, and we knew it at that point that it was over for that record. That was so disillusioning. It completely changed. It got to where if you were a band from the '80s, people were like, "Eh" — they didn't want anything to do with it.

For Skid Row, who had a number one Billboard album just a few months prior to *Nevermind*'s release, it must have seemed unfathomable that a changing of the guard could thwart the forward momentum the band had been enjoying since their debut. And yet . . .

Scotti Hill: It's just one of those things — you have to make it work, and we did for so long . . . and then *Nevermind* came out, right? Our sales were already starting to dwindle at that point, and then overnight the rug was pulled out, and it's like, "Why deal with any of this anymore? Nobody wants to see it or hear it." So we just went away.

Rudy Sarzo: I became associated with '80s music so there was, especially in the United States, very little interest in musicians of my genre who actually were successful in a certain era. Anything that had to do with that era became non grata in the following era. It's all the ebb and flow of time. You're not going to have the '90s without the '80s and the '70s and the '60s and the '50s. It's all a continuation. The music industry as we knew it, was destroyed, gone. It's like it imploded. It's one of those buildings that caves in, right? That's what happened and it was very difficult to release albums of the same caliber or the same filter that refined those gems of albums that become timeless, because back in the day you had the filter of the artist relations person in the music industry, you had the filter of the radio promotion guy, everybody in the record label somehow, some way, filtered that music through them and they made sure that it could be sold or played on the radio.

Some bands were seeing a more rough and ready trend about to happen, and the BulletBoys, on their 1991 sophomore release *Freakshow*, met the challenge head-on by staying true to the roots that had brought them gold success on their debut . . . roots that were already coming from a fairly raw and organic place.

Mick Sweda: We saw coming down the pike what was happening in the early '90s. It was pretty easy to see where music was going and where bands that sort of were thrown into our category were headed. It was, you could see the writing on the wall, in other words, and so our reaction to that was to get meaner. And you know, the choice of the first single from that record ["THC Groove"] was probably not the most commercially sensible one, but that was what we wanted to say. We wanted to say, "Look, we don't give a damn about singles and ballads and what is currently happening out there. This is our reaction to that." And yeah, we probably paid a price for doing that, but I stand by it at this point. It was a risk that we were willing to take at the time.

Bands were cognizant of a change on the horizon before the actual fall, and Frank Gryner offers a producer's perspective on how some of these bands who had dabbled in the excesses of hair metal were starting to strip back some of the paint.

Frank Gryner: [The bands] doing huge anthems and everything that we loved about the '80s, they knew that that had an expiration date and were like, "Let's go back." And that was something that was very common with the bands I worked with in the early '90s, it was like they were going back to their roots, and that was always part of the marketing. That was the intention when they went into the studio . . . "Let's make it organic, let's just do what we do. Let's not make it about production." If you really listen to the first Alice in Chains record, it sounded big, essentially it's all the same kind of ingredients [as earlier hard rock], it just got presented in a way that fit the grunge label.

Slaughter, who had taken a rocket ride to multiplatinum success with *Stick It to Ya*, saw their second album, 1992's powerfully well-crafted *The Wild Life*, sell a fraction of the amount of its predecessor, but by no means as a result of a product of lesser quality. Mark points instead to conscious business decisions by those on the other side of the music industry desks that helped to speed up the commercial decline of many artists.

Mark Slaughter: When the tides were changing, we were the last wave of, as they call it, the "hair band" era. [The year] '92 was the time that, you know, Nirvana was rumbling and the actual programmer of KROQ radio out of Los Angeles becomes the new president of MTV. And he says point blank in *Billboard* magazine, "I will no longer play Mötley Crüe, Slaughter, Poison, Ozzy." I mean, he literally just spelled it out that he would no longer play that music, and the largest radio station in the world turned its back on us. And ultimately, that's the first step in that change. But you can't blame it on that guy. The truth of the matter is that every 10 years there's a different cycle of music, a different thing, a different vibe, a different cultural movement. You've got to change and realize there's a different . . . you have a different market.

For a band like Skid Row, who had been on the verge of true icon status, the turning of the tides seems particularly cruel, especially when one considers the power and authentic aggression behind not only *Slave to the Grind*, but also 1995's excellent *Subhuman Race*, an album that still fought its way to gold status, despite the fact that many people had ignorantly relegated Skid Row's artistic contributions to some generic hair metal scrap heap. Years of nonstop touring and the strains of inner band tensions were as much at play in their deterioration as were the changing tastes of the music industry and consumers.

Scotti Hill: A lot of people liked that record [*Subhuman Race*], and for us . . . I can't speak for the other guys, but it was a hard record to make. It was a really hard record to make. It was different in the way that we weren't ready when we went into the studio, we didn't have all the songs, so we did a lot of writing in the studio. We were working with Bob Rock and that was . . . It wasn't the greatest experience for us. You know, his way of working just didn't really jive with our way of working. And there was just a massive amount of tension in the band. That's why we couldn't get the stuff written, because nobody wanted to show up. Nobody wanted to get in the room, man . . . You know, we just got off of 16 months on tour and then came home for a little while, made a record, and then 22 months on tour, and went back out, and then now we're making *Subhuman Race*, and . . . You know, pretty much everybody hates each other at that point.

You know, people are . . . they do what they're told . . . . "This is what you like now, and this is what you hate now, because this is the opposite of what you used to like." Every one of those motherfuckers has a fringe jacket hanging in the back of his closet, I don't care what you say. Just change it for a flannel shirt. You know, it's a different jacket, it's a flannel jacket, and, you know, no guitar solos. "Okay, we're going to eliminate guitar solos," so therefore we're going to lose a generation of guitar players. If you had tight pants and long hair, you were the fucking enemy. Hey man, I liked a lot of [grunge], and in my personal opinion, I think music may have needed that because it got really watered down and it got really gross and fucking sugar coated and bashful, bashful boys and their long hair . . . I mean, we not only went out of fashion, we were hated . . . People would be like, "You're in a band?" And I'd be like, "No, I work for a management company." I wouldn't even tell people what band I was in. It was funny, I watched the Bee Gees documentary, the three-parter. I think it was on HBO Max or something like that, and it was fantastic. And they go through the "disco sucks" era, and they were right in the middle of that. It reminded me so much of what we went through, only in their case much, much worse. But really, people not only weren't interested, they fucking hated us. They really did. I mean, just *hated* us.

I asked my friend Todd Kerns what it was like, as lead vocalist for the Age of Electric, a gold-selling act in their native Canada, navigating the changes of the early '90s. As an artist weaned on metal and equally informed by punk, pop, alternative music, and everything in between, Todd was able to comment in a spot-on illumination of the mercurial nature of relevancy in the music business, and the inevitability of change.

Todd Kerns: There was a line drawn, and people talk about it like it was the next day, but it wasn't. It sort of quietly happened. I think that it's true of almost every band or artist, they kind of grow up and become something different, or they just kind of grow like human beings grow. The one thing I will say for us is that we always loved music, and [it could be] fucking "Our Lips Are Sealed" by the Go-Go's or just weird pop songs. So things like the Pixies or things like Depeche Mode and all these things that sort of later on would become more like hipper things to reference, they just came more to the surface in a way. But being in a guitar rock band and having an interest in punk rock . . . I never got bitten by that sort of like, "I'm going to play like Eddie Van Halen." I would look at guys like Eddie Van Halen, and I'd go, "That's amazing. I'm going to play with somebody *like* Eddie Van Halen. I'm not going to be that fucking guy." I was more like, "Isn't Johnny Thunders the best? Isn't Rick Nielsen the king? That's what I would like to do." With that, having realized that I could sing kind of higher, it became very natural to just live in that world.

But when the '90s came along, there definitely became a line and there became, like everything, a uniform, and a real fear sort of started to set in. Age of Electric had already been kind of out there swinging and working and doing our thing, things started to change, and we slowly became what we became into the '90s. We were lucky enough not to have been really successful as the previous version of the band because that would have been the noose that hung us. But the fact that we just sort of kept growing and focusing on the other elements of what we do . . .

But I remember playing clubs and stuff like that and just goofing around . . . I think our drummer wrote Ozzy on my fingers, just like the old Ozzy tattoo that Ozzy used to have? It would make me laugh because guys would be like, "I've always been into the Melvins" and all these groups that they would start to kind of like be the touchstone that you were allowed to talk about. I'm like, "Dude, last year I was there when you had the big hair and you were listening to Warrant . . ." We all were, it's not a big deal. And I remember there specifically being a review in some kind of like way too hip magazine that had a real problem with the fact that I had Ozzy written on my fingers, and it was just the stupidest, funniest thing to us that having a couple of beers backstage and writing Ozzy on your fingers and going out and playing a show was like you didn't know the secret handshake. And to be honest, I never learned the secret handshake because I just love music. And I can talk about Abba for just as long as I can talk about anybody else, you know what I mean? And so when it started to become really militant, that's the stuff that turned me off.

The weird thing about the '90s is what was once cool was not cool so quickly. You had the gateway drugs like Alice in Chains and Soundgarden, which were essentially hard rock bands with a different spin on things. Looking back, I can't believe that we thought this was so radically different than what was going on in music previously. Soundgarden, I mean, Chris is a wailing rock singer, [there are] Sabbathy riffs and all that kind of stuff, but within that, heading into things like Nirvana and all that kind of stuff, which was way more from punk rock with pop-isms built in there, we loved that stuff immediately. We just thought these guys are amazing, and so were these songs. I think that was quite inspiring, but at the same time there was a real turn-off about like,

"You have to have this haircut" or "You can't have that haircut" more specifically. "You have to be wearing these kind of clothes." It just seems so silly now because it's such a blink of an eye when I look back on how quickly things had shifted out of whatever was cool into whatever the next thing was. It was happening under your feet and in real time. I honestly don't believe it will ever change that radically again, at least for me and probably for you, because we're not as subjected to it now because we do what we love to do [as opposed to what's commercially viable] and that's probably not going to change.

If we both were frozen in stasis in 1986, we would be really surprised to wake up today and realize that hip-hop or pop is the prevailing music, but when it happens in real time and you watch and feel it all kind of happening within a whole other conversation about the record industry itself, it all feels pretty natural . . .

A really gnarly story to me was when Moe Berg [lead vocalist of Canadian band the Pursuit of Happiness], and [Age of Electric] were in Toronto hanging out with the A&R guy and that shit, and he was taking us out on the town, and Moe goes, "Warrant's playing tonight." And he was genuinely excited about it. "Okay, cool." At that point that wasn't really a cool thing, but Moe was such a song guy, right? He looked past everything into the fact that these are good songs. And we went to some small club and it was just eye-opening because I'd never seen Warrant, but I'd seen one of their live home video type things in a hockey arena, and here they were in some small club, and there was four of them, and they'd cut their hair, and some plaid shirts going on . . . It wasn't a negative feeling toward them at all, it was a very eye-opening and sobering idea of this lifestyle we had chosen called music, because it's fucking hip today and it ain't hip tomorrow, and if you're not flowing with that, or if you represent too much of what the previous regime was, you're fucked. I think that's true of almost anybody. If you hang around long enough, you're cool again.

And we see that today, but a lot of the '80s new wave groups or pop stars, or anybody who was fortunate or unfortunate enough to become a *Teen Beat* magazine–something you stick on your wall for young girls, they would unfortunately be nailed to a cross for 10 years and then hopefully come out the other side. Like the Bay City Rollers. When I was kid, man, those guys . . . To this day, I have a soft spot for those guys, but those guys got eaten alive by an industry that was like, "No. No, this is not happening." And that's just the nature of the business that we're in and the same thing can be said for the grunge bands. They went through a phase of it all going away. A lot of that, unfortunately, was due to casualties and loss of life, but things just fall out of fashion so if we're looking back on hair metal falling out of fashion, it's like, "Yeah, well it all falls out of fashion."

Having worked with Gilby Clarke in a number of capacities, as a producer, as a songwriter, and having played in his touring band, I can say with a strong sense of conviction that he is one of the coolest human beings on the planet. Nothing seems to faze the guy, and he is always so authentically chilled out. But surely, as a rock'n'roll guitar player who cut his teeth on the '80s Sunset Strip . . . he must have at some point thought, Man, this grunge shit is *killing* me!

Gilby Clarke: No. No. No, once again, I think this is where the luck was involved. Like you said, I was in Guns N' Roses as it was happening. Oddly enough, Sean, I heard the Nirvana record, I think it was six months or so, maybe even more, before it came out. I was a writer with Virgin Records. I was the first American artist signed to Virgin America. I had a publishing deal early on. So Virgin was involved with Nirvana somehow, someway, and I got a cassette of that record, and I remember that the secretary there, her name was Dana, she was kind of like my everyday person I called and talked to and all that kind of stuff, and she goes, "Oh my God, you've got to hear this new record by Nirvana. Oh my God, they're going to be so big, they're awesome." And I got the record, and I was just like, "Oh, it just kind of sounds like more distinguished Ramones." I thought it was like pop-punk-rock . . . I didn't have a visual, I never saw a picture of them. I only heard it. And I thought, yeah, it's just a more sophisticated Ramones . . . Like even the D tuning [a trademark of the grunge sound] didn't throw me off or whatever, so my years during that era were strange.

I was in Guns N' Roses, like you said, and immediately was making a million-dollar solo record for Virgin and then [playing with] Slash. But I did start noticing during Slash's solo tour where I could feel things were changing. . . . For the most part, the tour did really well, but there were some spots where Slash was Slash, who just played, like you said, stadiums two years before. We had some light turnouts in some venues and stuff, so we could see it changing at that point, you know. But I think it wasn't until after the Snakepit Tour where I had to make my next solo record for Virgin . . . The first record, they didn't say a word to me, make the record you want to make. When it came to the second one, they had a very distinctive opinion of what they wanted me to sound like, and it was what everything else sounded like at 1996, '97. And I had to make that decision. "Can't do it." They wanted me to do all these [cowrites] . . . I'd always written by myself, you know, and they had all these cowriters and stuff, and all these people, and it was just weird. Even though those people had success, it wasn't really somebody that I would click with, you know? It's just the people they were suggesting to me weren't really right, and it just . . . Everything I was doing just didn't feel right. I felt like I was outside of my box, you know? And at that point, you just have to go, "Am I doing what I'm good at? Or am I doing this because it's my job now?" And granted, at that point I did have a wife, a house, a baby. I had to work and stuff, and that's when I actually said, "I can't do it. I can't do it." I definitely didn't get dropped, I definitely walked away from a deal, but they definitely also didn't want me to make the record I wanted to make. I gave them demos and they were, "No, no."

Many bands who had been arena-packing, multiplatinum album–selling superstars still continued to make albums and perform, albeit in drastically reduced commercial circumstances. Bon Jovi was the one band that somehow managed to stay relevant, never losing their arena rock status . . . Somehow any concessions in the sound of the band never felt forced and always managed to feel current as they retained a loyal audience while also connecting with a more youthful market with reinventions of their classic sound, as they did with 2000's "It's My Life." But Bon Jovi was definitely the exception, and many of these artists ended up recording for CMC International, a small label with major label distribution through BMG. Bands like W.A.S.P., Slaughter, Warrant, Kix, L.A. Guns, Dokken, and even the mighty Judas Priest released strong albums throughout the '90s, often reflecting a contemporary modernity while still retaining the core elements of their sound. Others labels like Spitfire Records, Sanctuary Music, and a revitalized Portrait Records (headed up by A&R guru John Kalodner) gave bands like Ratt, Great White, and Dio a vehicle for releasing new music, while also managing the rights and distribution of titles that had fallen through the cracks. Some bands, like Mötley Crüe and Def Leppard (both currently enjoying massive success on their hot-ticket Stadium Tour), were able to wrestle back the rights to their catalogs from their respective major labels, allowing them the freedom to have control over the commercial exploitation of their music.

Artists like Mr. Big directed their attention to markets overseas that were still hungry for their brand of rock'n'roll.

Paul Gilbert: Japan was like the life boat. In America, we were playing arenas as a support act, we weren't headlining.

But we were doing okay, I guess with *Lean into It*, we were headlining theaters, but when grunge came out, all of a sudden I remember the record label saying . . . We'd get the watered down version from management, but basically the idea was, "You guys just aren't cool anymore. There's a new trend and you're not it." But at the same time, our career in Japan was going through the roof, Southeast Asia was going great, and our manager just said, "Hey, play there," and so we did. It kept us busy, it wasn't like we sat around twiddling our thumbs with lots of time, we were totally busy with our career in that part of the world, still making records and touring, so because we were busy I didn't ruminate about it too much. It's hard to complain when you've got a gig anywhere.

Some of the bands fought through the hard times to eventually return as powerful headliners via selective dates that positioned them as high profile acts (Twisted Sister's rise to international heavy metal festival headliners is a prime example). Others, like Skid Row, endured the trials of personnel changes and humbling logistics to eventually build back their audiences.

Scotti Hill: We got a guy named Johnny Solinger [to replace vocalist Sebastian Bach]. We really liked him. He may not have been the perfect guy for the band, but we carried on, and we got on a Kiss tour and played 140 shows, I guess, with them. And then after that, sometime in late 2000, we got in a van and drove to Ohio and slept in sleeping bags, and then the next night we got in that van and drove somewhere else. And that went on for about four years. And we graduated to an RV, and then we graduated back to a bus with a trailer. And little by little we now play in front of a lot of people again. To achieve what we did achieve and headline and do all that cool shit, win awards, and be the toast of the town, and then lose it . . . And then go back to the very, very, very, very beginning and get back in a van and stay there, and drive around and break down and get bedbugs and fucking stay in hotels with blood on the floor and all that fucking shit. Grapple with the flu. Can't miss the gig. I got the flu, but we can't miss the gig because we won't have enough money for fucking gas to get us to wherever we need to be. It was the real trenches for a long time.

Just because the spotlight has faded, or more accurately, been refocused, does not mean that the creative impetus or artistic intention just goes away. Nor does the need to make a living and support oneself or one's family. And somewhere between these needs on the part of the artist and the desire for a once ravenous audience to connect with precious memories is the place many acts find themselves today.

Mark Slaughter: I realized that you're only as good as nostalgia is painting you, and you get stuck in that, but it's better to be stuck in that and have a career than not have anything. But . . . you still have those creative juices. You still want to go out there, and you still want to connect with people.

As we have seen countless times through movies, television, and advertising of all kinds, music of the past can be reinvented and reframed for new audiences. And because of its primary color vitality, perhaps there's no better music suited to this task than '80s rock. Let's give the last word on this subject to one of its most recognizable figures.

Dee Snider: Young people hear '80s music and they get turned on to it, and I think that '80s music is showing more staying power — you're seeing it used on [Netflix show] *Cobra Kai*, you're seeing young people who are discovering it and embracing it and enamored by it, the romance of it. They're romanticizing the *cool*. It's the middle finger factor. You've probably heard me say that before. I said we weren't complaining, we weren't whining. "We're Not Gonna Take It" wasn't complaining about my parents. It was giving them the finger and saying, "You can't fucking stop me. And you know, we're going to have a fucking good time." So it was a big reaction to the Reagan era, a very conservative time. And I would say for every action there's a reaction, and the decade of decadence, including the Madonnas and the Culture Clubs and all those people, was very reactive to a very Margaret Thatcher–Ronald Reagan conservative world we were in, and it grew, and young people were embracing something that was pushing back on this and saying, "Fuck you, fuck you. We're not gonna take it."

EPILOGUE

When I started writing this book, I wanted to point out the hypocrisy of all who dared to wag an elitist finger at hair metal. I believed that by examining its lineage and connections to music that has been accepted by music critics and cognoscenti at large as "cooler," "smarter," and just outright "better," I would unearth genuine revelations as to its artistic merit and historical value.

Reading over the introduction, I see that I sugarcoated my motivations, backtracking on my initial inspirational indignation and expressing a desire to make this a collegial experience. Essentially, this is what I usually end up doing when people make fun of this music. My book is called *Don't Call It Hair Metal*, and yet, I ended up using the term numerous times. It's hard not to, because the fact of the matter, the truth is, I wanted to shove "hair metal" down those people's throats and show them what a bunch of hypocrites they were. I was exhausted from the countless situations where I would end up in an argument over criticisms laced with generic categorizations and fallacy, fatigued at trying to point out the diversity and legitimate artistic intention that exists within this iteration of rock'n'roll. I have yet to find a professional working situation where there isn't at least one person in the group proffering a knowing smirk, smug condescension, or outright dismissal whenever a "hair metal" band or song is cited as an artistic reference. Personally, I've found that in these situations it's often easier just to play nice, perhaps suggest something was "Stones-y" or "Zep-like," knowing damn well my inspiration was coming from Cinderella or Whitesnake. Of course, the rock'n'roll highway is littered with refinements and appropriation. Maybe at the end of the day, we should all just cut to the chase and describe things in their root form. We could refer to all rock'n'roll riffs as "Muddy Waters–esque," all licks as "Chuck Berry–ish" or "Robert Johnson–inflected" (or, in the case of Yngwie, "Bach'n'Roll"?).

But I don't think we should do that, because it doesn't fairly represent the new fruit borne of the initial seed of inspiration. As I dug deeper and deeper into the evolution of not only '80s hard rock, but of my own development as a listener and creator, it struck me that some fruit is sweeter than others. And I also now truly understand that, from the perspective of a music lover moved by different elements and emphases of the rock'n'roll lineage than the ones that I have prioritized, one bad apple can spoil the whole damn bunch.

As I peeled back the layers of this onion, I was surprised at how painful it can be to look back with renewed perspective. The knowledge I have accumulated as a professional musician in many genres beyond rock and metal, including classical, country, hip-hop, and even jazz, has caused me to reconsider warm memories, the value I ascribed to some of the bands and artists in this genre and the experiences of my youth that were attached to their music. The same can be said of my own growth as a husband, a parent, an educator, and an ally to members of my community who have been slighted in the music that has been so important to me. I would find myself feeling a sense of loss at times throughout the process . . . akin to finding out that Santa Claus isn't real, or that social structures like family, school, and Church are fallible.

There is a duality of mind that I now engage when I listen to music that excites me on one level, yet challenges core moral and ethical values I have developed due to its lyrical content. The music often wins, its pull is too strong. That's neither a boast nor an admission of moral fault, it's just a fact. Fortunately, the positive influences and sense of empathy and justice instilled in me by the diverse communities in which I live and work fortify me when it's time to call bullshit on lyrics that are hurtful or degrading. I try to be careful what I make manifest in the world through sharing these days.

So yeah, a few illusions got smashed along the way. Maybe they have been smashed all along, and I've just been gluing them back together as I rewrite the script of my life in my own mind.

Or maybe not.

I've come to see the ultimate changing of the musical guard that came in the '90s as an inevitable reaction to formulaic refinement, yet my deep dive into the nuts and bolts of this stuff has also bolstered my overarching belief that the best of what the '80s subgenre known alternately as pop or glam or hair metal has to offer is nothing less than great rock'n'roll, a continuation of the authentic artistic work that came before. I may have run out of ways to describe the sound of an electric guitar, but in exhausting the possibilities and variations, I think I've made a damn good case that it isn't all the same. There was and is a connection in this music that goes beyond pale pastiche, and I believe that the cream of hair metal that has risen to the top in my consciousness (and hopefully yours) after writing this book is an important part of the greater rock'n'roll story.

I'm not much of a fighter, and I never have been. But I am proud to say I have never shied away from defending an underdog, and I feel that I did that with this book. I tried to honor and understand the intention behind all of these artists' work, the good and the bad, and to pay them back with a respect that is equal to the amount of inspiration they have given me. I believe we owe this to all artists, to fellow music lovers, and to ourselves, so that we may yield the best communal results from our subjective interpretations.

Finally, I think I've made peace with an insecurity that has plagued me, a need for validation in all areas of my life from people that I respect. That's a ridiculous and unfair thing to ask of anyone. First and foremost, *I* need to feel good about what I do in all areas of my life. I am who I am because of '80s hair metal — it has been one of the greatest influences in my life, second only (and not by much) to the influence of family. I think I have had a hard time *not* hearing any criticism of hair metal as a criticism of me as a person. Time to lose that.

I told you not to call it hair metal . . . but honestly, call it whatever you want. It's still rock'n'roll . . . and it doesn't have to matter to anybody else in the world. But I wanted you to know why it matters to me.

ACKNOWLEDGMENTS

I would like to send rock'n'roll regards to the following individuals for their efforts in making this book a reality:

Michael Holmes and everyone at ECW Press; thank you for taking a chance and allowing this not-so-young dude to carry the news. Shannon Parr, Jessica Albert, Jennifer Gallinger, Jen Albert, Emily Ferko, Emily Varsava, David Caron: it is an honor to be part of the ECW family!

Emm Gryner, thank you for introducing me to Michael Holmes, and for being someone I can share my unfiltered joy of '80s rock with.

Julie Gibb, thank you for your incredible transcriptions of the interviews I conducted.

To Erin, Des, and Jack Kelly, who support me unconditionally through all of my artistic endeavours: I love you all and am eternally grateful. Also, thanks to Angus Kelly, whose barking and "head bops" served as a reminder to take a break once in a while, and go for a walk!

To Dad, Mom, Pam, Kerry, Jim, Kevin, Dan, Melissa, and all the extended Kelly and Zucchiatti clan, for your lifelong love and support.

To Kevin Taylor, for allowing me access to his personal archive of amazing rock artifacts.

To my extended rock'n'roll family . . . Lee Aaron and band, Coney Hatch, Helix, Gilby Clarke, Alan Frew, Carole Pope and Rough Trade,

Trapper, Nelly Furtado, Crash Kelly, and everyone I have had the pleasure of making music with over the years, for the joy you have brought into my life.

To all my students, fellow staff members, and administrators at the Toronto Catholic District School Board for reminding me that rock'n'roll really does live and breathe in the hearts of the young, and the young at heart.

And of course, to all of the musicians and music industry professionals who shared their insights for the book, and their artistry with world . . . rock'n'roll is richer for your contributions.